DATE DUE

OCT 2 '84			
OCT 4 '84	JUN 27 1989		
OCT 29 '84	NO 29 '89		
NOV 23 '84	NO 23 '90		
DEC 7 '84	JY 30 '91		
JAN 2 '85	MR 31 '93		
JAN 23 '85			
JAN 28 '85			
AUG 5 '85			
AUG 19 '85			
JAN 30 '86			
FEB 13 '86			

GAYLORD 234 PRINTED IN U. S. A.

MAKE IT EASY ENTERTAINING

Also by Laurie Burrows Grad
Dining In—Los Angeles
Make It Easy in Your Kitchen

MAKE IT EASY ENTERTAINING

Laurie Burrows Grad

JEREMY P. TARCHER, INC.
Los Angeles
Distributed by Houghton Mifflin Company
Boston

Portions of this book have appeared in *Los Angeles Magazine*.

Library of Congress Cataloging in Publication Data

Grad, Laurie Burrows.
Make it easy entertaining.

Includes index.
1. Entertaining. I. Title.
TX731.G686 1984 642'.4 84-2751
ISBN 0-87477-289-3

Jeremy P. Tarcher, Inc.
9110 Sunset Blvd.
Los Angeles, CA 90069

Design by Thom Dower
Illustration by Tanya Maiboroda

Manufactured in the United States of America
A 10 9 8 7 6 5 4 3 2 1

First Edition

Once again, to my wonderfully supportive husband, Peter, and my understanding (even though he's a teenager) son, Nick—for putting up with my kitchen antics.

Contents

Acknowledgments

The author wishes to thank the following people for their contributions:

—Mary Carey, who has achieved sainthood in this life with her loyal friendship, dedicated patience, and constant support.

—Millie Loeb, my ingenious editor and good friend, who doggedly fought to keep my inspiration lit.

—Lea Chartok, for enduring my constant changes with a smile.

—My agent, Dominick Abel, for setting it all up.

—Beth Rawnsley, for her wealth of creative input under pressure.

—To all at Hour Magazine for their constant support, patience, and encouragement.

—Sandra Carter Collyer, for listening and understanding; Betsy Halpern Castenir, for her creative inspirations; and Diane Rossen Worthington, for pointing me on the positive road.

—Margy Newman, for her wonderful design for my kitchen, and Jane Mancbach, for helping me decorate the rest of the house.

—Tanya Maiboroda, for listening and transforming my ideas into beautiful illustrations.

—Deanna Fry, for excellent makeup artistry.

—Eric Serena, for hairstyling talents extraordinaire.

—Notable others: Herb Ball, Catherine Bergstrom, Bob Broder, Ellen Brown, Lucia Castaneda, Thom Dower, Kim Freilich, Derek Gallagher, Laura Golden, Barbara Greenebaum, Helen Haig, Barbara Marinacci, Jerry Mastin, Nena Prince, Irene Ramirez, Fred Roberts, Lorraine Shapiro, Barbara Tenenbaum, and of course, Jeremy Tarcher.

And my parents, for inspiring me to eat well and enjoy it.

Introduction

Make It Easy Entertaining is a complete menu cookbook. In contrast to my last book, *Make It Easy in Your Kitchen*, what you will find here is more than just soup to nuts: there are 40 unusual menus, with almost 200 new recipes divided into the five categories most requested by my viewers on *Hour Magazine*. On this nationally syndicated television show I have served as the resident Make-It-Easy cooking expert for the past five years. My weekly visibility on television and the kind of cooking information I offer make me a magnet—drawing requests for more than recipes. Both viewers and those who purchased my previous book constantly ask for the same kinds of advice: How can they take this style of cooking—which emphasizes simplicity, elegance, fresh and in-season ingredients, and every cooking trick that can be utilized without sacrificing quality—and use it when they entertain? Are there entertainment tips that are as easy and clever as the cooking hints that appeared in *Make It Easy in Your Kitchen*? Is this approach to food preparation appropriate for the most festive holiday occasions and the most important parties? Can Make-It-Easy cooking be lower in calories? Less expensive? Truly inflation fighting? Can it be adapted for breakfast, brunch, and lunch—categories not directly covered in the other book?

Make It Easy Entertaining is my response to these challenges.

I've observed our society in the midst of change. I've watched as new trends and lifestyles catch on—in food, fashion, and fitness. This leads to an intense interest in health and good, sound nutrition. In addition, we're becoming more casual—formality is quickly being replaced in all aspects of our lives. *Make It Easy Entertaining* parallels this change away from the formal, full-dress, heavy, complicated menu to a more relaxed atmosphere where the food is still primary.

The book is divided into five sections. The first explores daytime entertaining (with one exception) and offers menus for Festive Breakfasts and Brunches. It's a response to a demand for a more casual and inexpensive style of partying with some wonderful and new recipe ideas. *Breakfast Prepared the Night Before, A Casual Brunch Buffet, Picnic on the Grass,* and *A Midnight Breakfast* suggest a variety that moves way beyond the old bacon and eggs standard. They are all Make-It-Easy menus because you can prepare them almost totally in advance. The rest are also hassle-free and can be assembled in just a short period of time. Whether it's a relaxed *Sunday Football Brunch* that often lasts all day or the at-home *Business Breakfast,* more and more people are entertaining in this informal manner.

The second part, devoted to Inexpensive Feasts, is based on the assumption that less—in this case, less money—doesn't mean less quality. With the rising costs of food, we all have to become more creative and resourceful if we wish to entertain often. The clever use of soups, pasta, chicken, and vegetables can make your parties successful and memorable occasions. Just about everyone loves a *Hearty Winter Soup Supper,* consisting of an unusually spicy sausage soup coupled with a velvety rich carrot soup. *Just Desserts* is another winning menu—a wonderful assortment of taste-tempting sweets.

Sumptuous Slenderizing Parties, the third section in the book, is another instance in which less is preferable. I am constantly barraged with requests for delicious, low-calorie recipes. Everybody seems to be on a diet, about to go on one, or at least hoping to lose weight. These menus capitalize on the new trend toward fresher and lighter cooking without compromising quality. The *Midsummer Night's Supper* features poached halibut, fresh vegetables marinated à la Grecque, and a light Berry Whip—all easy recipes, but combined they form a delectable summer menu. The parties are designed to spark enthusiasm for dieting. Creating the right atmosphere helps, as in the *First Night of the Diet,* which combines great low-cal recipes and the buddy system as an inspirational start. Another secret to dieting is attractive food presentation. Especially see the *Dinner from the Famous Spas,* in which helpful tips on garnishing and table treatments set the mood of the menu. Also included is a supplement I call "Laurie's Larder," which lists special ingredients I've discovered that can help you shave calories.

The Holiday Celebrations section includes some wonderfully exciting, amazingly easy but traditional recipes. A Perfect Roast Turkey that needs no basting, all the trimmings, and, for the finale, a cool and refreshing Pumpkin Ice Cream Pie—all are designed to both simplify and guarantee success next Thanksgiving. A Halloween party with a variety of games, decorations, and incredible edibles (Make-Your-Own Pizzas and homemade fudge) is an exciting event to stage but, more importantly, it keeps the kids home and safe. A traditional Fourth of July barbecue is given a new twist with an unusual butterflied lamb dish, served with corn roasted in the coals and summer tomatoes combined with fresh Mozzarella cheese. All these menus, including a *Mother's or Father's Day Dinner* that the rest of the family cooks, are designed to reflect the Make-It-Easy style. Combined with party tips, these holiday celebrations are guaranteed to be memorable occasions.

Last, but certainly not least, come the Big Splashes—those major occasions and unique events that warrant special festivities and celebrations. Whether it's a traditional *Royal Tea Party* transformed into a wedding shower, a *Carbo-Loading Pasta Party*, or an *Open House Championship Chili Party*—these are the times to go "all out"—to celebrate with a special menu, music, and decorations, all tied together to present a festival of entertainment.

My philosophy of entertaining emphasizes comfort and relaxation. I want my guests to feel cared for. Whether it's a formal dinner for the boss or participation preparation of paella in the kitchen, the primary goal is to provide a casual, carefree atmosphere so that everyone has a good time—and that includes the cook. *Make It Easy Entertaining* is designed to help you organize and orchestrate your parties so that you need never have fears or anxieties about entertaining. This book also promises to break you out of old routines with a minimum of fuss. Try the Demi-Dinner or the dinner of recipes from America's most popular spas the next time you want to do something new and unusual. I guarantee your guests will be delighted.

Like most people, I abhor working against a clock. That is why there is no countdown, timetable, or time limit in *Make It Easy Entertaining*. This is a total menu cookbook, from appetizer to dessert. It is designed to be totally organized—to perform the cooking chores, to arrange the table, to decorate the house, and to completely set the scene with no guesswork. It should ease the fears of anxious party-givers by presenting a complete package.

I also believe that about the easiest route to go for larger parties is buffet entertaining. For the Big Splashes I have devised a number of one-fork recipes, such as the Easiest Championship Chili, Carbonnade à la Flamande, or the Ultimate Casserole, a wonderful baked pasta treat. These dishes can be balanced on a lap and conveniently eaten with a fork.

In my view, the most important ingredient of any successful party is wonderful food, splendidly presented. These menus are designed with an eye to color, texture, taste, and balance, as well as an awareness of seasonal availability. In each menu I try to include a salad, my California bias, because I feel it is a refreshing part of any meal.

When entertaining, I personally determine my guests' likes and dislikes and plan accordingly. I choose a wine or wines to accent the menu but also provide plenty of sparkling water plus limes and lemons for those who don't want alcoholic beverages. I also offer decaffeinated coffee and a variety of herbal teas as alternatives for those avoiding caffeine.

I promise that even a new cook can master these menus. With many tips on creative centerpieces, a dozen napkin-folding ideas, a number of suggestions about buffet serving, and, of course, hundreds of new Make-It-Easy recipes, even an inexperienced host or hostess can feel totally confident.

PLANNING THE PARTY

The fun of Make-It-Easy entertaining is getting into the spirit of each party, using the theme as inspiration for invitations, music, or unique table settings. One of the first steps is setting the scene. You will find real variety in this book's suggestions, ranging from a breakfast in bed for two to the most elegant sit-down dinner using your best china and crystal. In between there are casual and formal menus for almost any occasion.

The next step is one of the trickiest elements in successful party giving—selection and seating of guests. I try to be adventurous. I combine married couples and single men and women freely. I also mix people from varying occupations and of various ages. I intermingle them at the table—inspiring cross conversation for more stimulating and less "business"-oriented parties.

Unless parties are large, such as an open house or cocktail party, I generally telephone my guests to invite them. That way I get an instant response and don't have to follow up with calls. Once your party reaches 15 to 20 guests, however, I suggest sending out invitations. If I feel creative and have some time, I make my own invitations with marker pens on heavy white card stock. If not, I buy the simplest invitations available and fill in as necessary. I also send one to myself to make sure the mail gets through properly.

I find organization the key to successful entertaining. I write out a daily schedule of chores—those done ahead of time and those left for the last minute. I even keep a record of party menus so that repeat guests don't get repeat meals. I go through each recipe carefully, listing the necessary ingredients—including all the extras. I check the bar supplies and I freeze or purchase extra ice. I check on flowers or arrange to invade a neighbor's garden. I check my staples to be sure there is enough oil, vinegar, broth, coffee, tea, seasonings, and other necessities in the cupboard. I check the house for repairs and special cleaning jobs. (Now is the time to tackle those washing and dusting chores you keep putting off!) I freeze the dessert or any part of the meal that can be prepared earlier. I try to do as much in advance so I leave myself time to relax for a few hours just before the party.

After I've gotten organized, I can begin to set the scene. I clear out space in my living room, dining room, or bedroom. I move furniture back against the walls to make the floor space larger, especially for large buffets. I get rid of odd clutter and old magazines so that guests can have surfaces on which to set their plates or drinks. If seating space is limited, I place large pillows on the floor. If table space is short, I clear off dressers and bureaus, protect them with padding and cloths, and transform them into tables or bars.

Once the space is clear, I try to make the house as festive as possible by using plants or fresh flowers. In large cities, you can take advantage of inexpensive flower markets which open *very* early in the morning. I always enjoy the trip to the flower mart, and I have a good time creating my own arrangements by simply combining odd groups of flowers in vases, bowls, or even an old coffee urn. I own a few "frogs"—those wonderful porcupine-like devices that easily hold flowers at the base of a bowl. You can also lay a fresh flower at each guest's place or garnish all types of dishes with one rose, tulip, or whatever. When fresh flowers are unavailable, I substitute dried flowers, such as a big bowl of baby's breath or even brightly colored paper flowers. Silk flowers are another alternative, though typically more expensive.

When setting up any centerpiece, my rule of thumb is *Keep it low*! Guests shouldn't have to crane their necks to talk across the table. If you are using a centerpiece on a buffet, it should be low enough so that guests don't knock it over in their enthusiasm to get to the food. Centerpieces can be as simple as a bowl of apples combined with walnuts, a basket of vegetables, a collection of toys, or a bunch of balloons. The important thing is to make it pretty and colorful, yet not so massive that it distracts from the food. As another option, I lay fresh greens down the center of the table and reserve a few to garnish large platters and serving dishes.

The next step is setting the table. What I don't own myself I can generally borrow from my friends or neighbors. A solid white cloth always makes a table look elegant. I own a permanent-press one that saves time and money. I mix and match colorful plates. You don't need a perfect set of china, flatware, or glassware. I intermingle place mats, tie up glasses with napkins, or wrap silver with colorful ribbons to disguise mismatched sets. I prefer extra large napkins—actually I like to use colorful bandanas, especially for buffets. If the occasion is formal, I tie up the cutlery in the bandana and wrap it with white ribbon topped off with a sprig of baby's breath. For an informal party, I tie up the napkins with colorful yarn.

Party-style paper plates may appear to be both cheap and convenient but are actually expensive and ungainly. They're fine to use on a picnic, but when used in a buffet they become soggy, unattractive, and unmanageable for guests. Keep paper plates for outdoors, where they serve a great function.

Place mats are useful but large napkins, opened and laid flat, can substitute. They are especially eye-arresting if set down in an interesting geometric pattern over a tablecloth. This idea is particularly practical if you have an old cloth that you love which shows wear or tear from previous parties. I find baskets also extremely useful. I line them with foil, plastic, or napkins and fill them with breads, appetizers, or bowls of salads. The wicker ones are inexpensive, light, and decorative.

Lighting and music are integral parts of setting the scene. Soft lighting and lots of inexpensive votive candles dispersed around the room, combined with strains of Frank Sinatra or even classical music, create a romantic dining environment for the *Valentine's Dinner for Lovers* or *Dining European*. Upbeat rock music and bright lights befit the *Carbo-Loading Pasta Party* or the *First Night of the Diet*, giving you an extra charge for the upcoming race or diet.

A WORD ABOUT SEASONING

In all the recipes in this book, with the exception of the baked desserts and breads, I have recommended salt and freshly ground pepper to taste. Medical evidence suggests that salt is not very good for us. I've therefore left the choice open to the reader. Freshly ground pepper, lemon juice, and fresh herbs are my substitutes for heightening flavor.

Festive Breakfasts and Brunches

1. **An Intimate Breakfast in Bed**
   Orange Smash
   Berry-Filled Melon
   Honey French Toast
   Café Cinnamon

2. **Breakfast Prepared the Night Before**
   Iced Fruit Juice
   Memorable Breakfast Soufflé
   Baked Bacon
   *Brioches or Croissants
   Café au Lait

3. **Business Breakfast**
   Fruit Compote
   Infallible Cheese Soufflé
   *Breakfast Sausages
   Strawberry Loaf
   Strawberry-Honey Butter

4. **Mexican Fiesta Brunch**
   Sangrita
   Melon Wedges with Lemon and Lime
   Huevos a la Mexicana
   Ensalada
   *Warmed Corn Tortillas

5. **Sunday Football Brunch**
   Glazed Corn Beef
   Zucchini Pancakes
   Hot Irish Bread
   Chocolate Chip Squares
   *Fresh Fruit and Assorted Cheeses

6. **Picnic on the Grass**
   Chilled Guacamole Soup
   Sesame Chicken
   Icy Shrimp
   Cold Northern Italian Stuffed Tomatoes
   Apple-Nut Cake

7. **A Casual Brunch Buffet**
   Stuffed Cheese Bread
   Southern-Style Baked Ham
   Mustard Sauce
   Chutneyed Rice Salad
   Orange-Apricot Bread
   Orange-Honey Butter (see p. 253)

8. **A Midnight Breakfast**
   *Juices
   Joe's Special
   Smoked Salmon Spread
   Prosciutto Butter
   *Bagels
   Almond Pound Cake
   *Fresh Fruit

* Not a recipe

I THOROUGHLY ENJOY daytime entertaining, either early for breakfast or later for brunch. I find it a perfect way to give an informal or casual party easily, using creative food ideas and the simplest of surroundings.

The breakfast and brunches in this chapter have been set up to be assembled with a minimum of effort. Some—the *Business Breakfast*, *Casual Brunch Buffet*, and *Breakfast Prepared the Night Before*—can be totally prepared in advance. The others can be organized and prepped the day before, to be finished off early in the morning.

Not only do these menus make for relaxed celebrations, but they are also inexpensive ways to entertain, since economical ingredients like eggs, cheese, and salads are especially featured. Desserts are not essential here and are replaced with fruit compotes, light drinks, and a wonderful variety of sweet breads and cakes that have fruits and nuts as their primary ingredients.

Often breakfasts and brunches can revolve around an outdoor or indoor sporting event. The *Picnic on the Grass* can be set before a tennis match, golf game, or even a Little League game. The *Sunday Football Brunch* centers on indoor quarterbacks. It features hearty food for this often full-day affair of game after game after game. An assortment of extra bread, fruit, cheese, crackers, and desserts is a good idea for guests who manage to stay right through dinner.

The *Business Breakfast* is the only formal daytime event. Like the others, it can be assembled the day before. The food can be prepared and the table completely set. It's a wonderfully innovative way to conduct business in a congenial and hospitable environment—a positive step in entertaining new business acquaintances or making vital business decisions.

The *Mexican Fiesta Brunch* is a festive and colorful daytime party, no matter what the hour.

Breakfast Prepared the Night Before is a lifesaver for those who value weekend sleep. The soufflé can be prepared ahead and popped into the oven the next morning. Even the bacon is baked to save on messy cleanups.

A *Casual Brunch Buffet* consists of foods that travel well to a weekend home, on a trip, and as a house gift, or can be ready for drop-in weekend guests. Once the dishes are prepared, the relaxing part of the weekend can be thoroughly enjoyed. A *Midnight Breakfast* helps us make that late-night transition just a little bit easier with a variety of comforting foods.

Read the recipes for each menu carefully and plan the preparation accordingly. Baked desserts or breads can be cooked and frozen ahead of time. Butters and some sauces can be whipped up several days in advance. Even the fruit compotes can be cut up beforehand, covered, and stored overnight in the refrigerator.

The most fun about breakfast and brunch entertaining is being creative with the table settings. *An Intimate Breakfast in Bed* can be set on trays with a simple flower placed across each tray.

A few guidelines for early-morning entertaining: Have plenty of coffee, both decaffeinated and regular, on hand to wake up your sleepy crowd. A pot of hot water with assorted tea bags, or both regular and herbal varieties, is another thoughtful gesture.

An Intimate Breakfast in Bed

SERVES: 2
Orange Smash
Berry-Filled Melon
Honey French Toast
Café Cinnamon

The very idea of breakfast in bed is cozy and romantic. It's an ideal way to surprise your special someone on an anniversary morning—or any other time you want to say "I love you" in a special way.

But some people shy away from this luxurious treat, haunted by memories of cold toast, soggy cereal, and gelatinous lukewarm eggs. So here are some delicious alternatives for you—delicacies that must have been invented with breakfast in bed in mind.

The Honey French Toast is a delectable, nutty variation on an old favorite. It can be assembled in a matter of minutes and allowed to soak while the rest of the breakfast is prepared.

The Berry-Filled Melon may be prepared the night before. Just be sure to cover it tightly to keep the melon from absorbing odors.

Mix your Orange Smash beverage moments before serving so that the orange juice won't turn bitter. Meanwhile, brew a pot of coffee for the Café Cinnamon, or even a pot of your favorite tea.

The key to serving breakfast in bed is to keep things simple, uncluttered, and very, very pretty. Trays are a necessity, and bed trays work best by far. Line them with doilies or napkins for a delicate bit of luxury.

Flowers add color and a pleasant aroma. Standing elegantly in a bud vase, they take up little space. Better still, use an egg cup—it's harder to tip over. Or simply lay a single rose across each tray. You might even let a love note peek out from under the napkin or flower.

By all means, use your best china, glasses, and flatware to make this a truly special celebration.

Orange Smash

SERVES: 2
Preparation time: 5 minutes

The Ingredients:

- 12 ounces chilled orange juice
- 2 ounces vodka
- 2 teaspoons Grand Marnier
- ½ teaspoon Grenadine

The Steps:

1. In small pitcher, mix ingredients and stir until smooth.
2. Serve over ice.

Variations:

Tequila can be substituted for the vodka

Pineapple juice can be substituted for the orange juice.

For a nonalcoholic version, substitute Iced Fruit Juice (see page 16).

Berry-Filled Melon

SERVES: 2
Preparation time: 5 minutes
Chilling time: 1–2 hours

The Ingredients:

1 ripe cantaloupe, chilled
1 pint fresh blueberries
3 tablespoons Kirsch or Kirschwasser
3 tablespoons confectioner's sugar
1 teaspoon lime juice

The Steps:

1. Slice melons in half and scoop out seeds.
2. In bowl, gently toss berries with Kirsch, sugar, and lime juice.
3. Fill centers of melon halves with berries; chill for 1–2 hours prior to serving.

Variations:

Strawberries, raspberries, blackberries, or any other seasonal fruits can be substituted for blueberries.

Honeydew, Crenshaw, or any seasonal melon can be used.

Make-It-Easy Tips:

√ The recipe can be assembled earlier, covered, and refrigerated until ready to serve.

√ To keep melon half upright, cut a small piece from bottom.

√ Melons taste better when chilled; they need at least 36–48 hours to properly chill through the center.

Honey French Toast

SERVES: 2
Preparation time: 10 minutes
Cooking time: 5–7 minutes

The Ingredients:

½ cup milk
2 eggs
½ teaspoon cinnamon
½ teaspoon vanilla extract
4 slices sourdough bread, sliced 1″ thick
1 tablespoon unsalted butter
1 tablespoon vegetable oil

Topping:

3 tablespoons dairy sour cream
3 tablespoons honey
Chopped pecans (optional)

The Steps:

1. Whisk together milk, eggs, cinnamon, and vanilla until smooth.
2. Dip both sides of bread in mixture until soaked on both sides.
3. In large skillet, heat butter and oil together and sauté bread on both sides, about 2 minutes per side, or until golden brown.
4. In small bowl, whisk sour cream and honey together and serve over crisp French toast sprinkled with chopped pecans, if desired.

Variation:

Plain white bread, egg bread, or even raisin bread can be substituted for sourdough.

Make-It-Easy Tips:

√ Oil is added to butter to keep the French toast from burning.

√ When measuring sticky liquids like honey, wipe measuring spoon with oil or wash in very hot water to allow honey to freely fall off spoon.

Café Cinnamon

SERVES: 2
Preparation time: 5–10 minutes

The Ingredients:

1½ cups strong hot coffee
2 cinnamon sticks
½ cup sweetened whipped cream
½ teaspoon cinnamon
Accompaniment: Cinnamon sticks

The Steps:

1. Place hot coffee in 2 cups or mugs and add cinnamon sticks.
2. Top with sweetened whipped cream, sprinkle with cinnamon, and serve immediately with cinnamon-stick stirrers.

Variation:

½ cup hot milk can be added to coffee in cups for Café au Lait.

Make-It-Easy Tip:

√ If drip coffee maker is used, place a cinnamon stick in glass carafe during brewing cycle for added flavor.

Breakfast Prepared the Night Before

SERVES: 10
Iced Fruit Juice
Memorable Breakfast Soufflé
Baked Bacon
*Brioches or Croissants
Café au Lait

This breakfast is for a special occasion. It is especially appropriate when you're preparing a lively crowd for a day of skiing, hiking, fishing, or any other pleasurable activity. These recipes, assembled the night before, get

* Not a recipe.

your day off to an early start with a hearty, delicious meal that looks company-pretty on your table.

A cheerful table, decked out in lively, sunny colors, helps inject a mood of good feeling. Save steps in the morning by setting the table the night before. Better yet, get some "volunteers" to help while you assemble breakfast.

Bright place mats or crepe paper runners are a quick way to set a good-morning mood. Alternate colors for a fresh look and carry the color scheme to your napkins. A quick way to add splashes of sunshine is to easily fold each napkin into a lily shape fitted into a napkin ring. With the right side down, fold each napkin into quarters. Turn over with decorative or ornamental point up. (If there's no decorative tip, simply turn over). Fold back left and right corners, pleat softly and slip into napkin rings. (See illustration.)

Even a floral centerpiece can be prepared the night before and still look fresh. Cut blossoms with the stems very short, then float them in a sparkling glass bowl of water. Or refrigerate a bouquet of daisies overnight to keep it fresh until morning.

The Breakfast Soufflé has two big advantages. It can be assembled hours before baking—and it won't collapse even when a heavy-footed guest jumps out of bed in the morning. Bake it in one large casserole or in easy individual servings. Either way, it's pretty and tasty enough to tempt even the breakfast-skippers in your house.

Cooking the bacon in the oven is an extra help when you have a crowd to feed. The strips of bacon can be separated, arranged for baking, and refrigerated the night before. Then just pop them into the oven in the morning to bake with a minimum of attention. If you have only one

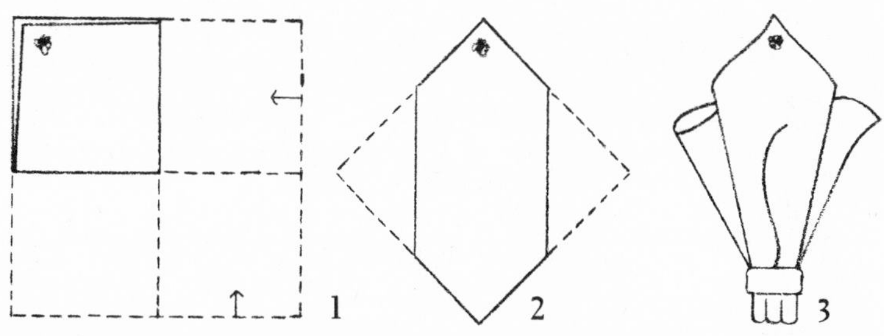

The Lily
1. With right side down, fold into quarters. 2. Turn over with ornamented point up. 3. Fold back L. and R. corners. 4. Pleat softly and even folds to shape. 5. Slip on napkin ring.

oven, prepare the bacon until almost crisp, remove excess grease, and set aside while the soufflé is baking. Once the soufflé is golden and puffed, place the bacon back into a hot oven, or even under a broiler, to just crisp before serving.

I always provide a supply of breakfast rolls such as brioches and croissants for those who prefer a Continental breakfast or are very hungry.

The Iced Fruit Juice is a cooling and refreshing morning treat. The juice can be poured and refrigerated in pitchers the night before. Tightly cover the juice to preserve the sweet taste. Just before serving time, pop the frozen fruit into each glass for a unique touch.

Café au Lait is a quick way to turn your morning coffee into a hearty beverage. Having all the ingredients measured in advance saves time in the morning. Top it with cinnamon for a warming beginning to an active weekend.

Iced Fruit Juice

SERVES: 10
Preparation time: 5 minutes

This refreshing combination of juice mixed with iced fruit can be assembled in a matter of minutes.

The Ingredients:

2 quarts orange juice
1 cup frozen unsweetened strawberries
1 cup frozen unsweetened peaches

The Steps:

1. Pour juice into pitcher and chill well.
2. At serving time, add iced fruit and serve immediately.

Variations:

Any variety of juice can be substituted for this morning refresher. Try pineapple, pear, apple, apricot, or even papaya.

Any variety of frozen fruit can be substituted to taste.

Make-It-Easy Tip:

√ To freeze fresh fruit easily, place cut up fruit on cookie sheet and freeze until firm. Place in airtight bag and store in freezer.

Memorable Breakfast Soufflé

SERVES: 10
Preparation time: 20 minutes
Cooking time: 35–40 minutes

The Ingredients:

1 cup dairy sour cream
¾ cup all-purpose flour
¼ pound butter, softened to room temperature
⅓ cup sugar
¼ cup orange juice
4 large eggs
1½ teaspoons baking powder
1 teaspoon grated orange rind
1 teaspoon vanilla extract
⅛ teaspoon cinnamon
⅛ teaspoon ground nutmeg
Pinch of salt

Filling:

8 ounces cream cheese
2 tablespoons dairy sour cream
2 tablespoons honey

Instant Apricot Sauce

1 12-ounce jar apricot preserves
1–2 tablespoons Grand Marnier or other orange liqueur

The Steps:

1. Preheat oven to 375°. Lightly butter, or spray with nonaerosol vegetable shortening, 10 small ramekin dishes or oven-proof custard cups.

2. In container of blender, food processor, or electric mixer, place sour cream, flour, butter, sugar, orange juice, eggs, baking powder, orange rind, vanilla extract, cinnamon, nutmeg, and salt. Beat until combined.
3. Empty batter into separate bowl and, without cleaning container, blend cream cheese, sour cream, and honey together until smooth.
4. Distribute half of batter in bottom of prepared dishes, add dollop of cheese mixture, and top with remaining batter. (Can be prepared ahead to this point, covered, and refrigerated until ready to bake.)
5. Place dishes on cookie sheet and bake for 35–40 minutes or until puffed and golden brown.
6. In small saucepan, melt apricot preserves over medium high heat. Add Grand Marnier or other orange liqueur and heat until hot and bubbly.
7. Serve hot soufflé immediately, topped with apricot sauce.

Variations:

Bake soufflé in one 9″ x 13″ x 2″ Pyrex baking dish (square or round) for 45–50 minutes or until puffed and golden.

Substitute raspberry, strawberry, blueberry, cherry, peach, or whatever fruit preserves desired for the sauce.

The sauce may be varied if desired. Try Crème de Cassis with blueberry preserves, or Cherry Herring with cherry preserves.

Make-It-Easy Tips:

√ The American Egg Board suggests that eggs be stored in their carton in the refrigerator—not in the egg tray that most refrigerators have. The carton protects the eggs from air and odors that can seep in through the delicate shell.

√ Avoid any raw eggs that are cracked. They can be unhealthy and must be discarded.

Baked Bacon

SERVES: 10
Preparation Time: 5 minutes
Cooking time: 12–15 minutes

The easiest way to cook bacon for a large group is to bake it in the oven, avoiding the constant monitoring usually needed to prevent burning and messy cleanup chores.

The Ingredients:

3 pounds bacon, regular sliced

The Steps:

1. Preheat oven to 400°.
2. Arrange cold bacon strips, fat edges overlapping, on broiler rack or cake rack set in roasting pan.
3. Bake for 12–15 minutes, uncovered and without turning, until crisp and brown.
4. Drain on paper towels and serve warm.

Variation:

Bacon can also be broiled for 2–3 minutes per side, or until crisp. Watch carefully to avoid burning.

Make-It-Easy Tips:

√ To reheat baked bacon, place on brown paper in 250°–300° oven for 5–10 minutes to warm through and get rid of excess grease.

√ Slab bacon (country-cured smoked pork) is often less expensive than presliced bacon, and butchers will slice it to your specifications.

√ Because of its high fat content, fresh sliced bacon stores poorly in the refrigerator. Freeze leftover bacon for longer storage.

√ Remember to line pan with aluminum foil to save on cleanup chores.

Café au Lait

SERVES: 10
Preparation time: 5 minutes

The Ingredients:

8 cups whole milk
8 cups strong freshly brewed coffee
Accompaniments: Cinnamon, cinnamon sticks

The Steps:

1. In large saucepan, scald milk by heating over medium heat until bubbles just begin to appear around edges. (Do not boil). Pour into pitcher.
2. Pour milk and coffee at same time into coffee cups. Serve immediately, sprinkled with cinnamon and with cinnamon stick stirrers.

Variation:

Decaffeinated coffee can be substituted for regular coffee.

Make-It-Easy Tips:

√ Milk can be scalded over boiling water in top of double boiler without having to worry about scorching. Scalding makes milk richer in taste.

√ A heated pitcher keeps the milk warm while pouring with the hot coffee.

Business Breakfast

SERVES: 8
Fruit Compote
Infallible Cheese Soufflé
Breakfast Sausages
Strawberry Loaf
Strawberry-Honey Butter

Here is a relatively new concept: an at-home business meeting that also works as a breakfast or brunch. It combines business with an informality that's particularly good for getting acquainted with new associates or making important decisions.

It's especially important that you yourself come across in a professional manner. That means not spending so much time preparing and serving that you have no time to talk business.

Doing as much in advance as possible lets you arrive at the table cool, calm, and relaxed. Nearly every item on this menu can be assembled the night before. Only the sausages need a last-minute sauté.

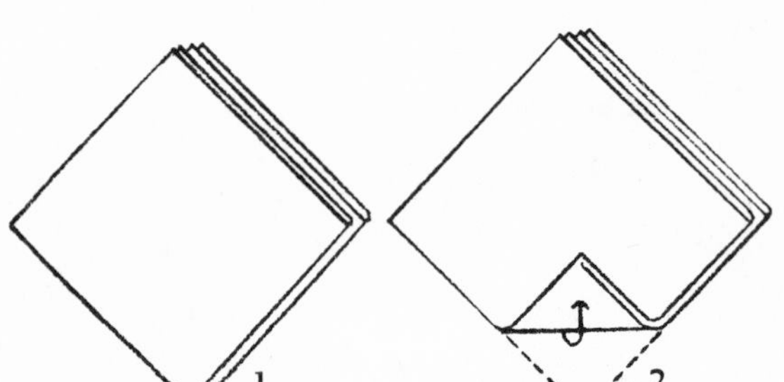

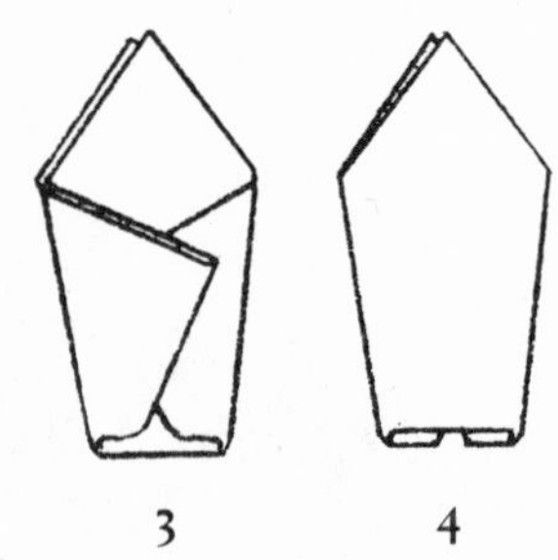

Folded Napkin
1. Fold the napkin into quarters. 2. Turn up the bottom corner. 3. Fold into thirds. 4. Turn the napkin over and lay it flat.

It's also a good idea to make up a pot of coffee, and perhaps a pot of tea besides. Strong varieties of coffee and fancy teas like Earl Grey or English Breakfast tea will complement the creamy cheese soufflé and the berry-sweet taste of the compote and strawberry loaf.

Both the compote and cheese soufflé are best served in individual dishes. This adds extra neatness and efficiency in serving—and cuts the risk of spilling sauce on someone's suit.

The emphasis here is on balancing business with hospitality. Blue, white, and gray are soft, pretty, and appropriately conservative colors for tablecloth and napkins. Napkins should be folded into quarters. Turn the bottom corner up, then fold into thirds. Turn the napkin over flat onto each plate. (See illustration.)

A cluster of bud vases filled with brightly colored flowers adds a note of good-morning freshness to the table. But you might also place a large, flat basket containing the *Wall Street Journal*, *Business Week*, *Fortune*, and other business magazines, neatly arranged, on the table.

The Strawberry Loaf will look neat and attractive already sliced and served on a breadboard or in a napkin-lined basket. The Strawberry-Honey Butter can be served in a mound of small scoops, shaped in a mold, or in a small crock.

Fruit Compote

SERVES: 8
Preparation time: 10 minutes
Chilling time: 2 hours

The Ingredients:

3 seedless oranges, peeled
1 20-ounce package frozen unsweetened peaches, thawed
1 tablespoon orange liqueur (Grand Marnier, Curaçao) (optional)
1 10-ounce package sweetened raspberries, thawed
Garnish: ⅓ cup pine nuts

The Steps:

1. Slice oranges and place in bowl. Drain peaches and add liqueur, if desired. Chill in refrigerator for 2 hours.
2. In food processor or blender, puree raspberries with liquid; strain.
3. Spoon oranges and peaches into individual dishes, top with raspberry puree, sprinkle with pine nuts, and serve.

Variation:

Substitute 1 tablespoon lemon juice for liqueur.

Make-It-Easy Tip:

√ To easily remove peel and membrane that cling to them, place oranges in bowl of boiling water; allow to stand 5 minutes, then peel.

Infallible Cheese Soufflé

SERVES: 8
Preparation time: 5–10 minutes
Cooking time: 50–55 minutes

This incredibly easy soufflé can be prepared in minutes in a food processor or blender and even assembled a day in advance.

The Ingredients:

10 slices white, whole wheat, egg, or sourdough bread (crusts removed)
½ pound sharp Cheddar cheese, roughly diced
2 cups whole milk
4 eggs
3 tablespoons unsalted butter, melted
1 teaspoon Worcestershire sauce
1 teaspoon Dijon mustard
½ teaspoon dry mustard
Salt and freshly ground pepper to taste

The Steps:

1. Preheat oven to 375°. Generously butter 8 ramekins or custard dishes or 1½ quart soufflé dish.
2. Place ingredients in food processor or blender (if necessary, do in 2 batches) and process until smooth.
3. Pour into small dishes or casserole, place on cookie sheet, and bake for 40–45 minutes for small dishes or 50–55 minutes for large casserole, or until set.

Variation:

Swiss, English Cheshire, or Monterey Jack cheese can be substituted for the Cheddar.

Make-It-Easy Tips:

√ Once cut, wrap cheese in aluminum foil, which keeps odors in and prevents drying out.

√ If assembling in advance, store in refrigerator, and bring to room temperature for 1 hour prior to baking.

Strawberry Loaf

YIELD: one 9″ loaf
Preparation time: 20 minutes
Cooking time: 1 hour

The Ingredients:

1½ cups all purpose flour
1 cup granulated sugar
1½ teaspoons cinnamon
½ teaspoon baking soda
½ teaspoon salt
2 eggs
⅔ cup vegetable oil
¾ cup chopped walnuts
1 heaping basket fresh strawberries, hulled and sliced

The Steps:

1. Preheat oven to 350°. Generously butter 9″ x 5″ x 3″ loaf pan.
2. Sift flour with sugar, cinnamon, baking soda, and salt.
3. In large bowl, beat eggs; add oil and sifted dry ingredients; stir until just mixed; stir in nuts and very gently fold in berries. Pour into prepared pan and bake for 60 minutes, or until inserted cake tester comes out clean.
4. Remove from oven and wait until completely cold before removing from pan.

Variation:

1 8-ounce package frozen strawberries, thawed but undrained, can be substituted for fresh.

Make-It-Easy Tips:

√ Do not buy strawberries more than a day or two in advance.
√ Do not wash until just before using.
√ Wash strawberries before hulling to prevent excess moisture from being absorbed once opened.

Strawberry-Honey Butter

YIELD: 2½ cups
Preparation time: 5–10 minutes

Strawberry-honey butter makes a wonderful topping for breads, waffles, and pancakes, or it can be used as a spread over warm croissants for breakfast. The recipe was inspired by a similar spread served at the San Ysidro Ranch in Montecito, California.

The Ingredients:

Strawberry Puree

10 medium-size ripe strawberries
3 tablespoons honey

1 pound unsalted butter, well chilled

The Steps:

1. Puree strawberries with honey in food processor or blender. Rinse out bowl or blender container and dry well.
2. Cut well-chilled butter into chunks, place in food processor or blender, and blend until light and whipped.
3. Add puree, a few tablespoons at a time, until butter is smooth and light pink in color.
4. Serve immediately in small round scoops, or chill in small mold and slice as needed.

Variations:

Fresh raspberries can be substituted for strawberries.

1 tablespoon Grand Marnier and 2 tablespoons powdered sugar can be substituted for honey.

Make-It-Easy Tips:

√ The butter must be well chilled or the mixture will separate.

√ Berry puree can be prepared well in advance and chilled until ready to use.

Mexican Fiesta Brunch

SERVES: 10–12
Sangrita (Mexican Bloody Mary)
Melon Wedges with Lemon and Lime
Huevos a la Mexicana
Ensalada
***Warmed Corn Tortillas**

Cooking Mexican style is a fabulous way to spice up breakfast standbys like eggs, cheese, and fruit. Add to that some lively, south-of-the-border color, and you have a brunch that says Wake Up to all your senses!

Take your choice of color schemes. You can choose the blue, pink, purple, and yellow of a piñata or the red, orange, yellow, and green of the foods themselves. Any bright cloth, including a sheet, can cover the table. Tea towels make excellent napkins and can be tied with thick, colorful yarn. Runners of crepe paper in hot spicy colors add to the fiesta look.

A bowl, basket, or even a large clay flowerpot can hold a variety of

* Not a recipe

fruits and vegetables for a centerpiece. You could use green, red, and yellow peppers, tomatoes, lemons, limes, avocados, gourds, or even red, white, and yellow onions. Or try filling flowerpots with bunches of piñata-colored paper flowers. Any dishes or utensils with the look of terra-cotta will fit right in, as will wooden salad bowls and spoons.

The Sangrita may be prepared through Step 2 the night before and left to chill overnight. Serve it in glasses or mugs—whichever you have plenty of.

Assemble the Huevos a la Mexicana in the morning. While it bakes, you have plenty of time to prepare the rest of your brunch. At the table, a lazy Susan is a big help for serving the toppings for the eggs—sour cream, salsa, bacon bits, and olives. Wrap the tortillas in aluminum foil and warm them in a 350° oven. Serve them in a large basket, wrapped in a colorful towel or napkin to keep them warm. Accompany the tortillas with lots of whipped sweet butter.

If you're clearly in an adventurous, fiesta state of mind, you might even complete the mood with some mariachi background music as guests arrive.

Sangrita

SERVES: 10–12
Preparation time: 10 minutes
Chilling time: 2–3 hours

A Sangrita is a Mexican version of a Bloody Mary. Traditionally, a Sangrita is imbibed by sipping alternately with a glass of tequila and halved limes and salt on the side to suck on between sips. In this version, 2 ounces of tequila to 6 ounces of the Sangrita are blended, then served well chilled.

The Ingredients:

48 ounces tomato juice
2¼ cups fresh orange juice (about 6–7 oranges)
6 tablespoons fresh lemon juice (about 2 lemons)

1¼ cup fresh lime juice (about 4 limes)
2 tablespoons minced onion
4 teaspoons sugar
1 tablespoon chili powder
2 teaspoons Worcestershire sauce
2 teaspoons white horseradish
Cayenne pepper to taste
Tabasco to taste
Salt and freshly ground pepper to taste
Tequila
Lime slices

The Steps:

1. Place all ingredients except tequila and lime slices in blender or food processor; blend until smooth. (If using blender, do in several batches.
2. Chill Sangrita 2–3 hours in pitcher or large bottle.
3. At serving time, blend 2 ounces of tequila, or to taste, with 6 ounces of Sangrita mixture. Serve in chilled glass garnished with slices of lime.

Variations:

The glasses may be chilled and the rims dipped in salt for an attractive presentation.

Sangrita may be served over ice if you prefer.

Tequila can be omitted if desired.

Make-It-Easy Tips:

√ The Sangrita may be prepared several days in advance and kept chilled in the refrigerator.

√ To increase the amount of juice and pulp from citrus fruits, keep at room temperature and then place fruits on a flat surface and roll with hand using slight pressure for a few seconds; then juice.

Melon Wedges with Lemon and Lime

SERVES: 10–12
Preparation time: 10 minutes
Chilling time: 2 hours

The easiest method of serving melons is cut into quarters or eighths, seeds removed, and simply garnished with lemons or limes.

The Ingredients:

2 cantaloupes
2 honeydew melons
1 lemon
1 lime

The Steps:

1. Slice melons into quarters or eighths, scoop out and discard seeds, and alternate attractively on large platter.
2. Surround with wedges of lemon and lime; cover tightly and chill for 2 hours or until ready to serve.

Variations:

If cantaloupes or honeydews are unavailable, substitute Casaba, Crenshaw, Persian, Santa Claus, Spanish, Sharlyn, or whatever melons are ripe and available.

If melons are totally out of season, prepare a simple fruit platter of seasonal fruits such as sliced oranges, kiwis, apples, pears, bananas, berries, etc. Remember to cover apples, pears, and bananas with a sprinkling of lemon juice to prevent discoloration.

Make-It-Easy Tips:

√ To avoid chilling step, keep melons in refrigerator for 2 days prior to serving. It takes at least 24–36 hours for cold to penetrate the center of a melon.

√ Cover cut melons tightly. Once cut, they tend to absorb other odors in the refrigerator.

Huevos a la Mexicana

SERVES: 10–12
Preparation time: 10–15 minutes
Cooking time: 50–60 minutes

Serve these baked eggs with mild or spicy salsa as desired.

The Ingredients:

2 cups (½ pound) shredded Cheddar cheese
2 cups (½ pound) shredded Monterey Jack cheese
1 7-ounce can diced green chilies, drained
1 2-ounce jar diced pimientos, drained
2 cups half-and-half
2 cups whole milk
1 cup all-purpose flour
6 eggs
Salt and freshly ground pepper to taste
Accompaniments: Spicy or mild salsa (see page 264), dairy sour cream, bacon bits, and sliced ripe olives

The Steps:

1. Preheat oven to 350°. Generously butter a 9″ x 13″ x 2″ baking dish.
2. In large bowl, mix cheese with chilies and pimientos; combine and place on bottom of dish.
3. In bowl, whisk half-and-half, milk, flour, eggs, salt, and pepper until smooth; pour over cheese.
4. Bake for 50–60 minutes or until set in center and lightly golden.
5. Serve immediately with spicy or mild salsa, sour cream, bacon bits, and olives.

Variations:

All Cheddar or all Monterey Jack cheese can be substituted for the combination.

Diced bacon bits, chopped scallion greens, or sliced ripe olives can be added in Step 2 to taste.

Make-It-Easy Tips:

√ Make sure soft cheese like Monterey Jack is thoroughly chilled before grating.

Ensalada

SERVES: 10–12
Preparation time: 15 minutes

The Ingredients:

1 large head lettuce, shredded
4 tomatoes, cut into small wedges
4 scallions thinly sliced (green and white parts included)
1 2.2-ounce can sliced ripe olives
¾ cup grated Cheddar cheese

Avocado Dressing:

1 ripe avocado, peeled and seeded
¼ cup mayonnaise
2 tablespoons lemon juice
1 scallion, cut in small pieces
1 tablespoon honey
½ teaspoon chili powder
½ teaspoon finely minced garlic
⅛ teaspoon cayenne pepper
3 or 4 shakes Tabasco
Salt to taste
Garnish: Dairy sour cream, crushed tortilla chips

The Steps:

1. In large salad bowl, place lettuce, top with tomatoes, scallions, ripe olives, and sprinkling of cheese.
2. In food processor or blender, process dressing ingredients until smooth.
3. Drizzle dressing on top of salad, garnish with sour cream and chips and serve.

Variations:

Green pepper strips, shredded carrots, sliced radishes, and other salad ingredients can be added.

Make-It-Easy Tips:

√ To prepare homemade tortilla chips, cut flour or corn tortillas into wedges with kitchen scissors, fry in hot vegetable oil until crisp and golden, drain on paper towels, and salt as desired. (Tortilla chips can also be baked in 400° oven for 10 minutes or until crisp.)

Sunday Football Brunch

SERVES: 8
Glazed Corned Beef
Zucchini Pancakes
Hot Irish Bread
Chocolate Chip Squares
*** Fresh Fruit and Assorted Cheeses**

One thing's certain about football fans—their minds are on the game, not the decor. And they'll surely work up an appetite from their armchairs as ravenous as any quarterback on the field. So keep the table-trimming simple and serve lots of solid, no-nonsense food. And since there's no rule against the cook enjoying the game, the meal shouldn't require a lot of fuss.

You might be able to persuade folks to sit at the table at half-time, but if they're replay fans or overly fond of John Philip Sousa, serve this meal buffet-style and let them hurry back to the TV. It's a one-fork meal easily balanced on one's lap, with or without a tray.

Of course, if you want to get into the spirit of the day even more, why not dress up your table with these unusual ideas—the football fans will enjoy it even if they're too glued to the TV to say so. Spread a stadium blanket across the table—protected with placements or runners. Or cover the table with a green cloth (burlap or felt work well too). Then tape or pin some white yard lines on the cloth with a big paper "50" in the middle. Top it off with a football—unless your crowd is likely to get carried away with an indoor impromptu game.

The Glazed Corned Beef, Zucchini Pancakes, and Hot Irish Bread with the addition of a tossed green salad make a simple, hearty, and uncluttered buffet. A lazy Susan helps organize condiments like mustard, sour cream, and chives, but no one will mind if you dollop and mound them into saucers or small dishes. Forks wrapped in napkins and laid neatly in a row are quick and easy to grab.

* Not a recipe

If you're not a fan yourself, the pancakes can be served throughout the day, cooked in relays and served on salad plates. Just be prepared for a run on the kitchen during a time-out. A round of pancakes can be done in advance and kept warm on brown paper in a slow oven.

The Hot Irish Bread, like almost any bread, is most delicious served fresh from the oven, cooled just enough for easy handling. But it can be baked ahead and rewarmed if you like—the football fans won't mind a bit. Serve it already sliced on a breadboard, or in a basket. Nestling it in napkins or a tea towel helps keep it warm. Or follow this special tip: Put one napkin in the bottom of the basket, place a piece of foil warmed in the oven next, and follow with another napkin on top. The foil will insulate and help keep the bread warm. Whipping the butter with an electric mixer, food processor, or blender lets impatient fans spread it quickly.

Top off the day's goodies with Chocolate Chip Squares and a large bowl of fresh fruit and assorted cheeses. The squares can be baked ahead of time, are faster to make than cookies, and make perfect finger food. And don't forget an extra supply of assorted breads and crackers to have on hand for guests who manage to stay through dinner.

One more tip: Make sure to have plenty of soft drinks or beer on hand all day—it's amazing what a thirst people can work up from sitting down.

Glazed Corned Beef

SERVES: 8
Preparation time: 10 minutes
Cooking time: 45 minutes

The Ingredients:

1 cooked 4-pound brisket of corned beef
1/4 cup dark brown sugar, firmly packed
2 tablespoons Dijon mustard
1 cup orange juice
Accompaniment: Mustard sauce (see page 50)

The Steps:

1. Preheat oven to 325°.
2. Place corned beef in shallow roasting pan and score fat by making crisscross slashes with paring knife.

3. Combine sugar with mustard; paint over top of corned beef.
4. Pour juice into pan and bake for 45 minutes, basting occasionally.
5. Serve hot, sliced with Mustard Sauce.

Variation:

An assortment of interesting mustards make a wonderful accompaniment.

Make-It-Easy Tip:

√ To boil uncooked corned beef, cover with cold water, bring to a boil, cover and cook over low heat 3 hours. Allow to cool ½ hour in the liquid, drain, and proceed with the recipe.

Zucchini Pancakes

YIELD: 20–24 pancakes
Preparation time: 15 minutes
Cooking time: 5 minutes

These small round variations on the potato pancake make a wonderful brunch dish topped with sour cream and chives, or they can be served as a side dish for roast meats or poultry.

The Ingredients:

3 cups (1¼–1½ pounds) grated zucchini
½ cup all-purpose flour
½ cup freshly grated parmesan cheese
½ cup mayonnaise
¼ cup finely chopped scallions (green and white parts included)
4 eggs, lightly beaten
1 teaspoon lemon juice
Salt and freshly ground pepper to taste
2 tablespoons vegetable oil (or more)
1 tablespoon butter (or more)
Garnish: Dairy sour cream and chopped chives or scallion greens

The Steps:

1. Place grated zucchini between layers of paper towels and blot dry.
2. In large bowl, combine zucchini with flour, Parmesan, mayonnaise, scallions, eggs, lemon juice, and salt and freshly ground pepper to taste; mix until smooth batter is formed.
3. On griddle or in large skillet, heat oil and butter, and spoon out 2 tablespoons batter for each pancake.
4. Brown well on each side for 2 minutes, flattening out with spatula on second side. Drain for a minute on paper towels to avoid excess grease.
5. Finish up remaining batter, adding more oil and butter as necessary.
6. Serve hot garnished with sour cream and chives.

Variation:

Pancakes can be topped with Italian tomato sauce and grated Parmesan cheese, or served Mexican-style with guacamole, sour cream, and salsa.

Make-It-Easy Tips:

√ Zucchini may also be squeezed through several layers of cheesecloth to extract excess moisture and keep batter a smooth texture.

√ As you prepare pancakes, keep the finished ones hot in a warm oven on sheets of brown paper to absorb the excess grease.

√ Zucchini are at their best when only 6–8 inches long. The larger sizes are often tasteless, with a woody texture.

Hot Irish Bread

YIELD: 8″–9″ round loaf
Preparation time: 15 minutes
Cooking time: 50–55 minutes

Hot Irish Bread is best baked the traditional way, in a cast-iron skillet.

The Ingredients:

4 cups all-purpose flour
¾ cup sugar

4 teaspoons baking powder
½ teaspoon salt
¼ pound unsalted butter
1½ cups whole milk
1 cup currants
2 eggs
1 tablespoon caraway seeds
Accompaniment: Whipped sweet butter

The Steps:

1. Preheat oven to 350°. Generously butter 8″–9″ cast-iron skillet, 9″ round cake pan, or similar size soufflé dish.
2. In large bowl, sift flour, sugar, baking powder, and salt together.
3. With electric beater, or by hand, cut in butter until crumbly.
4. Add milk, currants, eggs, and caraway seeds; mix well to make a soft dough.
5. Spoon into prepared skillet and make impression on top of loaf in sign of cross (⅛″ deep). Bake for 50–55 minutes, or until inserted knife comes out clean.
6. Remove from oven, allow to sit for 5 minutes, and turn out onto rack. Allow to cool an additional 5–10 minutes before slicing.
7. Serve warm with whipped sweet butter.

Variations:

Leftover Irish bread may be rewarmed or even toasted, sliced, and served with whipped sweet butter.

Raisins can be substituted for currants.

Reduce milk by ¼ cup and add ¼ cup Irish whiskey if desired.

Make-It-Easy Tips:

√ After opening a package of currants, store in refrigerator.

√ Store caraway seeds, as with any other spice, in a dark, cool area. They will keep for about a year. If seeds begin to harden, they are still good to use in cooking or baking.

Chocolate Chip Squares

YIELD: 24–36 cookies
Preparation time: 15 minutes
Cooking time: 20–25 minutes

The Ingredients:

- ¾ cup (1½ sticks) unsalted butter, softened
- 1 cup dark brown sugar, firmly packed
- 1 egg, lightly beaten
- 1 teaspoon vanilla extract
- 1½ cups all-purpose flour
- ½ teaspoon baking soda
- ½ teaspoon baking powder
- Pinch of salt
- 1 6-ounce package semisweet chocolate chips

The Steps:

1. Preheat oven to 375°. Generously grease 9″ x 13″ x 2″ baking pan.
2. In large mixing bowl, cream butter with sugar until smooth and fluffy. Add egg and vanilla; continue to beat until well combined.
3. In separate bowl, sift flour, baking soda, baking powder, and salt together.
4. Combine sifted dry ingredients with butter mixture; beat until smooth. Stir in chocolate chips.
5. Spread in prepared baking pan and bake for 20–25 minutes or until golden on top. Allow to cool slightly; cut into squares.

Variation:

½ cup chopped walnuts or pecans can be added if desired.

Make-It-Easy Tip:

√ If brown sugar has hardened, place it in a jar with half an apple, seal, and let stand a day. The moisture from the apple will soften the sugar.

Picnic on the Grass

SERVES: 4
Chilled Guacamole Soup
Sesame Chicken
Icy Shrimp
Cold Northern Italian Stuffed Tomatoes
Apple-Nut Cake

A picnic is always a great way to spend a sultry summer day, far away from a hot kitchen. This one has a Make-It-Easy menu that's out of the ordinary and very, very cooling.

At this picnic, the birds and the trees provide most of the atmosphere, while you spread a simple cloth on the grass. The mood is outdoors and rustic, so use a blanket, a sheet, or a red checked tablecloth. If a table is available, try colorful wallpaper remnants as a fun tablecloth. Use the Apple-Nut Cake for an edible and appetizing centerpiece.

Forks and soup spoons are all you need for flatware. These organize easily rolled up in napkins. The chicken is finger food, so a Wash'n Dri packet slipped into each bundle will be much appreciated. Use paper napkins, or substitute terry hand towels or even washcloths for some pretty practicality. The bundles can be tied with ribbon or heavy yarn in festive colors.

Cool is the key word in your packing plan. For the most refreshment and, more importantly, for health reasons, be sure the shrimp, soup, and chicken stay chilled. Thermos containers come in a great variety of shapes and sizes for easy packing. If you don't have them, substitute other containers and nestle them among bags of ice. Or use the blue, plastic-covered packs of "artificial ice" that provide lots of cold without the mess of melting ice cubes.

The Chilled Guacamole Soup requires no cooking at all and can be made the morning or the night before. (Do not prepare much further ahead than this or the soup will discolor.) Carry it in a thermos, or improvise with a large jar or juice bottle. Just test the jar first by filling it with water to make sure it won't leak. Small jars or plastic containers can hold a selection of garnishes for people to choose from. Hot and cold paper cups or mugs are a handy way to serve the soup.

The Icy Shrimp cooks in minutes, then cools in the refrigerator while the day warms up. Pack it in a thermos container, or use the plastic containers available at delicatessens or restaurant supply stores. It's extra important that the shrimp and mayonnaise keep cold to stay fresh, so eat this dish first as an appetizer with crackers alongside.

Bake the Sesame Chicken during the cool of the evening the night before, then let it chill in the refrigerator until lunchtime. Baking the chicken avoids the splatters of frying, and the sesame-herb-cheese combination makes this an unusual picnic entrée.

The Northern Italian Stuffed Tomatoes are another no-cooking delight. Depending on the size of the tomatoes, you can pack them in an egg carton or muffin tin to protect them.

Like the chicken, the Apple-Nut Cake is a bake-ahead treat. Once the cake is cool, put it back in the baking pan and cover it with foil for easy packing. To keep it looking pretty, save the slicing until you're ready to eat. And, while you're baking, double the recipe and freeze an extra cake for a future occasion.

For a beverage, take your choice. Go with fruit juice, lemonade, sparkling water, a bottle of chilled white wine, beer—whatever suits your mood.

But getting back to the practical side, don't forget the insect repellent—or the litter bag. They're not as charming to think about as the wonderful food, but the seconds it takes to pack them help make sure everyone has a good time.

Chilled Guacamole Soup

SERVES: 4
Preparation time: 15 minutes
Chilling time: 4–6 hours or overnight

The Ingredients:

2 large ripe avocados
2 cups chicken broth
1/3 cup dairy sour cream
1/4 cup mayonnaise
2 tablespoons lemon juice
2 scallions, chopped (green and white parts included)
1 teaspoon chili powder
1/2 teaspoon freshly minced garlic
1/2 teaspoon Worcestershire sauce
Pinch of Tabasco, or to taste
Salt and freshly ground pepper to taste
Garnish: Chopped scallions (green and white parts included), chopped tomatoes, crushed taco-flavored chips

The Steps:

1. In food processor or blender, add all ingredients; process until smooth; chill 4–6 hours or overnight.
2. Taste for seasoning, adjust to taste with salt, pepper, and Tabasco, and serve garnished with chopped scallions, tomatoes, and crushed taco-flavored chips.

Variation:

Lime juice can be substituted for lemon juice.

Make-It-Easy Tips:

√ The ripening process begins after avocados leave the tree, which is why they are often hard when sold at the market. A hard avocado will ripen in a few days in a warm, dark place.

√ Squeeze lemon juice on avocado immediately after cutting to prevent discoloration.

√ If using a blender, process mixture in 2 or 3 batches.

Sesame Chicken

SERVES: 4
Preparation time: 15 minutes
Cooking time: 45–55 minutes

The Ingredients:

1 cup finely crushed soda crackers (about 20–25, depending on the size)
1 cup freshly grated Parmesan cheese
2 tablespoons finely minced scallions (green and white parts included)
2 tablespoons freshly chopped parsley
½ teaspoon paprika
Salt and freshly ground pepper to taste
8 chicken thighs, washed and patted dry
¼ pound (1 stick) salted butter, melted
2 tablespoons sesame seeds, lightly toasted

The Steps:

1. Preheat oven to 375°. Lightly butter shallow baking pan.
2. In small bowl, mix cracker crumbs, cheese, scallions, parsley, paprika, salt, and pepper.
3. Dip chicken in butter and then roll each piece in cracker mixture to form thick coating.
4. Arrange chicken pieces in single layer in baking pan, sprinkle with sesame seeds, and dot with butter. Bake for 45–55 minutes or until tender and golden.
5. Cool, wrap in aluminum foil, and chill until ready to serve.

Variations:

1 whole chicken cut up in 8 pieces or quartered chicken breasts can be substituted for chicken thighs.

Poppy seeds can be substituted for sesame seeds.

Make-It-Easy Tips:

√ Coat chicken on a surface covered with waxed paper for easy cleanup.

√ Crumbs are easily crushed in food processor or blender. They can also be placed between layers of waxed paper or foil and crushed with a rolling pin.

Icy Shrimp

SERVES: 4
Preparation time: 15 minutes
Cooking time: 5 minutes
Chilling time: 2–4 hours

This recipe comes from a friend, Michelle Naumburg, who serves it as an appetizer, lunch dish, or cold summer supper.

The Ingredients:

1½ pounds raw, cleaned and shelled medium shrimp.

Sauce:

¾ cup mayonnaise
¼ cup minced onion
¼ cup minced celery
2 tablespoons vegetable oil
2 tablespoons chili sauce
1 tablespoon lemon juice
½ teaspoon celery seed
Salt and freshly ground pepper to taste
Garnish: Lettuce leaves
Accompaniment: Crisp toasted pita bread

The Steps:

1. Bring large pot of salted water to a boil, add shrimp, and continue to cook over high heat for 3–5 minutes or until done. (DO NOT OVERCOOK.) Run under cold water in colander and drain. Cool slightly.
2. In food processor, blender, or by hand, process sauce ingredients until smooth and toss with shrimp.
3. Chill for 2–4 hours and serve icy cold on bed of lettuce accompanied by crisp toasted pita bread.

Variation:

Crabmeat or even lobster can be substituted for the shrimp.

Make-It-Easy Tips:

√ 2 pounds raw shrimp in shells equals about 1½ pounds cooked cleaned shrimp.

√ Ask your local fish dealer to clean and shell the shrimp for you. If he's not too busy, he will often oblige. If not, find a wonderful tool called a shrimp deveiner, or use the sharp tip of a paring knife to easily shell the shrimp.

Cold Northern Italian Stuffed Tomatoes

SERVES: 4
Preparation time: 15 minutes
Chilling time: 2 hours or overnight

Cold Northern Italian Stuffed Tomatoes are a combination vegetable and salad. Serve this dish in the summer when tomatoes are ripe and plentiful. I always prepare a few extra for a picnic since the outdoors seems to enhance people's appetites.

The Ingredients

6 large tomatoes
2 cups cooked rice
4 slices prosciutto ham, chopped
2 tablespoons freshly chopped parsley
2 tablespoons minced scallions (green and white parts included)
3 tablespoons olive oil
1½ tablespoons red wine vinegar
½ teaspoon Dijon mustard
Salt and freshly ground white pepper

The Steps:

1. Cut tops off tomatoes, scoop out pulp, and reserve ½ cup chopped pulp for stuffing.
2. In bowl, combine tomato pulp with rice, prosciutto, scallions, and parsley. In separate bowl, whisk oil, vinegar, mustard, salt, and pepper. Toss rice with dressing.
3. Stuff mixture into tomatoes and chill for 2 hours or overnight.

Variations:

Chopped chives or scallion greens can be added if desired.
The new Balsimico vinegar adds extra flavor to the stuffing.
Westphalian ham can be substituted for prosciutto ham.

Make-It-Easy Tips:

√ A serrated grapefruit spoon makes a great tool for scooping out tomatoes.

√ Once scooped out, turn tomatoes cut-side down on paper towels to drain before stuffing.

Apple-Nut Cake

YIELD: 1 large loaf or 4 mini-loaves
Preparation time: 15 minutes
Cooking time: 55–60 minutes for large loaf or 45–50 minutes for mini-loaves

Bake this cake in mini-loaves so that each picnic guest can receive his or her own.

The Ingredients:

2 cups all-purpose flour
¾ cup sugar
1 tablespoon baking powder
1 teaspoon salt
½ teaspoon baking soda
½ teaspoon cinnamon
¼ teaspoon ground nutmeg
1 cup unsweetened applesauce (chunky or smooth)
2 tablespoons vegetable oil
1 egg
1 teaspoon vanilla
½ cup dairy sour cream
1 cup chopped walnuts

The Steps:

1. Preheat oven to 350°. Generously butter and lightly flour a 9″ x 5″ x 3″ loaf pan or four 6″ x 3½″ x 2″ mini-loaf pans.
2. In large bowl, combine flour, sugar, baking powder, salt, baking soda, cinnamon, and nutmeg.
3. In separate bowl, beat applesauce, oil, egg, and vanilla. Add to dry ingredients along with sour cream and nuts; stir well until smooth.
4. Pour into prepared pan and bake for 55–60 minutes for large loaf or 45–50 minutes for mini-loaves, or until inserted knife comes out clean.
5. Remove from oven and allow to cool for 10 minutes; turn out onto rack and finish cooling.

Variation:

Raisins can be substituted for nuts, or a combination of ½ cup nuts and ½ cup raisins can be used.

Make-It-Easy Tip:

√ For a flavorful addition to any recipe calling for nutmeg, buy nutmegs whole and grate quickly and easily with a fine grater.

√ Ground nutmeg sold in spice jars doesn't have the zest of the freshly ground, but it can be substituted.

A Casual Brunch Buffet

SERVES: 8

Stuffed Cheese Bread
Southern-Style Baked Ham
Mustard Sauce
Chutneyed Rice Salad
Orange-Apricot Bread
Orange-Honey Butter (see page 253)

Here is brunch in the broadest sense of the word—something you can start eating sometime in the late morning and keep reaching for as long as someone's hungry. It's the answer for weekend guests, or the visitors who say, "You'll see us when you see us." These foods travel well, so you can use them as instant refrigerator fillers for a weekend at a vacation home.

The look is as casual as the timing. Pack the foods picnic-style in containers that double as serving dishes. Food can be served family- or buffet-style, if everyone lands in the kitchen at roughly the same time. A simple checkered tablecloth makes the kitchen cheerful. If you like, decorate the Orange-Apricot Bread with nuts and slivered apricots as an edible centerpiece. Or pack along a basket of fresh seasonal fruit.

All the cooking is done in advance, with one small but worthwhile exception. The Stuffed Cheese Bread is prepared ahead of time, but bakes to crusty perfection just before serving.

The Baked Ham makes great sandwiches, so keep some rolls or assorted loaves of bread nearby. Arranging overlapping slices of ham in rows, circle, or spirals takes seconds and makes for both a pretty presentation and easy serving.

The Chutneyed Rice Salad complements the ham, helps use up leftover rice, and provides a delicious surprise for people who don't expect an unusual, piquant dish like this on a casual table. It makes a zesty change of pace from the usual mundane potato or macaroni salads.

You may need a few little extras on hand, too, like cream cheese and butter for the Orange-Apricot Bread or other breads. Pack them in crocks or small plastic dishes, depending on how fancy or casual you want to be.

People will be as thirsty as they are hungry. Depending on their likes and dislikes, keep on hand lots of hot coffee, a variety of juices, a pitcher of iced tea, chilled wine, cold beer, and a big jug of milk.

This complete menu is so versatile that I find it can be used as a festive Easter brunch. I've even served it as a Sunday supper with the addition of some freshly steamed broccoli.

Stuffed Cheese Bread

SERVES: 8
Preparation time: 15 minutes
Cooking time: 20 minutes

This stuffed French bread can be served as a luncheon sandwich, as an accompanying bread, or as an hors d'oeuvre when cut in thinner slices.

The Ingredients:

4 ounces Swiss cheese, grated (1 cup)
4 ounces Mozzarella cheese, grated (1 cup)
4 ounces Parmesan cheese, grated (1 cup)
¼ pound baked ham, diced
¼ bottle beer (3 ounces)
2 eggs, lightly beaten
2 tablespoons unsalted butter, softened
¼ teaspoon freshly ground pepper
1 loaf crusty French, sourdough, or Italian bread

The Steps:

1. Preheat oven to 375°.
2. In bowl, combine cheese, ham, beer, eggs, butter, and pepper and mix well.
3. Split bread lengthwise and remove the soft doughy interior.
4. Stuff cheese mixture in crust and close carefully.
5. Wrap in foil and bake for 20 minutes.
6. Unwrap, cut into 2″-thick slices, and serve as luncheon dish; or, cut in 1″-thick slices, as hot hors d'oeuvre.

Variation:

Use small individual sourdough or French rolls and reduce baking time to 10 minutes. The small rolls save time because they do not need to be sliced after baking.

After bread has been stuffed, leave the loaf open and bake the two halves open-faced, for a crispy variation.

Make-It-Easy Tips:

√ Prepare bread, wrap in foil, and refrigerate overnight or until ready to bake.

√ Before grating a soft cheese like Mozzarella, brush grater with a little oil so that the cheese will not stick to the grater.

Southern-Style Baked Ham

SERVES: 8–10
Preparation time: 10 minutes
Cooking time: 1 hour 35 minutes
1 hour 45 minutes

The Ingredients:

1 5-pound canned ham
10–12 cloves

Glaze:

1¼ cup brown sugar
¼ cup orange juice
2 tablespoons Dijon mustard (grainy type is preferable, if available)
1 tablespoon cider vinegar
Garnish: Orange slices
Accompaniment: Mustard Sauce

The Steps:

1. Preheat oven to 325°. Place ham fat side up on rack in foil-lined pan.
2. With sharp knife, lightly score top of ham in diamond pattern; decorate each diamond center with a clove.
3. Bake ham for 1 hour, remove from oven, and increase heat to 350°.
4. Combine glaze ingredients together in bowl, stir well, spread over ham, and continue to bake, basting occasionally, for 35–45 minutes, or until ham is cooked (thermometer registers 160°).
5. Slice and serve garnished by orange slices with accompanying mustard sauce.

Variation:

Apple juice or even applesauce can be substituted for orange juice.

Make-It-Easy Tips:

√ It is easier to slice the ham when slightly chilled.
√ The heavier the orange, the juicier it is. Always buy thin-skinned oranges, which are generally the juiciest.

Mustard Sauce

YIELD: 1½ cups
Preparation time: 5 minutes

The Ingredients:

1 cup mayonnaise
2 tablespoons Dijon mustard (smooth or grainy)
1 teaspoon lemon juice
½ teaspoon freshly ground white pepper

The Steps:

1. Combine mayonnaise, mustard, lemon juice, and pepper in bowl and mix until smooth.
2. Serve immediately, or chill until ready to use.

Variation:

2 tablespoons minced cornichons (sour pickles) and 2 tablespoons freshly chopped parsley may be added if desired.

Chutneyed Rice Salad

SERVES: 8–10
Preparation time: 15 minutes
Chilling time: 2–4 hours

The Ingredients:

Dressing:

¾ cup chopped chutney
½ cup peanut or vegetable oil
2 tablespoons lemon juice
1 teaspoon freshly grated ginger or ½ teaspoon ground ginger
Salt and freshly ground pepper to taste

Salad:

6 cups cold cooked rice (2 cups raw)
2 cups peeled and chopped tart apples
1 cup chopped celery

½ cup raisins
¼ cup minced scallion greens
¼ cup toasted slivered almonds
Garnish: Coriander leaves or watercress

The Steps:

1. Combine dressing ingredients together in large bowl; stir to combine.
2. Add remaining salad ingredients, stir well, cover and refrigerate for 2–4 hours or overnight to blend flavors.
3. Serve garnished with coriander leaves or watercress.

Variations:

Chopped peanuts, chopped bacon bits, mandarin orange segments, or other condiments can be added. Use your imagination to create a wonderfully tangy salad.

Make-It-Easy Tips:

√ Chop the apples first, cover with the lemon juice to keep from browning, and stir into dressing.

Orange-Apricot Bread

YIELD: 1 large loaf
Preparation time: 15 minutes
Cooking time: 50–55 minutes

The Ingredients:

3 cups all-purpose flour
⅓ cup granulated sugar
4 teaspoons baking powder
1 teaspoon salt
4 tablespoons unsalted butter, softened to room temperature
1 egg
1 cup whole milk
½ cup apricot preserves
Rind of 1 orange
Juice of 1 orange or ½ cup fresh orange juice

The Steps:

1. Preheat oven to 375°. Generously butter and lightly flour 9″ x 5″ x 3″ loaf pan.
2. In large bowl, sift flour with sugar, baking powder, and salt.
3. With electric beater, or by hand, mix in butter and egg.
4. Add milk, preserves, rind, and juice; continue to beat until smooth.
5. Pour into prepared pan and bake for 50–55 minutes, or until inserted knife comes out clean.
6. Remove from oven, allow to cool in pan for 5–10 minutes, and invert onto rack to finish cooling.

Variations:

Serve with Orange-Honey Butter if desired (see index).

Chopped nuts, such as walnuts or pecans, or raisins may be added, to taste.

Can also be baked in 4 mini-loaf pans for 40–45 minutes.

Make-It-Easy Tip:

√ Grate extra orange rind, dry in slow oven or in warm area, and store in small jars ready for use.

A Midnight Breakfast

SERVES: 8–10

***Juices**
Joe's Special
Smoked Salmon Spread
Prosciutto Butter
***Bagels**
Almond Pound Cake
***Fresh Fruit**

What do you serve when it's too late for dinner, after a long night of charades, Scrabble, or even a game of Trivial Pursuit? After a late-night party, an evening at the theater or movies, or even after a wedding? My answer is A Midnight Breakfast. It's the perfect menu to appease overtired guests

*Not a recipe

who are hungry. It's less formal than a Midnight Supper and emphasizes comforting foods.

Since the hour is late, this menu is served buffet-style, and participation from guests is encouraged. Set a relaxed and casual table, using everyday dishes and pretty paper napkins.

A variety of juices served in pitchers should start off the breakfast, especially tomato, orange, grapefruit, or pineapple. A large pot of brewed decaffeinated coffee can follow. I sprinkle a little cinnamon in with the ground coffee as a special treat before brewing. Since avoiding caffeine is important at the midnight hour, a pot of hot water and a basket of assorted herb teas is another thoughtful accompaniment.

The Almond Pound Cake is a sweet treat that freezes beautifully, sparing you last-minute work. Bagels can similarly be purchased earlier and frozen. It's easiest to slice them before freezing, then pop them into the toaster when you need them. No bagels handy? Substitute hearty rye or pumpernickel bread.

The Smoked Salmon Spread and Prosciutto Butter are quick to fix, but can be prepared in advance to allow extra time to put together Joe's Special. Shape the spreads into logs, or serve them in pretty crocks or mugs. And if you want to simplify things even more, substitute cream cheese and smoked salmon with bagels, served "as is" with sprigs of parsley and wedges of lemon.

That leaves only Joe's Special to be cooked up fresh at the last minute. Serve it straight from the skillet, set on a trivet to protect the table. Place the Joe's Special alongside a basket of assorted citrus fruits. This simple centerpiece combining oranges, lemons, limes, and kumquats, with an accent of a few daisies, adds color to the table.

A Midnight Breakfast is designed to make that P.M. to A.M. transition just that much easier.

Joe's Special

SERVES: 8–10
Preparation time: 15 minutes
Cooking time: 8–10 minutes

Joe's Special is a dish originating in San Francisco. It is a combination of ground beef, spinach, and eggs that can be served as a quick main course, hearty lunch, or brunch dish.

The Ingredients:

2 tablespoons unsalted butter
2 tablespoons olive oil
1 medium onion, finely minced
2 pounds lean ground beef
2 10-ounce packages frozen chopped spinach, thawed and thoroughly squeezed dry
½ teaspoon dried oregano, crumbled
½ teaspoon dried basil, crumbled
¼ teaspoon dried thyme, crumbled
Salt and freshly ground pepper to taste
8 eggs, beaten
¼ cup half-and-half
4–5 tablespoons freshly grated Parmesan cheese
Garnish: Cherry tomatoes

The Steps:

1. In large, heavy-bottomed 10″ or 12″ stainless or enameled skillet, heat butter and oil together; when hot, add onion; sauté over medium heat until just soft, about 5 minutes.
2. Add ground beef and cook over high heat, separating with fork, until crumbly. Pour off excess grease, add spinach, and stir to combine.
3. Season with oregano, basil, thyme, salt, and pepper; cook over medium heat for 1 minute, stirring often.
4. Beat eggs with half-and-half and pour over meat mixture; stir often to keep eggs from accumulating on bottom of skillet.
5. Cook until set, sprinkle with Parmesan cheese, and serve hot, garnished with cherry tomatoes.

Variation:

For a pancake version, sprinkle with grated cheese and run under a broiler until the top is golden and bubbly.

Make-It-Easy Tips:

√ It is important to squeeze spinach thoroughly dry of moisture before adding to skillet.

√ Do not cook spinach in aluminum or iron pots, which give it a metallic taste. The new anodized aluminum cookware is permissible, however.

Smoked Salmon Spread

YIELD: 2 cups
Preparation time: 10–15 minutes

The Ingredients:

1 1-pound can salmon, drained with skin and bones removed
1 8-ounce package cream cheese
1 small onion, finely chopped
1 tablespoon lemon juice
1 tablespoon freshly snipped dill or 1 teaspoon dried dill weed
1 teaspoon white horseradish
1 teaspoon Worcestershire sauce
½ teaspoon liquid smoke
Salt and freshly ground pepper to taste

The Steps:

1. In food processor, blender, or by hand, process ingredients until a smooth spread.
2. Chill until ready to serve.

Variation:

Spread can be chilled for several hours to firm, shaped into a ball or log, rolled in chopped parsley or chopped walnuts, and served as an appetizer.

Make-It-Easy Tip:

√ Liquid smoke is available under several brand names. I use the one from E. H. Wright, made by distilling wood. It can also be used in barbecue sauces and for flavoring grilled meats, poultry, or fish.

Prosciutto Butter

YIELD: 1 cup
Preparation time: 5–10 minutes

The Ingredients:

6 ounces (1½ sticks) unsalted butter, softened to room temperature
3–4 ounces (about 6 thin slices) prosciutto, trimmed of fat

The Steps:

1. In food processor or blender, chop prosciutto finely. Add butter and continue to process until smooth.
2. Pack into crock or shape into log, cover, and refrigerate until ready to serve.
3. Serve chilled or at room temperature.

Variation:

1 teaspoon chopped chives or ½ teaspoon grated lemon rind can be added if desired.

Make-It-Easy Tips:

√ If you have forgotten to soften the butter, do not fret—grate it or dice it and process as above.
√ Prosciutto butter can be frozen.

Almond Pound Cake

YIELD: 1 bundt cake
Preparation time: 15 minutes
Cooking time: 1 hour

This cake is a variation on a traditional pound cake recipe that calls for a pound of butter, flour, and sugar.

The Ingredients:

1 cup (1 2½-ounce package) sliced almonds
12 ounces (3 sticks) unsalted butter, at room temperature

2¼ cups sugar
3 cups sifted all-purpose flour
¾ cup whole milk
6 eggs
1 tablespoon baking powder
2 teaspoons almond extract
1 teaspoon vanilla extract
1 teaspoon freshly grated lemon peel

The Steps:

1. Preheat oven to 350°. Generously butter and lightly dust with flour a large bundt pan.
2. Evenly distribute almonds over bottom of prepared pan.
3. In large bowl, beat butter and sugar together with electric mixer until light and smooth. Add remaining ingredients and beat thoroughly for 5–10 minutes, or until creamy.
4. Pour into prepared pan and bake for 1 hour, or until inserted cake tester comes out clean.
5. Cool slightly, invert onto rack and continue to cool for 15 minutes.
6. Serve warm or at room temperature, thinly sliced.

Variations:

1 cup slivered almonds or 1 12-ounce package semisweet chocolate bits can be folded into batter before baking.

Cake can be baked in large loaf pan.

Make-It-Easy Tips:

√ Since this pound cake is so rich, slice it very thin. Freeze any extra for future use.

√ The potency of baking powder diminishes with age and therefore becomes ineffective as a leavening agent. To test to see if powder is effective, place ½ teaspoon of powder in ¼ cup hot water. If powder is fresh, water will bubble actively. If no reaction, time to head to the store for a new supply.

Inexpensive Feasts

1. **Hearty Winter Soup Supper**
   Zuppa Salsiccie
   Potage Crécy (Cream of Carrot Soup)
   Cheese Wafers
   *Crusty French Bread
   Old-Fashioned Gingerbread
   Whipped Apple Cream

2. **Leftovers for the Connoisseur**
   Leftover Vegetable Soup
   Curried Chicken
   Apricot Chutney
   *Plain White Rice
   Cucumbers in Sour Cream
   Banana Mousse

3. **Far Eastern Delights**
   Kung Pao Chicken
   *White Rice
   Spicy Chilled Chinese Noodles
   Stir-Fried Zucchini and Water Chestnuts
   (It Doesn't Matter That It Isn't Chinese) Strawberry Fool

4. **Limited-Funds Feast**
   The Ultimate Casserole
   Radish, Cucumber, and Fennel Salad
   Onion Bread
   Make Your Own Sundaes
   Hot Fudge Sauce/Hot Butterscotch Sauce

5. **Just Desserts**
   Royal Ice-Cream Torte
   Glazed Oatmeal Cake
   Cocoa Brownies
   Apricot Bars
   Irish Coffee

6. **Country Fare**
   Tortilla Baskets
   Addy's Chicken
   Green Bean and Onion Salad
   *Bread
   Light Lemon Pie

7. **Reinventing the Fondue Party**
   Swiss Cheese Fondue
   Spinach Salad with Almonds
   Icy Lemon-Raspberry Delight

8. **Dining European**
   Czechoslovakian Vegetable Soup
   Pork Chops and Apple Rings
   *Brown Rice
   Two Greens Salad with Red Bell Peppers
   Cloud Pie

* Not a recipe

THE MENUS IN THIS SECTION are designed to utilize economical ingredients, transforming them into festive events. Memorable parties need not be expensive affairs.

The *Hearty Winter Soup Supper* features a whole meal in your most attractive soup bowls or mugs—easy, inexpensive, and, best of all, comforting on a cold winter's night. Soup is a great filler-upper. I offer three in the other menus in this section, allowing for smaller main-course portions. Remember, if you prepare soup ahead and leave it in the refrigerator for any length of time, simmer it for at least 5 minutes every 2 or 3 days to keep it fresh. Soups freeze beautifully as well, so double quantities to save on extra chores.

There are other ways to economize without sacrificing quality. For example, *Leftovers for the Connoisseur* revitalizes cooked vegetables in soup, poultry in curry, and an abundance of bananas in Banana Mousse. *The Limited-Funds Feast* capitalizes on one of my favorite inexpensive ingredients—pasta. Pasta is so versatile it can stretch the smallest amount of meat into a nutritious main course.

Asking people over for *Just Desserts* is not only an acceptable way to entertain at minimum cost, but it also makes many guests feel very comfortable because they can reciprocate in a similar manner. A feast of sweets is perfect for late-night parties and calls for a minimum of last-minute effort.

You will also find a menu in the section called *Reinventing the Fondue Party*. This menu not only revives cheese fondue but also encourages group participation and stimulates lively conversation to ensure a successful evening.

Perhaps the most important secret to dollar-saving entertaining is good planning. Follow your menus to the letter. Avoid impulse buying. If, however, pork chops are "on special" while you're preparing for *Dining European*, buy double the amount and freeze them for a future dinner.

There are many tried-and-true tips on how to save money at the supermarket, but they are worth repeating because they work. Try to consolidate marketing trips to save on gas and avoid impulse purchases. Buy "on special" but investigate prices in the weekly food section of your local newspapers to save costly trips and Make-It-Easy on your shopping chores. Also remember to shop after eating rather than before. It's obviously easier to give in to temptation if you're hungry.

When purchasing produce, look for locally grown vegetables and fruits, which are fresher, tastier, and less expensive than the shipped varieties. Buy produce in season and ask the greengrocer for advice about what's best. If, for example, green beans are unavailable for the *Country*

Fare dinner, by all means substitute broccoli, asparagus, or whatever is in season and freshest. When preparing salads, always make your own dressing. It has the advantages of being both less expensive and free of additives. Made properly, it always tastes infinitely better!

Fortunately, just about everybody likes chicken, and it is the least expensive meat you can use. In this inflation-fighting section, I emphasize its versatility. You will find it in *Far Eastern Delights* as Kung Pao Chicken, as Curried Chicken in *Leftovers for the Connoisseur* and in a one-pot recipe called Addy's Chicken in *Country Fare*. If time and energy permit, buy whole, uncut chickens and chop them yourself. It's quite a money-saver.

When purchasing beef, buy on special and select the leaner meats, which are less expensive and better for your health. Tenderize them in marinades or by long and slow cooking. Slab bacon is much more economical than the sliced variety and can be frozen for future use.

The most important tip in purchasing meats, poultry, or fish at the market is to make friends with the butcher. Very often he or she will be more than happy to cut up a chicken, bone a leg of lamb, or even fillet a fish for no charge at all.

There are some excellent, inexpensive jug wines available. Again, your local wine merchant is the person to turn to for advice. For an extra-special presentation, decant red wine into a carafe a few hours before serving to allow it to "breathe." Chill white wine in a carafe or decanter to keep it icy cold.

Inflation-fighting parties require some easy table-setting tips and clever handiwork to create attractive presentations. Perrier bottles as individual bud vases, tiered plates of desserts, or an edible bread centerpiece are all wonderful ideas to make these menus appealing.

Don't be shy about sharing or borrowing coffee pots, platters, serving pieces, tables, chairs, flowers from a garden, or other necessities. Friends and neighbors are usually delighted to oblige, especially if you offer to reciprocate.

Hearty Winter Soup Supper

SERVES: 8
Zuppa Salsiccie
Potage Crécy
Cheese Wafers
*** Crusty French Bread**
Old-Fashioned Gingerbread
Whipped Apple Cream

Whether you're warming up winter travelers or skiers, hot soup is a great way to chase away the cold. It's also an economical way to feed a crowd, especially when the budget has been stretched thin by holiday expenses.

Here two hearty and savory soups are served: one meaty, the other creamy vegetable—both rich enough to fill up and warm a large group. The Cheese Wafers and Crusty French Bread lend the perfect crunchy texture to accompany the soups.

You can accent the peasant theme by draping a shawl across the tablecloth. Flowers—fresh, dried, or cloth—will look country-pretty clustered

* Not a recipe

in a pitcher, or here and there in jars or tumblers. Or set candles on a tray or plate and surround them with pinecones.

The Cheese Wafers and sliced Crusty Bread piled in a basket lined with napkins and two tureens full of steamy soup complete the table setting. A crock-pot or bean pot makes a nice substitute for a tureen.

This meal is ideal for buffet serving, since each person needs only a soup spoon for dinner and a teaspoon for dessert. The soup spoons can be rolled up in napkins and tied with yarn, macrame cord, or even burlap twine for a rustic effect. Place them in a basket or a flowerpot to finish off the country look. Serve the soup in mugs on plates large enough to hold the bread. Have extra mugs handy, since people will very likely want to try both soups. And, if your kitchen is large enough, try serving the soup in an attractive pot, kept warming on the range. All the accessories and mugs can be placed alongside or arranged decoratively on a kitchen counter or table.

The Whipped Apple Cream can be prepared an hour or two ahead and chilled. The Zuppa Salsiccie can be made a day earlier and refrigerated or even frozen well in advance. Then simply reheat it while the Potage Crécy simmers, the gingerbread bakes, the French bread toasts, and your whole house fills with the most incredible homemade aromas.

Zuppa Salsiccie

SERVES: 8
Preparation Time: 15 minutes
Cooking time: 1½ hours

This hearty Italian sausage soup has a wonderful spiciness.

The Ingredients:

2 tablespoons olive oil
1 pound hot Italian sausage, sliced in ½″ circles
1 pound sweet Italian sausage, sliced in ½″ circles
2 large onions, chopped
1 green pepper, chopped
2 cups red wine
1 28-ounce can crushed tomatoes packed in puree

5 cups canned beef broth
2 tablespoons freshly chopped parsley
1 teaspoon finely minced garlic
½ teaspoon dried basil, crumbled
½ teaspoon dried oregano, crumbled
Salt and freshly ground pepper to taste
1 7-ounce package bow-tie noodles
Garnish: 1–1½ cups freshly grated Parmesan cheese

The Steps:

1. In large deep saucepan or Dutch oven, heat oil and sauté sausages until lightly browned over high heat. Discard excess grease, leaving 2 tablespoons in pan.
2. Add onions and green pepper and sauté until soft, about 5–7 minutes. Add wine and allow to boil for two minutes.
3. Add tomatoes, broth, parsley, garlic, basil, oregano, salt, and pepper. Bring to a boil, reduce heat, cover, and simmer slowly for 1 hour.
4. Add noodles, cover, and continue to simmer for 20 minutes or until noodles are tender.
5. Serve in deep soup plates garnished with Parmesan cheese.

Variations:

All hot or all sweet Italian sausages can be substituted for the combination. Polish *kielbasa*, Mexican *chorizo*, or Portuguese *linguiça* can be substituted as well.

If fresh herbs are in season, substitute 1 tablespoon fresh herbs for 1 teaspoon of the dried.

Additional vegetables such as diced celery or carrots can be added with the onions in Step #2.

Diced potatoes or kidney or white beans can be substituted for the pasta.

If a thinner soup is desired, add an additional cup of beef broth.

If tomatoes packed in puree are unavailable, use regular whole juice-packed tomatoes; chop, drain off most of the liquid. Return tomatoes to can, and fill to the top with canned tomato puree.

Make-It-Easy Tips:

√ To further reduce the fat level, parboil the sausages for 15 minutes before sautéing.

√ Prepare the soup a day in advance and refrigerate so that excess grease can be easily removed the next day.
√ Refrigerate canned stocks so that when they are opened, any excess fat can be easily removed.

Potage Crécy (Cream of Carrot Soup)

SERVES: 8–10
Preparation time: 15–20 minutes
Cooking time: 1 hour

This recipe is an adaptation of one taught to me by cooking teacher Ann Roe Robbins. The French call this soup Crécy because their best carrots grow in the town of this name.

The Ingredients:

4 tablespoons (½ stick) unsalted butter
10 medium carrots, peeled and thinly sliced
1 large onion, thinly sliced
2 leeks, white part only, carefully washed and thinly sliced
10 cups chicken broth
¼ pound whole slab bacon, cut into large chunks
1 teaspoon sugar
Salt and freshly ground pepper to taste
⅓ cup raw rice
1 cup heavy cream
Garnish: Freshly chopped parsley

The Steps:

1. In large saucepan, heat butter; when melted, sauté carrots, onion, and leeks over medium-low heat, until soft, about 10–15 minutes.
2. Add broth, bacon, sugar, salt, and pepper. Bring to boil, cover, and simmer slowly for 20 minutes, or until carrots are tender.
3. Add rice and continue to cook an additional 20 minutes.
4. Purée in food processor or blender until smooth.
5. Return to saucepan, add cream, and heat just until warmed through. Adjust seasonings to taste and serve hot, garnished with freshly chopped parsley.

Variations:

Bacon can be omitted if desired.
Two large scallions can be substituted for leeks.
Beef broth can be substituted for chicken broth.

Make-It-Easy Tips:

√ Store unwashed leeks with roots attached in paper towels to keep dry. If wet, they rot quickly.

√ Leeks' wide flat leaves pick up dirt and grit easily, so they must be carefully washed before use. Cut off roots, leaving a thin layer of the vegetable's base intact. Cut off tops just above junction with the white stem.

√ Do not store carrots with apples. Apples release a gas that gives carrots a bitter taste.

If desired, the chunks of bacon can be boiled for 3–5 minutes, drained, and then added in Step #2 to reduce excess fat.

Cheese Wafers

YIELD: 36–40
Preparation time: 15–20 minutes
Cooking time: 14–16 minutes

The Ingredients:

6 ounces (1½ sticks) unsalted butter, softened
1¼ cups grated Swiss cheese
¼ cup grated Parmesan cheese
1 teaspoon Dijon mustard
1 cup all-purpose flour

The Steps:

1. In food processor, electric mixer, or by hand, combine butter with Swiss cheese, Parmesan cheese, and mustard. Add flour and continue to process until well blended.
2. Shape dough into a large circle, wrap in plastic wrap, and refrigerate for 1 hour.
3. Preheat oven to 350°. Lightly butter a cookie sheet.

4. Pinch small pieces of dough, roll into ½″ balls, and place on cookie sheet. Flatten with palm of hand and bake for 14–16 minutes or until golden brown.
5. Remove from spatula, allow to cool, and serve.

Variation:

1½ cups Cheddar cheese can be substituted for Swiss and Parmesan.

Make-It-Easy Tips:

√ If you've forgotten to soften the butter, grate it and it will soften quickly and easily.

√ Store baked wafers in sealed containers and they will keep for several days. Wafers can also be frozen successfully.

Old-Fashioned Gingerbread

YIELD: 4 mini-loaves or 1 large loaf
Preparation time: 15–20 minutes
Cooking time: 35–55 minutes

This traditionally spicy cake is especially wonderful served warm, topped with Whipped Apple Cream or even vanilla ice cream.

The Ingredients:

¾ cup molasses
1 cup light brown sugar, firmly packed
¼ pound (1 stick) unsalted butter, melted
2 eggs
2½ cups all-purpose flour
2 teaspoons ginger
1 teaspoon cinnamon
1 teaspoon ground nutmeg
½ teaspoon ground cloves
½ teaspoon mace
½ teaspoon baking powder
½ teaspoon salt
2 teaspoon baking soda

1 cup boiling water
Accompaniments: Whipped Apple Cream (recipe follows) or vanilla ice cream

The Steps:

1. Preheat oven to 350°. Generously butter one 9″ x 5″ x 3″ or four 6″ x 3½″ x 2″ mini-loaf pans and lightly dust with flour.
2. Combine molasses and brown sugar in bowl of food processor, strong blender, electric mixer, or by hand in mixing bowl.
3. Add butter and process for a few seconds; add eggs and mix well.
4. Combine flour, ginger, cinnamon, nutmeg, cloves, mace, baking powder, and salt; stir and add to molasses mixture.
5. Dissolve baking soda in boiling water, stir, and add, continuing to beat until smooth.
6. Pour into prepared pans and bake for 50–55 minutes for large loaf or 35–40 minutes for mini-loaves.
7. Allow to cool slightly. Serve warm, accompanied by Whipped Apple Cream or vanilla ice cream.

Variation:

½ cup chopped walnuts or pecans can be added to the batter after Step 5.

Make-It-Easy Tips:

√ To avoid residue when measuring sticky liquids such as molasses, rinse the measuring cup in very hot water first.

√ Baking powder's potency diminishes with age and thus loses its effectiveness as a leavening agent. To test to see if your supply is still good, place ½ teaspoon of powder in ¼ cup of hot water. If active, bubbles will appear; if no bubbles appear, it's time to buy a new supply.

Whipped Apple Cream

SERVES: 8
Preparation time: 10 minutes

Serve this chilled cream with the squares of gingerbread.

The Ingredients:

2 cups unsweetened applesauce, well-chilled
Sugar to taste
2 cups heavy cream, well chilled
1 teaspoon vanilla extract
Garnish: Cinnamon

The Steps:

1. Sweeten applesauce with sugar to taste.
2. Whip cream until it begins to thicken. Add vanilla and continue to whip until soft peaks form. Gently fold into applesauce, sprinkle with cinnamon, and serve immediately, or chill for 1–2 hours before serving.

Variation:

Homemade applesauce, easy to prepare, can be substituted. Simply core, slice, but do not peel 4–6 large, tart Pippin, Granny Smith, or even McIntosh apples. Simmer with a few tablespoons apple juice until soft, strain through food strainer, discard peels, and fresh sauce is ready to use.

Make-It-Easy Tips:

√ Applesauce is sweetened to taste rather than the presweetened applesauce available at the market which is loaded with sugar.

√ When whipping cream, chill bowl and beater so that cream will not turn while beating. The applesauce must also be cold so that the cream can hold its stiffness.

Leftovers for the Connoisseur

SERVES: 4
Leftover Vegetable Soup
Curried Chicken
Apricot Chutney
*** White Rice**
Cucumbers in Sour Cream
Banana Mousse

Leftovers for company? Why not? Just serve them up with that extra something special—in this case a sprinkling of curry powder. You might even find yourself cooking extra meat, rice, and vegetables just so you can cook this meal anytime.

Select a colorful tablecloth or an assortment of brightly colored place mats as the basis for the table setting. A bouquet of wildflowers will brighten the table further. Daisies and asters last longer than many wildflowers and are extremely economical. They don't even need a fancy vase—leftover jars and bottles will do fine. Or place a few potted plants in a basket for an easy table decoration.

A variety of small candles, perhaps of different colors, give a pretty light. Tiny candles that come in colored glass holders are inexpensive and easy to find at supermarkets. Just be sure they're unscented so they don't interfere with the taste of the food.

The chutney can be prepared weeks in advance and refrigerated until serving time. Both the Leftover Vegetable Soup and the Cucumbers in Sour Cream can also be made ahead of time and chilled. On a cold night, the soup can be warmed and served piping hot. And if you want to skip the first course, feel free to omit the soup.

For a lighter and lower-calorie accompaniment to curry, substitute plain yogurt for the sour cream, seasoned with a touch of cumin. Either way, the cucumbers provide that cooling taste in contrast to the hot curry. The banana mousse supplies an additional creamy, cool, and smooth taste after a spicy meal.

* Not a recipe

Leftover Vegetable Soup

SERVES: 4
Preparation time: 10 minutes
Chilling time: 2 hours or overnight

This calls for cooked vegetables and turns them into a wonderfully flavorful chilled or hot soup. I serve this chilled in summer, hot in winter. The best vegetables to use are carrots, broccoli, zucchini, asparagus, squash, or even potatoes. The vegetables should be well cooked. If not, cook them for a few minutes longer in the broth and process, liquid and all.

The Ingredients:

2 cups leftover vegetables, cooked until soft
1 cup chicken broth
1 cup half-and-half
1–2 tablespoons fresh herbs (chives, parsley, basil, dill)
Salt and freshly ground pepper to taste
Garnish: Dairy sour cream or yogurt and freshly chopped parsley

The Steps:

1. In food processor or blender, process vegetables with broth until just combined.
2. Add half-and-half and continue to process until smooth.
3. Season to taste with herbs, salt, and pepper and chill for 2 hours or overnight.
4. Just before serving, adjust seasonings and serve garnished with dollop of sour cream or yogurt and freshly chopped parsley.

Variations:

Be creative with seasonings. Here are some suggestions:
Carrots—ground ginger, ground nutmeg, and chopped parsley
Broccoli—chopped chives and chopped parsley
Zucchini—chopped basil, chopped parsley, and chopped chives
Asparagus—chopped chives and chopped parsley
Squash—ground nutmeg, chopped chives, and chopped parsley
Potatoes—heavy cream instead of half-and-half for a richer vichyssoise; 3 tablespoons chopped chives, with extra chopped chives for garnish.
Beef broth can be substituted for chicken broth.

Make-It-Easy Tips:

√ Cook the vegetables in broth for increased flavor.

√ Remember to add more seasonings after chilling, since cold diminishes the intensity of the flavors.

Curried Chicken

SERVES: 4
Preparation time: 15 minutes
Cooking time: 8–9 minutes

I suggest chicken curry only because it tends to be the most reasonable in price. However, this basic recipe will rejuvenate just about any type of leftover available. Cooked meat, fish, or seafood in the same amount can be turned into a fabulously easy main course. Vary the amount of curry powder for spiciness as desired. I suggest using chicken broth with poultry, fish, or shellfish and beef broth with meat.

The Ingredients:

3–4 tablespoons unsalted butter
1 cup peeled and finely chopped tart apple (1 large)
2 cloves garlic, finely minced
4–5 teaspoons curry powder dissolved in 2 tablespoons broth plus 1 teaspoon lemon juice
Salt to taste
2 tablespoons all-purpose flour
1⅓ cups chicken broth
1½ pounds (about 2 cups) cooked chicken, cut in bite-size pieces

Condiment Garnishes: Chopped scallions, chopped hard-cooked eggs, chopped bacon, chopped peanuts, chopped coconut, raisins, and Apricot Chutney (recipe follows)
Accompaniment: White rice

The Steps:

1. In large skillet, heat butter and sauté apple, onion, and garlic over medium heat until just soft, about 5 minutes.
2. Add curry powder (dissolved in liquid), and salt to taste. Stir until smooth. Add flour, stir, and cook 2 minutes longer.

3. Add broth and chicken, stir well, heating to warm through.
4. Serve hot over white rice with several condiment garnishes.

Variation:

½–1 cup whipping cream can be added to the finished curry and warmed through for a creamier version.

Make-It-Easy Tips:

√ Curry powder is not a spice by itself. It is a blend of herbs and spices that varies in intensity and strength. Try several brands to find one that best suits your taste.

√ If you prefer a milder curry, begin with a paste of 2 tablespoons curry powder plus 2 tablespoons broth mixed with 1 teaspoon lemon juice. Taste sauce and continue to add a paste of curry mixed with broth until desired taste is achieved.

Apricot Chutney

YIELD: 1 quart
Preparation time: 15 minutes
Cooking time: 1½ hours

A food processor allows you to easily prepare this wonderful preserved fruit accompaniment. Seal the chutney in glass jars and give it as a thoughtful house gift.

The Ingredients:

12 ounces (2 cups) coarsely cut dried apricots
1 cup golden raisins
1 large onion, finely chopped
1 cup dark brown sugar, firmly packed
1½ cups cider vinegar
½ cup orange juice
¼ cup minced candied ginger
1 tablespoon grated lemon rind
1 tablespoon grated orange rind
1 teaspoon minced garlic
½ teaspoon crushed dried red pepper flakes

¼ teaspoon ground allspice
Salt to taste

The Steps:

1. In large saucepan, combine ingredients and bring to boil; reduce heat, cover, and simmer 1 hour.
2. Uncover and continue to simmer 30 minutes longer, or until thickened.
3. Cool, then chill until ready to use.
4. Serve at room temperature as a side dish for curry.

Variations:

Chutney can also be served as an accompaniment to poultry or meat, used as a glaze for roasting poultry or meats, or added to a salad as a flavoring.

Chopped apples, pineapple, mangoes, pears, peaches, and other fruits can be added to the chutney as desired.

Make-It-Easy Tip:

√ Chutney will keep in the refrigerator for several weeks or can be frozen for future use. To preserve in jars, pour hot chutney into sterilized jars, adjust caps according to manufacturer's directions; process in a hot water bath 10 minutes, and store on the shelf.

Cucumbers in Sour Cream

SERVES: 4
Preparation time: 15 minutes
Chilling time: 1 hour

The Ingredients:

2 medium cucumbers, peeled and thinly sliced
½ teaspoon salt

Dressing

½ cup sour cream
1 tablespoon freshly snipped dill or 1 teaspoon dried dill
2 teaspoons lemon juice

Pinch of sugar
Salt and freshly ground white pepper to taste

The Steps:

1. Place cucumber slices in bowl, sprinkle with salt, and refrigerate 30 minutes. Drain well and pat dry on paper towels.
2. In small bowl, combine dressing ingredients; whisk until smooth.
3. Add cucumbers to sour cream mixture, toss gently, and chill 1 hour before serving.

Variations:

A pinch of cayenne pepper can be added to taste.
Yogurt can be substituted for sour cream.

Make-It-Easy Tips:

√ Cucumbers are sprinkled with salt to extract excess moisture and make them crisper.

√ If using a hothouse cucumber, eliminate salting and refrigerating step. Slice, pat dry on towels, and proceed.

Banana Mousse

SERVES: 4
Preparation time: 15–20 minutes
Chilling time: 6 hours or overnight

I've included a banana mousse in this menu because I always seem to have a surplus of ripe bananas. It is an unusual dessert. Prepare it the morning it is to be served, or the night before, but not any earlier.

The Ingredients:

2 teaspoons unflavored gelatin
3 tablespoons cold water
1⅛ cups heavy cream
3 large, ripe bananas
1 tablespoon lemon juice

¼ cup granulated sugar
1 teaspoon vanilla extract
Garnish: Whipped cream and/or sliced strawberries, raspberries, or blueberries

The Steps:

1. Soften gelatin in water in Pyrex cup for 5 minutes.
2. Meanwhile, whip cream until stiff with electric beater and place in covered bowl in refrigerator.
3. Without cleaning beaters, mash bananas and beat with lemon juice until smooth. Add sugar and vanilla and continue to beat until smooth.
4. Place Pyrex cup of softened gelatin in small pan of simmering water and heat, stirring until gelatin is dissolved.
5. Add dissolved gelatin to banana puree; fold in whipped cream and pour into 2-quart soufflé dish or 8 little ramekins or custard dishes; chill for 6 hours or overnight.
6. Serve mousse chilled, garnished with additional whipped cream and sliced strawberries, raspberries, or blueberries.

Make-It-Easy Tips:

√ Lemon juice is added to keep banana from discoloring.

√ To get the foamiest whipped cream, chill bowl and beaters before beating. Use a deep and narrow bowl to prevent splatters. Whip slowly at first and then speed up until foamy.

√ Ultra-pasteurized cream has a longer storage life than regular pasteurized cream, but it has a poorer whipping quality and is a less effective sauce thickener.

√ If powdered gelatin is added to hot water directly, some of the granules will lump and not properly dissolve, thereby reducing the gelatin's thickening power. Once softened in cold water, the moistened crystals can easily dissolve.

√ Make sure that gelatin is thoroughly dissolved in Step #4, with no graininess, before adding remaining ingredients.

Far Eastern Delights

SERVES: 4
Kung Pao Chicken
***White Rice**
Spicy Chilled Chinese Noodles
Stir-Fried Zucchini and Water Chestnuts
(It Doesn't Matter That It Isn't Chinese) Strawberry Fool

Chinese cooking is a lifesaver when it comes to saving time *and* saving money. So when you're busy and on a budget, it's time to whip out the nearest wok and whip up some Oriental delights.

Chinese presentation is as uncomplicated as the cooking is speedy. Loaded with bright, glossy vegetables, the dishes look pretty in themselves and don't need a lot of extra fuss.

But a few extra touches can be inexpensive and fun. For instance, chopsticks add authenticity, and smiles, at low cost. Don't omit the forks, though—most Westerners will break down and use them before the meal is over.

Red is the traditional Chinese good-fortune color. If you have red napkins left over from Christmas or Valentine's Day, now is the time to use them. Fold like fans to enhance the Oriental mood, then stand them in goblets or tea cups.

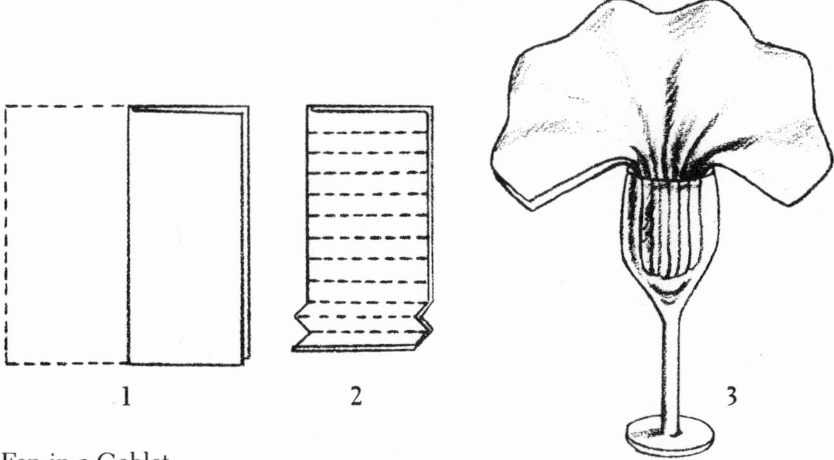

Fan in a Goblet
1. Fold the napkin in half. 2. Pleat in 1-inch accordion pleats all the way to the top. 3. Slip one end into a glass and allow the other to open up.

* Not a recipe

Chrysanthemums symbolize immortality to the Chinese—usually they are inexpensive, so they'll leave some life in your budget, too. You can bunch them in a bouquet, or arrange three blossoms floating in a recycled fish or punch bowl to liven up your table.

For serving dishes, any bowls, platters, or plates are fine. Footed bowls, if you have them, accent the Chinese look, but plain oval platters follow the custom of most Chinese restaurants. A vividly colored bowl sets off white rice with a striking contrast.

Chili peppers brighten both the color and the flavor of the zippy Kung Pao Chicken. Season it as you like, cutting down on the peppers for people who prefer a milder taste. You can even use a bunch of dried red peppers as part of the table decor. By all means be flexible with the Stir-Fried Zucchini and Water Chestnuts. Substitute other seasonal vegetables as desired.

Was it the Chinese who taught pasta to the Italians, or vice versa? Either way, the Spicy Chilled Chinese Noodles combine chewy and crunchy textures with a classic Chinese blend of flavors. Punctuate this dish with an easy garnish of scallion brushes.

It's doubtful, anyway, that the Europeans learned Strawberry Fool from the Chinese. Nevertheless, it's so cool and refreshing after a spicy meal that no one will waste time arguing about its origins.

Because these recipes cook so quickly and should reach the table shortly after they leave the stove, organizing ingredients is a must. Do all the chopping and measuring ahead of time and line up the ingredients in the order in which you will need them.

Have the noodles and their sauce ready to assemble. Cook the chicken dish first, then slip it into a warm oven for a few moments while you stir-fry the zucchini dish. Since the zucchini sits covered for a few moments, you'll have the perfect opportunity to assemble the noodle dish. And in minutes dinner is ready for the table.

Kung Pao Chicken

SERVES: 4
Preparation time: 20 minutes
Cooking time: 5–6 minutes

This spicy hot chicken dish can be toned down easily by limiting the amount of hot peppers.

The Ingredients:

½ cup raw peanuts
2 cups boneless chicken (approximately 2 breasts cut into 1¼ inch cubes)
1 tablespoon soy sauce
1 tablespoon cornstarch
6 whole dried red chili peppers, or to taste
3 scallions, cut into ¼″ slices (green part only)
1 clove garlic, finely minced
1 teaspoon finely minced ginger

Seasoning Sauce:

2 tablespoons soy sauce
1 tablespoon dry sherry
2 teaspoons sugar
1 teaspoon white vinegar
1 teaspoon toasted sesame oil
¼ cup peanut oil

The Steps:

1. While readying other ingredients, roast nuts in a 400° oven for 15 minutes or until golden.
2. In small bowl, combine chicken with soy sauce and cornstarch; mix well and set aside.
3. Wipe chili peppers with dampened towel, remove tips, and set on plate. Place scallions, garlic, and ginger on separate plate near cooking area; place roasted peanuts alongside other ingredients.
4. Combine soy sauce, sherry, sugar, vinegar, and sesame oil and stir to form seasoning sauce.
5. Heat wok, add peanut oil, and when hot, stir-fry red peppers until they turn dark red; add chicken and continue to stir-fry over high heat for 3 minutes or until chicken turns opaque. Remove chicken with slotted spoon, leaving excess oil in pan.

6. Add scallions, ginger, and garlic; stir-fry for 1 minute. Return chicken, add seasoning sauce, and stir-fry for 1 minute to combine flavors.
7. Add peanuts, stir, and serve immediately over white rice.

Variations:

Soaked Chinese mushrooms can be squeezed dry, cut into small triangles, and added with scallions.

Stir-fried noodles can be added in Step #7 and served instead of rice.

Nuts can be used untoasted to save time.

Make-It-Easy Tips:

√ Any type of chicken, dark or light meat, can be used.

√ Make sure to assemble all ingredients around the cooking area before heating the wok.

√ The dried red chili peppers used in this recipe can be found in Chinese, Italian, Greek, and Mexican stores. They are very hot, so proceed with caution. Store in a tightly covered jar at room temperature.

Spicy Chilled Chinese Noodles

SERVES: 4–6
Preparation time: 15–20 minutes
Cooking time: 10–15 minutes

The Ingredients:

1 pound spaghetti, spaghettini, or capellini
1½ tablespoons toasted sesame oil
¼ pound baked ham, shredded
1 8-ounce can water chestnuts, drained and diced
4 scallions, cut into ¼ inch pieces (green part only)

Sauce:

¼ cup soy sauce
¼ cup beef or chicken broth
3 tablespoons sesame seed paste or peanut butter
3 tablespoons Japanese rice or white wine vinegar

2 tablespoons toasted sesame oil
1 tablespoon sugar
1 teaspoon grated ginger
Tabasco to taste
Garnish: 2 tablespoons toasted sesame seeds

The Steps:

1. Drop noodles in boiling salted water, and cook until just tender, *al dente*. (Cook fresh noodles for 1–2 minutes, and dry according to package directions.) Drain well and sprinkle with 1½ tablespoons toasted sesame oil.
2. Place cooked noodles in serving bowl and garnish with ham, water chestnuts, and scallions.
3. In food processor, blender, or electric mixer, combine sauce ingredients until smooth.
4. Pour over noodles, top with sesame seeds, toss, and serve immediately, garnished with scallion brushes.

Variation:

Hot chili oil can be added to sauce for spiciness with Tabasco omitted.

Make-It-Easy Tips:

√ Do not assemble salad until just before serving or noodles may become gummy. Sauce and noodles can be readied in advance and assembled at last minute.

√ Tiny cooked shrimp, shredded chicken, diced pork, or whatever fish, poultry, or meat desired can be added to salad.

√ If substituting fresh pasta, either Italian or Chinese, cook no longer than 1–2 minutes or it will become gummy and pasty. If fresh pasta is frozen, cook without thawing.

√ Chinese sesame seed paste, prepared from toasted sesame seeds, has a nuttier and more pronounced flavor than the Middle Eastern tahini, which is prepared with untoasted sesame seeds.

√ Sesame seeds can turn rancid if stored at room temperature. For long storage, keep in refrigerator or freezer; thaw, toast, and proceed with recipe.

√ To make a scallion brush easily, cut off root end of onion and top part; leave piece 2½″–3″ long. With sharp paring knife make many crisscross incisions in each end. Soak in cold water for several hours and they will "flower." (See illustration.)

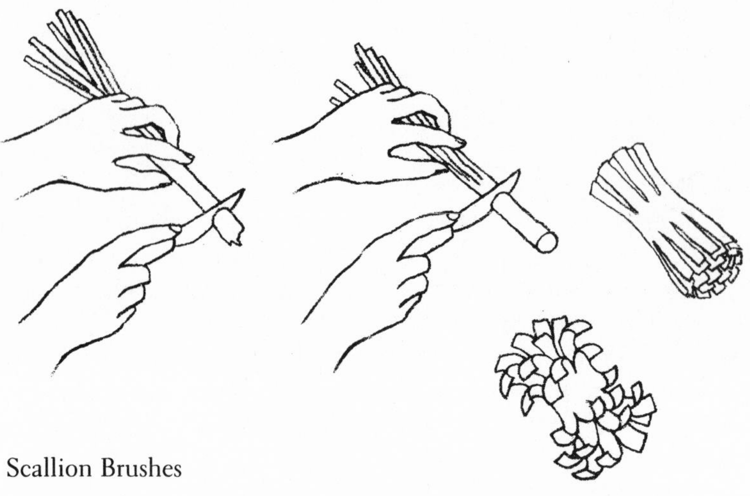

Scallion Brushes

Stir-Fried Zucchini and Water Chestnuts

SERVES: 4
Preparation time: 10–15 minutes
Cooking time: 5 minutes

The Ingredients:

1 pound zucchini, sliced in ¼″ thick rounds
1 8-ounce can sliced water chestnuts, drained (or use one 5-ounce can whole water chestnuts, drained and sliced in half vertically)
¼ cup chicken broth
1 tablespoon soy sauce
½ teaspoon sugar
3 scallions, cut in ¼″ pieces (green part only)
2–3 tablespoons peanut oil
Salt to taste

The Steps:

1. Assemble zucchini and water chestnuts in bowls near cooking area; mix broth, soy sauce, and sugar together and also set near cooking area.
2. Heat wok and add oil; when hot, add scallions and stir-fry for 30 seconds; add salt and stir.
3. Add zucchini and stir-fry for 1–2 minutes, coating well with the oil; add water chestnuts.
4. Add soy sauce mixture, stir, cover, reduce heat to medium-low and cook 2–3 minutes, or until zucchini is tender but still crunchy in texture.
5. Taste for seasonings, adjust to taste, and serve zucchini hot.

Variations:

Substitute parboiled broccoli or asparagus for the zucchini.

Substitute shredded Jerusalem artichokes (sunchokes) or the Mexican root vegetable jicama for the crunchy texture of water chestnuts.

Low sodium soy sauce may be substituted for those who wish to restrict their salt intake.

Make-It-Easy Tip:

√ Select fresh, firm, young zucchini. Avoid limp ones with blemishes. Zucchini are quite perishable. Keep in refrigerator in a plastic bag for only 1–2 days before using.

(It Doesn't Matter That It Isn't Chinese) Strawberry Fool

SERVES: 4
Preparation time: 20 minutes
Chilling time: 2–3 hours or overnight

The name "fool" originated from the French word "foulé," meaning crushed. It is a dessert made of any cooked fruit and cream.

The Ingredients:

½ pound fresh strawberries, hulled, or equivalent amount frozen strawberries, thawed

¼ cup granulated sugar
1½ cup heavy cream
¼ cup confectioner's sugar, or to taste

The Steps:

1. In small saucepan, heat berries with granulated sugar until boiling. Reduce heat and simmer slowly, stirring often, for 8–10 minutes.
2. Remove from heat and puree in food processor, blender, or through food mill. Chill for 2–3 hours or overnight.
3. Whip cream until just stiff. Add confectioner's sugar and continue to beat until stiff peaks form.
4. Fold into chilled fruit puree so that fruit streaks through cream, place in parfait glasses or desert dishes, and serve immediately.

Variation:

Blackberries, blueberries, raspberries, peaches, or any seasonal fruit can be used and sweetened to taste.

Make-It-Easy Tips:

√ To whip cream easily, chill bowl and beaters for half an hour prior to whipping.

√ When selecting a basket of blackberries, avoid any with stains, a sure sign the berries are softening or decaying.

Limited-Funds Feast

SERVES: 6–8
The Ultimate Casserole
Radish, Cucumber, and Fennel Salad
Onion Bread
Make Your Own Sundaes
Hot Fudge Sauce
Butterscotch Sauce

This menu is perfect when there are more guests than money available. It allows you to entertain graciously and successfully on a shoestring budget.

Casseroles are great standbys since they are both economical and easy. The trick is to keep them interesting. The Ultimate Casserole is full of surprises and guaranteed to feed a hungry crowd of family and friends. It's also designed to be served with just a fork and to be balanced on a lap when you have more company than table space.

Since this is a relaxed, informal meal, decorating is extra easy. Small flowering plants make an instant centerpiece—just reach for the nearest pot of African violets or begonias to brighten the table.

As always, plan ahead for a no-hassle buffet. Do as much cutting, chopping, and assembling as possible in advance. Now you are ready to begin the evening with uncluttered counters and an empty sink—which makes cleanup a snap. Assemble the casserole in advance, or even bake it, freeze it, then reheat it at dinnertime. Try doubling the recipe and freezing an extra for a future dinner. Assemble the salad and prepare the dressing earlier, too—just save the tossing for the last minute. You can also prepare the butter for the Onion Bread ahead of time, as well as the sundae sauces, which refrigerate successfully.

Line up the buffet as follows: plates, food, cutlery, and napkins. As an alternative, create a cutlery holder out of a napkin. Fold the napkin in half, fold the top flap back, one half again. Turn the napkin over, fold into quarters, and insert the utensils. (See illustration.)

A basket for the casserole is an inexpensive, pretty way to protect fingers, and a trivet protects your table top. Cutting the casserole into squares makes one-handed serving easy. Tongs do the same for the salad, and tossing in the dressing makes one less step—and one less potential spill—than serving salad dressing on the side. Pile the Onion Bread high for a bountiful look in a basket lined with a napkin or pretty dish towel.

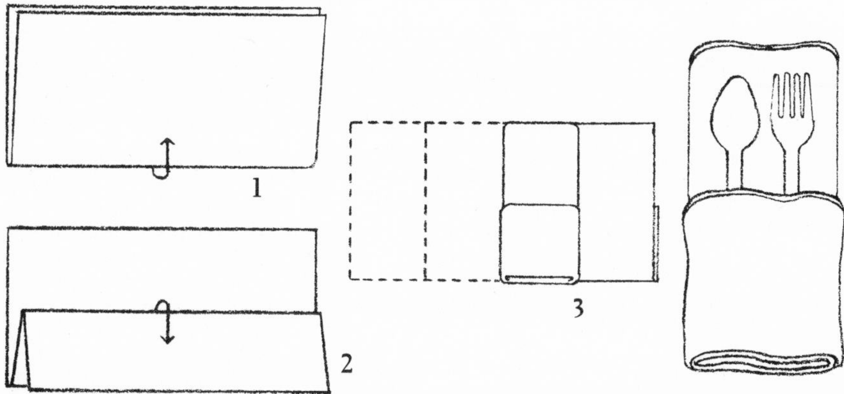

The Cutlery Holder
1. Fold the napkin in half. 2. Fold the top flap back one half. 3. Turn the napkin over, fold it into quarters and insert the utensils.

Make Your Own Sundaes are a treat for kids of all ages. Choose whatever toppings suit your taste and your budget. The fun additions let you go with a "bargain brand" ice cream. Save this buffet-style dessert for a grand finale after all the dinner dishes are cleared out of your way.

The Ultimate Casserole

SERVES: 6–8
Preparation time: 20 minutes
Cooking time: 1 hour, 15 minutes

The bacon-based tomato sauce combined with the olives, chicken, cheese, and pasta will delight even those who usually avoid casseroles.

The Ingredients:

6 slices bacon, diced
1 large onion, thinly sliced
10 large mushrooms, sliced
1 28-ounce can crushed tomatoes, packed in puree, drained
1 cup pimiento-stuffed olives, sliced
Salt and freshly ground pepper to taste
3 cups cooked chicken, diced in large cubes
1 pound spaghetti, cooked
3 cups grated Cheddar cheese

The Steps:

1. Preheat oven to 350°. Lightly butter large lasagne-style baking dish, approximately 11″ x 14″ x 3″.
2. In large skillet, sauté bacon over medium-high heat until browned; remove bacon to paper towels to drain.
3. Remove all but 2 tablespoons grease from pan, and sauté onions and mushrooms until golden.
4. Add tomatoes, olives, bacon, salt, and pepper; bring to a boil and simmer 10 minutes. Add chicken and stir until thoroughly combined.
5. Meanwhile, boil pasta in salted boiling water until *al dente*; drain and rinse under cold water.

6. On bottom layer of prepared casserole, place half of spaghetti, half of chicken, and half of cheese. Repeat layers ending with cheese on top, and bake for 1 hour, or until hot and bubbly.
7. Serve cut in squares.

Variations:

Grated Swiss, Monterey Jack, or Muenster cheese can be substituted for Cheddar.

1 tablespoon chopped parsley, ¼ teaspoon dried basil, and ¼ teaspoon dried oregano can be added to taste.

If tomatoes packed in puree are unavailable, use regular whole juice-packed tomatoes; chop, drain off most of the liquid. Return tomatoes to can, and fill to the top with canned tomato puree.

Make-It-Easy Tips:

√ Pasta is rinsed under cold water to stop the cooking immediately and wash off excess starch.

√ Store mushrooms in paper bag in refrigerator, which allows air to circulate and keep them fresh.

√ Bacon dices easily if frozen.

√ Casserole can be cooked in advance and frozen for future use. Reheat frozen in 325° oven for 1 hour, or until hot and bubbly.

Radish, Cucumber, and Fennel Salad

SERVES: 6–8
Preparation time: 10 minutes

This salad also works well as part of an antipasto platter with Julienne of Carrot Salad and Green Bean and Onion Salad.

The Ingredients:

1 large cucumber, peeled, seeded, and thinly sliced
1 bulb fennel, thinly sliced with feathery top included
2 bunches radishes, thinly sliced
1 tablespoon freshly chopped parsley

Dressing:

⅓ cup olive oil
3 tablespoons lemon juice
⅓ teaspoon freshly minced garlic
⅛ teaspoon oregano, crumbled
Salt and freshly ground pepper to taste

The Steps:

1. Place cucumber, fennel, radishes, and parsley in salad bowl.
2. Combine dressing ingredients in screw-top jar and shake well to combine.
3. Pour dressing over salad ingredients, toss, and serve.

Variations:

Salad can be prepared in advance and allowed to chill for several hours.

Sliced celery can be substituted for fennel.

Make-It-Easy Tips:

√ Fennel, also called finocchio, fenucchi, or anise, resembles celery in appearance and texture but has an anise or licorice flavor. Select compact, greenish-white bulbs with crisp green stalks. If you refrigerate bulbs in perforated plastic bags, they will keep for 5–7 days.

√ Select firm, medium-sized radishes with good red color. Avoid overly large ones, which tend to have a woody or spongy texture.

Onion Bread

YIELD: 1 loaf
Preparation time: 10–15 minutes
Cooking time: 20 minutes

The Ingredients:

Onion Butter:

2 tablespoons unsalted butter
½ cup finely chopped onion
¼ pound (1 stick) unsalted butter

Salt and freshly ground pepper to taste
1 loaf French, Italian, or sourdough bread

The Steps:

1. In skillet, heat 2 tablespoons butter; add onions and sauté over medium heat until soft and just golden; allow to cool slightly.
2. Preheat oven to 375°.
3. In food processor, blender, electric mixer, or by hand, combine onions with ¼ pound butter, salt, and pepper until just smooth.
4. Slice bread horizontally, spread with onion butter, reform into loaf, loosely wrap in aluminum foil and bake for 10 minutes.
5. Open up foil and continue to bake for an additional 5–10 minutes or until crisp and golden.
6. Serve immediately, cut in slices.

Variations:

Scallions or shallots can be substituted for onions.
¼ cup freshly grated Parmesan cheese can be added to butter mixture.

Make-It-Easy Tips:

√ It is easier to butter bread lengthwise and then cut into small slices after baking.
√ Slice bread easily with a serrated-edged knife.
√ If preparing butter by hand, make sure to soften the butter first. If you've forgotten to soften the butter, simply grate it and it will soften in a minute.

Make Your Own Sundaes

SERVES: 6–8
Preparation time: 5

A variety of sauces, ice creams to taste, and a few toppings make this a festive and inexpensive way to end this casual dinner.

The Ingredients:

2 pints vanilla ice cream
1 pint chocolate ice cream

Sauces:
Hot Fudge Sauce (recipe to follow)
Hot Butterscotch Sauce (recipe to follow)

Optional Toppings (select two or three):
Chopped nuts
Chopped toffee
Chopped fresh fruits
Liqueurs (coffee, chocolate, almond)
Cookie crumbs or granola
Shredded coconut
Chocolate chips
Whipped cream

The Steps:

1. Place scoops of ice cream in large bowl.
2. Place sauces nearby and surround with bowls of toppings.
3. Ask everyone to make his or her own sundae.

Variation:

Use all vanilla or vary ice cream flavors to taste.

Make-It-Easy Tip:

√ To scoop out ice cream easily, dip ice cream scoop in hot water before each scoop.

Hot Fudge Sauce

YIELD: ¾ cup
Preparation time: 5 minutes

The Ingredients:

6 ounces real semisweet chocolate chips
3 ounces butter
2 tablespoons heavy cream
½ teaspoon vanilla extract

The Steps:

1. In double boiler over simmering water, or heavy saucepan over low heat, melt chocolate and butter together until soft, smooth, and shiny.
2. Add cream and vanilla and continue to stir until smooth.
3. Remove from heat, stir well, and serve warm.

Make-It-Easy Tips:

√ The sauce can be made in advance and kept warm in the double boiler.

√ Never cover a pot in which chocolate is melting. Any excess moisture or condensation will "stiffen" the chocolate and prevent it from combining easily with the rest of the ingredients.

Hot Butterscotch Sauce

YIELD: 1¼ cups
Preparation time: 5 minutes
Cooking time: 5–10 minutes

The Ingredients:

⅓ cup (5 tablespoons plus 1 teaspoon) unsalted butter
1 cup light brown sugar, firmly packed
⅓ cup heavy cream

The Steps:

1. In small saucepan, heat butter over low heat; when melted, stir in sugar and cream.
2. Bring to a boil, reduce heat, and simmer for 3–5 minutes, without stirring.
3. Remove from heat, stir well, and serve warm.

Variation:

Sauce can be kept in refrigerator and served chilled or reheated.

Make-It-Easy Tip:

√ Remember to firmly pack brown sugar down. (One pound of brown sugar equals 2¼ cups firmly packed.)

√ As the sauce cools, it continues to thicken.

Just Desserts

SERVES: 8–10
Royal Ice Cream Torte
Glazed Oatmeal Cake
Cocoa Brownies
Apricot Bars
Irish Coffee

It is perfectly permissible to cut down on entertainment expenses by skipping the main meal entirely and starting with dessert. It's a great accompaniment to an evening of cards, or just a friendly celebration.

A simple buffet arrangement works best, allowing people to help themselves. Put plates on one end of the buffet, followed by the desserts, napkins, silverware, and coffee. People appreciate a pot of plain and brewed decaffeinated coffee or tea as an alternative to the whiskey-spiked Irish treat.

Since the Irish coffee needs no spoon, most people will require only a fork. The forks can be rolled in napkins, then arranged in an interesting pattern on the table. Cups, saucers, and spoons for those who choose plain coffee or tea can be placed nearby.

An added advantage to serving desserts is that they are decorative in themselves. When you prepare the brownies, you might save a few walnuts to sprinkle on top before baking. The apricot bars might be dressed up similarly with slivers of dried apricots. Extra apricots left over will add bits of edible color placed here and there on the serving plate. The torte and oatmeal cake look picture pretty without extra dressing up. You might even place a large jar or canister of multicolored jelly beans on the table as a colorful addition.

Tiered cake plates add height that shows off dainty items like the brownies and apricot bars. Stacking the brownies or apricot bars in mounds or pyramids also adds height, while lining the plates with paper doilies lends an expensive but pretty touch.

People can enjoy the desserts comfortably in the living room if coffee tables or end tables provide enough space. But bridge tables can also be decked out for double-duty, with open napkins for place mats. Or try crisscrossing runners in different colors of crepe paper.

Amidst all these sweets, a very simple centerpiece provides all the extra accent necessary. Consider a few candles on the buffet, a recycled candy jar filled with dried flowers, or a tiered arrangement of candies—anywhere you please.

And don't forget a large bowl of fresh fruit for those limiting their sweet intake. It's a thoughtful gesture, bound to be appreciated.

Of course, serving dessert after you've just served your own family dinner does not allow you much preparation time. Luckily, every item in this menu—except the coffee—can be made in advance and frozen. Slightly thawed, they will slice easily, then warm to room temperature. The exception here is the Royal Ice Cream Torte. Remove it from the freezer minutes before serving, then give it a grand last-minute entrance.

Royal Ice Cream Torte

SERVES: 8–10
Preparation time: 12–20 minutes
Cooking time: 8 minutes
Freezing time: 3–4 hours or longer

The Ingredients:

1 8½-ounce package chocolate wafers, crumbled
2 tablespoons unsalted butter, melted
1½ pints chocolate ice cream, softened
2 cups prepared chocolate fudge topping or Hot Fudge Sauce (see page 90)
1½ pints mint chocolate chip ice cream, softened
6 Heath Bars or similar toffee candy, crushed
Accompaniment: Chocolate fudge topping

The Steps:

1. Preheat oven to 350°. Lightly oil 8″ springform pan or spray with nonaerosol vegetable shortening.
2. Moisten crumbs with melted butter and mash with fork. Place in springform mold. Bake crust for 8 minutes; cool.
3. Place softened chocolate ice cream over crushed wafers. Spoon 1 cup fudge sauce over chocolate ice cream; top with mint ice cream and spoon remaining fudge sauce over.
4. Sprinkle top with crushed Heath Bars, cover with foil, and place in freezer for at least 3–4 hours before serving. Remove from freezer 10–15 minutes before serving, place on platter, unlock springform sides, and remove. Serve with additional fudge sauce on the side.

Variation:

Ice cream flavors can be varied to taste. Try raspberry sherbet and chocolate ice cream, or vanilla with strawberry, or whatever creation desired.

Make-It-Easy Tips:

√ Torte can be made in advance and frozen for several weeks.
√ Crush candy easily by chilling first and then crushing in food processor. If doing by hand, freeze first, place in strong plastic bag, and bang with hammer until crushed.

Glazed Oatmeal Cake

SERVES: 10–12
Preparation time: 15 minutes
Cooking time: 40 minutes

The Ingredients:

1 cup oatmeal
1 cup brown sugar, firmly packed
¾ cup all-purpose flour
¾ cup whole wheat flour
½ cup white sugar
1½ teaspoons baking soda
1 teaspoon cinnamon
½ teaspoon ground nutmeg
Pinch of salt
2 eggs
1 cup whole milk
½ cup vegetable oil
2 tablespoons molasses

Frosting:

1¼ cups brown sugar
1 cup shredded coconut (optional)
1 cup chopped pecans
4 ounces (1 stick) unsalted butter, melted
6 tablespoons half-and-half

The Steps:

1. Preheat oven to 350°. Generously butter 9″ x 12″ x 2″ baking pan.
2. In large bowl, mix oatmeal, brown sugar, flours, white sugar, baking soda, cinnamon, nutmeg, and salt; stir to combine.
3. In separate bowl, beat eggs, add milk, oil, and molasses, and continue to beat until smooth.
4. Add egg mixture to flour mixture and combine until smooth; pour batter into prepared pan and bake for 35–40 minutes or until inserted knife comes out clean.
5. Remove cake from oven and turn heat to broil.
6. Combine frosting ingredients in bowl, mix until smooth, spread on baked cake, and broil 4″ from heat for 2–3 minutes, watching carefully until just glazed and golden.

7. Allow to cool, cut into squares, and serve warm or at room temperature.

Make-It-Easy Tips:

√ Cake can be frozen successfully uncut. Thaw slightly and easily cut into squares.

√ Whole wheat flour is more nutritious but has a shorter shelf life, so purchase in small quantities.

√ When measuring molasses, lightly oil the spoon prior to measuring and the sticky liquid will fall off more easily.

√ When measuring brown sugar, always pack firmly into measuring cup.

Cocoa Brownies

YIELD: 16 bar cookies
Preparation time: 10–15 minutes
Cooking time: 35–40 minutes

The Ingredients:

2 cups sugar
1 cup vegetable oil
1½ cups all-purpose flour
½ cup (2 ounces) cocoa
4 eggs, lightly beaten
1 teaspoon vanilla
1 cup chopped walnuts (optional)

The Steps:

1. Preheat oven to 350°. Generously butter 9″-square baking pan.
2. In large mixing bowl, beat sugar and oil together; add flour, cocoa, eggs, and vanilla and continue to beat until smooth.
3. Add optional nuts, pour into prepared pan, and bake 35–40 minutes or until just set but not overbaked.
4. Allow to cool slightly, cut into squares, and serve.

Variation:

Brownies can also be baked in an 8″ square pan but cooked 5–10 minutes longer.

Make-It-Easy Tip:

√ Light or excessive heat causes deterioration in vanilla. Store bottle in box in which it comes.

Apricot Bars

YIELD: 16 bar cookies
Preparation time: 20 minutes
Cooking time: 50–55 minutes

The Ingredients:

6 ounces dried apricots
4 ounces (1 stick) unsalted butter
¼ cup dark brown sugar, firmly packed
1⅓ cups all-purpose flour
½ teaspoon baking powder
Pinch of salt
1 cup dark brown sugar, firmly packed
2 eggs, lightly beaten
1 teaspoon vanilla extract
Garnish: Confectioner's sugar

The Steps:

1. Place apricots in small saucepan and add water to cover; bring to a boil, cover and simmer for 10 minutes or until apricots just begin to soften. Drain, cool slightly, and finely chop.
2. Preheat oven to 350°. Generously butter 8″-square baking pan; dust lightly with flour.
3. In large mixing bowl, cream butter with ¼ cup of the brown sugar with electric beater until light and fluffy. Add 1 cup of the flour and mix until crumbly.
4. Spread batter in prepared pan and bake for 20 minutes or until lightly golden.

5. Meanwhile, sift remaining ⅓ cup flour, baking powder, and salt together into bowl. Add remaining 1 cup brown sugar, eggs, vanilla, and chopped apricots, and mix well.
6. Spread over baked layer and continue to bake for 20–25 minutes or until lightly golden.
7. Cool in pan. When slightly cool, cut into bars, sprinkle with confectioner's sugar, and serve.

Variation:

⅓ cup chopped walnuts or pecans can be added to taste.

Make-It-Easy Tip:

√ Once opened, a package of dried apricots should be stored in a tightly covered container in the refrigerator to preserve color and moisture. Frozen dried apricots will keep indefinitely.

Irish Coffee

SERVES: 1
Preparation time: 5 minutes

Recipe is given for a single serving. Multiply as necessary.

The Ingredients:

1–2 teaspoons sugar (or 1 lump)
1 jigger Irish whiskey (about 1½ fluid ounces)
½ cup strong black coffee
2–3 tablespoons sweetened whipped cream

The Steps:

1. Put sugar into large goblet (about 6–7 ounce size).
2. Pour whiskey over sugar and fill glass to within ½″ of top with strong black hot coffee.
3. Stir together to dissolve sugar.
4. Top with sweetened whipped cream but do not stir. The fun is sipping the hot coffee and whiskey through the cool cream.

Variation:

Grated chocolate or cinnamon can be used as a topping if desired.

Make-It-Easy Tip:

√ A jigger container—either metal, glass, or plastic—resembles a small whiskey glass and is often called a "shot glass." There seems to be no universal agreement on the amount of liquid that goes to make up a jigger. Generally 1½ fluid ounces is considered to be the correct amount, although there are large jiggers of 2 ounces and small jiggers of 1 ounce.

Country Fare

SERVES: 4
Tortilla Baskets
Addy's Chicken
Green Bean and Onion Salad
Bread
Light Lemon Pie

This budget-minded dinner saves you preparation time and cleanup chores, as well as money. It's hearty country fare, with a bit of a Mexican accent.

A simple table also saves you decorating time. Aim for a stylishly rustic look. Use any tablecloth you like, or none at all if the tabletop is pretty by itself. Napkins, opened and laid out like diamonds, make improvised place mats. Turn part of the meal itself into a centerpiece by serving the bread on a board right in the middle of the table. A round or braided loaf adds a festive flair of its own.

The breadboard and rustic motif make this a perfect time to use any wooden utensils you have—wooden dishes, salad bowls, napkin rings, or even wooden spoons for serving.

If you want to add a little more "special occasion" atmosphere, candles dress up the countryside theme with soft, old-fashioned light. Votive candles are inexpensive; they can shine on the table, or here and there around the room, in candlesticks, saucers, or even ashtrays. A selection of dried flowers or branches such as dogwood, lilac, or pussy willow enhance the country mood.

The Tortilla Baskets add the option of an unusual but budget-smart appetizer. People can enjoy them served on small plates in the living room. Remember to include little forks and lots of napkins.

The Green Bean and Onion Salad perks up the table with its splash of color. It's also a make-ahead dish that can sit in the refrigerator from two hours to two days.

Addy's Chicken teams up those classic budget-stretchers—chicken, potatoes, and onions—all in one dish for a supper-satisfying meal. Save extra money by buying a whole chicken instead of a package of higher-priced cut-up parts. It takes almost no time to easily hack a chicken into pieces with a Chinese cleaver or chef's knife. You can show off this tasty combination of flavors on an oval platter, ringed with sprigs of parsley.

Butter for the bread can get an extra touch, too. Soften it and pack it in a crock, a mug, even a wide-mouthed sugar bowl. Or put it on a plate, and brighten it with sprigs of parsley or a few leaves of watercress.

Dessert won't wear out your budget or you when it's Lemon Pie with an easy crumb crust. Bake it while the chicken simmers, or freeze it days ahead. And as long as you're using the lemon juice, you might take a minute to use the peel as a garnish. Remove the peel in a long strip with a vegetable peeler. Then wind the peel into curls or spirals to top each slice of pie.

Tortilla Baskets

SERVES: 4
Preparation time: 5–10 minutes
Cooking time: 2–3 minutes

Serve these broiled crisp appetizers piping hot.

The Ingredients:

4 snack-size flour tortillas
1 cup (4 ounces) grated Cheddar cheese
2 tablespoons green chile salsa
2 teaspoons freshly grated onion
Garnish: Dairy sour cream

The Steps:

1. Preheat broiler.
2. Place each tortilla in small tart pan, or shape heavy-duty aluminum foil into mini-tart pan shape. Push down in center so tortilla forms shell.
3. Sprinkle each tortilla with 1½ teaspoons salsa, ⅓ teaspoon onion, and 2 tablespoons cheese. Repeat layers, ending with cheese on top.
4. Broil 3″ from heat until hot and bubbly, and tortilla is crisp and golden. Serve immediately with dollop of sour cream.

Variations:

Use green chile salsa available in the market or prepare salsa (see page 264).

If snack-size tortillas are unavailable, substitute the larger tortillas and increase cheese and salsa.

Monterey Jack cheese can be substituted for Cheddar cheese.

Make-It-Easy Tips:

√ When placing tortillas in tart pans, push down gently to avoid ripping the tortillas.

√ If mold forms on the surface of hard cheese, just scrape it off. The cheese is still good.

Addy's Chicken

SERVES: 4
Preparation time: 15–20 minutes
Cooking time: 35–40 minutes

Although the ingredients are more French than Mexican, this recipe comes from a Mexican woman who serves this inexpensive dish frequently.

The Ingredients:

1 3-pound chicken, cut into 8 pieces
Salt and freshly ground pepper to taste
2 tablespoons unsalted butter
2 tablespooons olive oil
2 large onions, thinly sliced
1 cup dry white wine or dry vermouth
¾ cup chicken broth
2 teaspoons oregano, crumbled
2 large potatoes, thickly sliced
Salt and freshly ground pepper to taste

The Steps:

1. Wash chicken, pat dry, and lightly season with salt and pepper.
2. Heat butter and oil together in large deep skillet and brown chicken over high heat until golden. Remove chicken and set aside.
3. Add onions and sauté over medium heat for 3–4 minutes, scraping up browned particles from bottom of pan.
4. Add wine, allow to boil for a minute, and then add broth and oregano.
5. Return chicken to pan, arrange potatoes on top, cover, and simmer slowly for 30–35 minutes or until chicken is tender.
6. Adjust seasonings with salt and pepper to taste and serve immediately.

Variations:

Chicken thighs, chicken breasts, or a combination of both can be substituted for the whole chicken.

Sliced carrots can be added and sautéed with onions.

Make-It-Easy Tips:

√ Dish must be served immediately or the potatoes will become mushy. If preparing in advance, complete cooking through Step #4 and refrigerate the chicken and sauce separately. Reheat both, add chicken, arrange potatoes on top, and proceed with recipe.

√ Store potatoes in a cool, dry, well-ventilated place. Do not store in refrigerator. The potato starch will convert to sugar and result in an overly sweet-tasting potato. To reverse this problem, remove potato from refrigerator and sugar will convert back to starch.

Green Bean and Onion Salad

SERVES: 4
Preparation time: 15 minutes
Cooking time: 2–3 minutes
Chilling time: 2 hours or overnight

The green beans can be cooked and marinated one or two days in advance.

The Ingredients:

1½ pounds fresh green beans
½ cup olive oil
3 tablespoons white wine vinegar
2 tablespoons roughly chopped parsley
1 tablespoon freshly snipped dill or 1 teaspoon dried dill weed (optional)
2 scallion greens, roughly chopped
1 teaspoon Dijon mustard
Pinch of sugar
Salt and freshly ground pepper to taste
1 medium-size sweet Bermuda onion
1 cup cherry tomatoes

The Steps:

1. Trim ends off beans, place in large saucepan of boiling salted water, and cook for 3–5 minutes, depending on size of bean, or until just tender. Drain in colander and immediately place under cold running water.

2. In food processor or blender, process olive oil, vinegar, parsley, dill, scallions, mustard, sugar, salt, and pepper until smooth.
3. Pour dressing over beans, toss well, cover and chill for 2 hours or overnight.
4. One hour before serving, thinly slice onion, cut cherry tomatoes in half, and add to beans; gently toss and refrigerate until ready to serve chilled.

Variation:

Small tomato wedges can be substituted for cherry tomatoes; if out of season, omit entirely.

Make-It-Easy Tips:

√ When adding beans to boiling water in Step #1, add beans gradually to keep water boiling constantly.

√ Green beans should be rinsed under cold water to stop cooking process and ensure a bright green color.

Light Lemon Pie

YIELD: Two 9″ pies
Preparation time: 20 minutes
Cooking time: 30 minutes

This Lemon Pie is so creamy it resembles a cheesecake. The recipe is for two pies since it is easier to prepare two at one time. Freeze the other for a great dessert ready for last-minute company.

The Ingredients:

3 cups chocolate wafer crumbs (about 45–50 wafers)
10 tablespoons (5 ounces) unsalted butter, melted
¼ cup sugar

Filling:

1 14-ounce can sweetened condensed milk
Juice of 2 lemons (about 4–6 tablespoons)
4 eggs, separated
Pinch of salt
Garnish: Spirals of lemon peel or thinly sliced lemons

The Steps:

1. Preheat oven to 350°. Lightly butter two 9″ pie plates.
2. In bowl, mix cookie crumbs, butter, and sugar together. Spoon into prepared pans and, using back of spoon, firmly press against bottom and sides of pan. Bake 8–10 minutes. Cool slightly before filling.
3. In large bowl, mix milk with lemon juice; whisk in egg yolks until smooth.
4. In separate bowl, whip egg whites until slightly stiff. Add salt and continue to beat until stiff peaks form.
5. Gently fold beaten whites into lemon mixture, pour into prepared pie pans and bake for 20–25 minutes or until lightly golden and inserted knife comes out clean.
6. Remove from oven, cool slightly, and chill. Serve chilled with a garnish of spirals of lemon peel and thinly sliced lemons.

Variations:

To cut down on preparation time, substitute 2 prepared graham cracker crusts.

Graham crackers, ginger snaps, vanilla wafers, or any type of cookie can be used for crust.

Make-It-Easy Tips:

√ Crust can be frozen for 20 minutes, instead of baking.

√ Egg whites will not whip stiffly, if there is even a trace of egg yolk. If any yolk should fall into the whites, scoop it out with a large piece of egg shell.

√ Do not beat egg whites in an aluminum bowl or they will develop a grayish tint, unless the bowl is the new anodized aluminum.

√ If sweetened condensed milk is unavailable, substitute the following mixture: In food processor or blender, combine 1 cup instant nonfat dry milk solids, ⅔ cup granulated sugar, ½ cup boiling water, and 3 tablespoons melted unsalted butter. Process until smooth and store in covered container in refrigerator until ready to use.

√ Pie is best when served chilled. If freezing, remember to leave at room temperature for 15 minutes prior to serving.

Reinventing the Fondue Party

SERVES: 8–10
Swiss Cheese Fondue
Spinach Salad with Almonds
Lemon-Raspberry Delight

I think it's time to revive the fondue party. It's truly fun, inexpensive, and an instant way to turn guests into a group. With everyone dipping into one pot, it's a great icebreaker. Besides, Swiss cooks have been balancing budgets and pleasing palates with fondue for generations, so who's to call it passé?

I also love fondue's versatility. A number of cheeses can replace the Swiss, so buy one that's on sale this week. You can use up stale bread with fondue, or use raw vegetables for a lower-calorie alternative. Or you can offer both. If you're short of fondue forks, skewers will do—or any fork with a long handle. In place of wine, beer can be used. Even the pot itself need not be an "official" fondue pot. A crock-pot will work, or serve the fondue in an earthenware bowl. The idea is just to keep it warm.

Salad is the traditional accompaniment for fondue. It provides color, texture, and a fresh, zesty taste to contrast with the creamy cheese sauce. The cooling sherbet with its colorful raspberry topping makes a bright, refreshing finale after the hot fondue.

Setting the table for fondue is especially easy, since the fondue pot itself becomes the centerpiece. Bread cubes look pretty in baskets lined with bright napkins or checkered cloths, and you can show off vegetables in baskets or bowl lined with curly red or green lettuce leaves. It can help to use a few small bowls or baskets instead of one large one to keep their contents within easy reach. Cutlery can be bundled by wrapping each place setting in a napkin, tying with bright yarn or ribbon, and placing in a basket or bowl.

Most importantly, everyone should be able to reach the pot of fondue without stretching. A round table works best, but you can substitute two bridge tables, each with its own pot.

Bread can be cubed and popped into a plastic bag until needed. Vegetables can be cut, wrapped, and chilled ahead of time. The cheese can be shredded and even the sauce for dessert prepared beforehand and refrigerated. Then, when it's time to cook, get some volunteer help in the kitchen—perhaps the best icebreaker of all.

Swiss Cheese Fondue
(Fondue Neufchâteloise)

SERVES: 8–10
Preparation time: 15 minutes
Cooking time: 10 minutes

The secret of a successful fondue is the grains of starch in the potato flour, which hold the cheese in suspension in the wine and help keep the mixture stable by acting as a binder.

The Ingredients:

1 pound Gruyère cheese, shredded
1 pound Swiss (Emmentaler) Cheese, shredded
2 tablespoons potato starch flour
2 cloves garlic, cut and sliced in half

4 cups dry white wine
6 tablespoons Kirsch or Kirschwasser
Freshly ground nutmeg to taste
Freshly ground white pepper to taste
2 large loaves French, Italian, or sourdough bread, with crust left on, cut into 1″ cubes (with crust on each piece); and/or *crudités* (see Variations).

The Steps:

1. In large bowl, toss cheeses with flour.
2. Rub inside of large fondue pot or any two-quart flameproof cocotte or similar heavy cooking vessel with cut sides of garlic.
3. Pour in wine and heat until tiny air bubbles rise to the surface (almost to the boil).
4. Gradually add coated cheese, by handfuls, stirring constantly over low heat with wooden fork or spoon, until cheese is melted.
5. Reduce heat and stir in Kirschwasser; season with nutmeg and pepper and serve immediately with speared bread cubes or crudités.

Variations:

Varieties of cheese that may be substituted: Appenzeller, Cheddar (cook with beer), Edam, Fontina, Gouda, Jarlsberg, Mozzarella, and Muenster.

For wine, substitute beer, dry vermouth or even champagne.

For Kirschwasser, substitute cognac, brandy, or even whiskey.

1 tablespoon cornstarch or all-purpose flour may be substituted for potato starch. It may also be dissolved in Kirschwasser and added in Step #5.

In place of bread cubes, substitute *crudités* such as sliced broccoli florets, carrots, celery, cherry tomatoes, raw mushrooms, green pepper, and scallions, or even cooked shrimp, ham cubes, or boiled potatoes.

Make-It-Easy Tips:

√ The only necessary utensils for preparing fondue are a heavy cooking vessel, a supply of long forks or spears, and a portable heat source such as a fondue pot, an electric hot plate, an electric crock-pot, a Bunsen burner, a Sterno ("canned heat") stove, or even a small electric frypan.

√ Stale bread is ideal for use in fondues.

- √ If fondue is too thick, add a few drops of white wine, stirring constantly.
- √ If fondue is too thin, dissolve 1 teaspoon cornstarch in white wine and add, stirring constantly.
- √ When purchasing cheese for fondue, always select the natural cheese. Although it may be slightly more expensive than the processed varieties, in the long run the natural cheese is healthier for you and easier to use when cooking.
- √ The easiest way to shred cheese is in a food processor, using a well-chilled cheese. If doing by hand, remember to brush a little oil on the grater to make cleanups easier.
- √ The cheese must be melted as gently as possible to prevent the fat and protein in the cheese from separating.
- √ As each diner stirs the fondue with a fork, it will keep the consistency smooth.

Spinach Salad with Almonds

SERVES: 8–10
Preparation time: 10–15 minutes

The Ingredients:

2 pounds fresh spinach, washed and dried with stems removed
1 bunch radishes, thinly sliced
2 eggs, hard-cooked
½ cup slivered almonds, toasted

Dressing:

½ cup vegetable oil
3 tablespoons fresh lemon juice
½ teaspoon freshly grated lemon rind
¼ teaspoon dried tarragon, crumbled
Pinch of grated nutmeg
Salt and freshly ground pepper to taste

The Steps:

1. Break up spinach leaves into bowl; distribute radishes on top, grate egg over leaves, and top with nuts.

2. In screw-top jar, combine dressing ingredients and shake until smooth.
3. Pour dressing over spinach, toss well, and serve immediately.

Variation:

Substitute chopped walnuts, pecans, pine nuts, or Spanish peanuts for almonds.

Make-It-Easy Tip:

√ Purchasing spinach in cellophane bags often saves washing and removing stems but it is often less fresh than loose spinach. Avoid bags that are soft, containing leaves with dark, wet spots.

Icy Lemon-Raspberry Delight

SERVES: 8–10
Preparation time: 5–10 minutes

This quick and easy refreshing dessert is the perfect follow-up to hot fondue.

The Ingredients:

2 10-ounce packages frozen raspberries in syrup, thawed and drained
3 tablespoons fresh orange juice
3 pints lemon sherbet

The Steps:

1. In food processor or blender, place berries and orange juice, and process until smooth. Strain through fine sieve.
2. Scoop sherbet into individual dishes or one large attractive bowl, drizzle with sauce, and serve immediately.

Variations:

Frozen strawberries can be substituted for raspberries.

1–2 tablespoons Grand Marnier or some other liqueur can be added to sauce.

Any refreshing sherbet, ice cream, or frozen yogurt desired can be substituted for lemon sherbet.

Make-It-Easy Tip:

√ Sauce can be prepared in advance and chilled until ready to serve.

Dining European

SERVES: 6
Czechoslovakian Vegetable Soup
Pork Chops and Apple Rings
Two Greens Salad with Red Bell Peppers
***Brown Rice**
Cloud Pie

Here is a hearty but dressy meal, guaranteed to please your guests and take the nip out of autumn or the chill out of winter. It's also one of those slow-cooking meals that warms your kitchen and greets friends with welcoming aromas.

The ingredients suggest a rustic and Bohemian theme that can carry over to your table setting. A bunch of tall breadsticks clustered in a basket can accent the table. Or use bud vases or empty Perrier bottles with sprigs of flowers, fresh or dried.

If the trees haven't yet lost all their leaves, borrow a few for place cards. A gold marking pen can be used to engrave names impressively right on the leaves. Do you remember the trick children use to keep leaves from wilting? Place the leaves between sheets of waxed paper, then press them with a warm iron. When the paper is removed, wax will adhere to the leaves. Writing on the leaves, however, will be easier before waxing them. Fold napkins quickly and prettily into a candle shape. Then the leaves or a sprig of dried flowers can be slipped into the fold at the base.

Dessert is made ahead of time, awaiting only its garnish. The salad dressing can be prepared in advance, the greens crisped and refrigerated before the final toss. I also chop the soup vegetables earlier and set them aside. The apples for the pork chops can also be mixed with lemon and spices ahead of time, and the pork chops themselves prepared for baking. While they bake, you can start the rice and finish putting the soup together. Then, as it simmers, start the rice. Add the apples to the pork

*Not a recipe

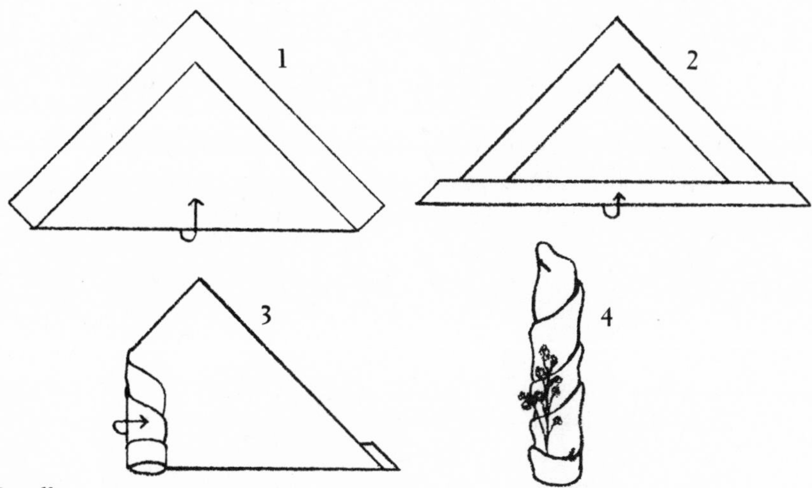

Candle
Use 15- to 17-inch napkins with border, plain color or double-sided print.

1. Fold up into a triangle, leaving a border. 2. Fold bottom up 1 inch.
3. Fold napkin over. Roll from left, tack end in. 4. Stand napkin on a plate.

chops, and while they finish baking serve the soup as a first course. The scent of simmering spices wafting from your oven completes the atmosphere of this inexpensive and elegant dinner for six.

Czechoslovakian Vegetable Soup

SERVES: 6
Preparation time: 15 minutes
Cooking time: 45–50 minutes

The Ingredients:

4 tablespoons (½ stick) unsalted butter
5 carrots, peeled and thinly sliced
2 medium onions, thinly sliced
1½ cups shredded cabbage (green, red, or a combination of both varieties can be used)
4¾ cups chicken broth
¼ cup freshly chopped parsely
Salt and freshly ground pepper to taste
½ pound (2 cups) grated Cheddar cheese
Accompaniment: Slices of crusty French bread

The Steps:

1. In large, deep saucepan or Dutch oven, heat butter and sauté carrots, onions, and cabbage; cook covered over medium heat for about 15–20 minutes, stirring occasionally.
2. Add broth, parsley, salt, and pepper; bring to boil, cover, and simmer slowly for 30 minutes, or until vegetables are fork-tender.
3. Spoon cheese into soup bowls, ladle soup over, and serve immediately with slices of crusty French bread.

Variation:

To make a one-pot dinner, after soup is cooked, add 1 cup thinly shredded chicken or beef and heat to warm through.

Make-It-Easy Tips:

√ When selecting cabbage, avoid those with separate leaves growing from main stem below the head; the texture of these cabbages is often coarse, and the flavor too strong.

√ Always slice cabbage with stainless knives. Carbon steel may blacken the leaves.

Pork Chops and Apple Rings

SERVES: 6
Preparation time: 15 minutes
Cooking time: 1 hour, 10 minutes

The Ingredients:

10 pork chops, cut ¾″ thick
Salt and freshly ground pepper to taste
2 tablespoons vegetable oil
1 tablespoon unsalted butter
¾ cup apple juice
¾ cup golden raisins
¾ cup dark brown sugar, firmly packed
¼ teaspoon ground cinnamon
¼ teaspoon ground nutmeg
4 tart apples, peeled and thickly sliced

2 tablespoons lemon juice
½ cup apple juice

The Steps:

1. Preheat oven to 350°.
2. Lightly season chops with salt and pepper to taste. Heat oil and butter together in large skillet and sauté chops, 4–5 at a time, over medium-high heat until browned; arrange chops in large baking dish.
3. Add ¾ cup apple juice in skillet, scrape up browned particles from bottom of pan, and pour over chops; cover dish and bake for 45 minutes. Turn chops.
4. In separate bowl, combine raisins, sugar, cinnamon, and nutmeg.
5. Toss apples with lemon juice, then toss with sugar mixture, coating well. Add apples to baking dish, pour remaining ½ cup apple juice over all, cover, and return to oven for an additional 15 minutes.
6. Serve hot, piling apples and raisins atop each chop.

Variation:

Pears can be substituted for apples.

Make-It-Easy Tips:

√ Sauté no more than 4–5 chops at a time; otherwise, the heat of the pan will not stay constant so that the chops will not brown well.
√ An apple-slicing gadget provides an easy method to perform this tedious chore.
√ The lemon juice prevents the apples from discoloring.

Two Greens Salad with Red Bell Peppers

SERVES: 6
Preparation time: 5–10 minutes

The Ingredients:

1 large head butter lettuce
1 large head red or leaf lettuce
2 medium red bell peppers, cut into julienne matchstick strips

Mustard Vinaigrette:

6 tablespoons olive oil
2 tablespoons red wine vinegar
1 teaspoon Dijon mustard
1 teaspoon freshly chopped parsley
¼ teaspoon honey
Salt and freshly ground pepper to taste

The Steps:

1. Break up lettuce into large salad bowl and top with peppers.
2. Combine vinaigrette ingredients in small bowl, whisk until smooth.
3. Pour dressing over greens and peppers, toss to combine, and serve immediately.

Variations:

Any seasonal greens can be substituted for lettuce.

Select salad accents by seasonality and cost factors. If red bell peppers are not in season, use green bell peppers or even slices of raw jicama as a colorful addition to the greens.

Make-It-Easy Tip:

√ Always tear greens into pieces instead of cutting with a knife, which can cause the leaf edges to brown.

Cloud Pie

SERVES: 6–8
Preparation time: 15 minutes
Cooking time: 35–45 minutes

The Ingredients:

Crust:

4 egg whites
18 soda crackers, crushed
1 cup finely chopped walnuts
1 cup sugar

1 teaspoon vanilla
½ teaspoon baking powder

Filling:

1 cup heavy cream
2 tablespoons sugar
1½ tablespoons coffee liqueur
1 teaspoon vanilla

Garnish: Shaved chocolate

The Steps:

1. Preheat oven to 325°. Generously butter 9″ pie plate.
2. In metal bowl, beat egg whites until stiff.
3. In separate bowl, combine crackers, nuts, sugar, vanilla, and baking powder. Gently fold into egg whites until thoroughly combined, spread evenly in prepared plate, and bake for 35–45 minutes. Cool.
4. Whip cream until almost stiff. Add sugar, liqueur, and vanilla and continue to whip until stiff and well mixed.
5. Pour filling into cooled crust, garnish with shaved chocolate, and serve sliced in wedges.

Variation:

Substitute chocolate almond, orange, or any other liqueur desired for filling.

Make-It-Easy Tips:

√ Always beat egg whites in metal bowl to get extra volume. Do not use aluminum or you will have a grayish tint. (The new anodized aluminum cookware is permissible, though.) The whites should also be at room temperature for increased volume. If not, pop the whole eggs, in their shells, into a small bowl of warm water.

√ To easily prepare chocolate curls, place chocolate bar in warm spot for 15 minutes, or until it can be shaved without crumbling. Press firmly with vegetable peeler, placing curls on plate. Refrigerate for 15 minutes to harden.

Sumptuous Slenderizing Parties

1. **First Night of the Diet**
   Hungarian Potted Chicken
   Toasted Rice
   Broccoli with Carrot and Lemon Garnish
   Light Apple Mousse

2. **Midsummer Night's Supper**
   Iced Curried Zucchini Soup
   Poached Halibut with Mustard Dill Sauce
   Vegetables à la Grecque
   Berry Whip

3. **Cocktail Party for the Calorie Conscious**
   Warm Bloody Bull Shot
   Creamy Herb Dip
   *Vegetable Basket
   Light Liver Pâté
   Romanian Eggplant "Caviar"
   Chinese Marinated Bay Shrimp

4. **Dinner from the Famous Spas**
   Toasted Potato Shells (La Costa)
   Game Hens à l'Orange (The Canyon Ranch)
   Skinny Spinach Salad (The Oaks and The Palms)
   Mango-Lime Paradise (The Golden Door)

5. **Gourmet Vegetarian**
   Individually Baked Vegetable Terrines au Gratin
   Bulgur Pilaf
   Coleslaw with Buttermilk Dressing
   Marinated Oranges and Strawberries

6. **Dinner from the Orient**
   Chinese Steamed Fish
   *Steamed White Rice
   Stir-fried Snow Peas, Mushrooms, and Water Chestnuts
   Frozen Fruits

7. **Elegantly Light Dinner**
   *Chilled White Wine
   Seviche
   Poulet Citron
   Parsleyed Brown Rice
   Poireaux Braises (Braised Leeks)
   Minted Melon

8. **Outdoor Barbecue on Skewers**
   Chinese Grilled Shrimp
   Shish Kebab in Mustard Marinade
   Skewered Vegetables
   Iced Pineapple Sherbet

* Not a recipe

HEALTHFUL LIVING, a desire for increased physical fitness and longevity, and a high regard for what we eat has produced a new wave of lighter cooking. There's less fat, less refined sugar, and less protein content to meals. This cuisine is delicate in flavor, uses a great deal of chicken and fish, and emphasizes fresh ingredients.

Entertaining in this lighter style requires inventiveness in preparation as well as presentation. The menus in this chapter are designed to convey this new fresh and wholesome approach to low-calorie entertaining. They are not limited to dieters. Attractively garnished and presented, the recipes can appeal to just about anyone as slimming alternatives.

If, however, nondieters are present, they can certainly be treated to a side dish of sour cream, some slices of bread, or even a scoop of ice cream while the dieters hopefully stick by the rules.

When preparing main dishes, such as the Individually Baked Vegetable Terrines au Gratin for the *Gourmet Vegetarian* menu, double the ingredients, and freeze the extra in individual containers as instant homemade frozen low-calorie meals.

Nonalcoholic beverages such as the Warm Bloody Bull Shot in the *Cocktail Party for the Calorie Conscious* actually take the edge off hunger pangs. Guests can totally enjoy themselves eating all the light hors d'oeuvres such as the Creamy Herb Dip prepared with yogurt instead of sour cream.

Soups such as the Iced Curried Zucchini prepared with buttermilk instead of cream in the *Midsummer's Night Supper*, or appetizers such as the Seviche in the *Elegantly Light Dinner*, or the Chinese Grilled Shrimp in the *Outdoor Barbecue on Skewers* are also low-calorie fillers.

As we have learned from the health spas in this country, garnishing, presentation, and portion control are essential to the appeal of low-calorie cooking. A forlorn piece of dried-out fish on a large empty plate will discourage the most steadfast of dieters—who will surely leave the table hungry and may reach for the nearest junk food for comfort. The same fish steamed Chinese-style as in the *Dinner from the Orient*, presented on a large platter, and beautifully garnished with greens, will appease both the eye and the appetite of a dieter.

The *Elegantly Light Dinner* emphasizes presentation of the food as well as elegance on the table. The setting of the scene can enhance the enjoyment of the evening. The freshest of flavors are combined in the Poulet Citron, using lemon juice and garlic as substitutes for salt to achieve a natural and delicate taste. The pace of this meal, as with any of the others in the chapter, should be slow and leisurely. The more time spent dining, the more satisfied the appetites, especially when the most filling ingredient is the conversation.

Poultry entrees are featured in four of the eight menus, fish and seafood in three. And Lamb Shish Kebab in the *Outdoor Barbecue on Skewers* is from the leg, the leanest cut of the lamb.

Carbohydrates are no longer a taboo for calorie counters. The Toasted Rice in the *First Night of the Diet*, the Bulgur Pilaf in the *Gourmet Vegetarian* dinner, the Toasted Potato Shells in the *Dinner from the Famous Spas*, the Parsleyed Brown Rice in the *Elegantly Light Dinner*—all make clear the idea that nutritious carbohydrates should be enjoyed as part of a well-balanced low-calorie menu.

Help and support are key factors in any low-calorie regime. The *First Night of the Diet* describes the enthusiasm we can use to help each other achieve weight loss. The background workout music, weigh-in, "before" photos, and charts can create a fun environment for guests.

Desserts in this chapter concentrate on fruit. Refined sugar provides empty calories. Honey has the same amount of calories but is considerably sweeter, so less is necessary. The real answer to dieters' desserts is to readjust the taste buds to naturally sweet fruits—plain, in compotes, whipped with yogurt, or even frozen for a cooling treat.

The following is a brief list I call Laurie's Low-Cal Larder. It includes those special ingredients I have discovered to shave off just a few more calories. I keep them in the house at all times. Remember to read the ingredient list on the package carefully before purchasing any canned, dried, or frozen foods. I make it a point to avoid those products listing sugar, salt, or MSG as a primary ingredient.

LAURIE'S LOW-CALORIE LARDER

Fresh lemon juice and vinegar
Fresh garlic or onions
Fresh herbs (I purchase when available, chop, and freeze in small plastic bags)
Variety of dried herbs and spices
Dry white wine
Mexican salsa (low-sodium)
Mustards (especially the new grainy varieties)
Unsweetened fruit juices
Milder soy sauce (salt-reduced)
No-salt canned tomatoes or tomato paste
Undiluted canned chicken or beef broth, preferably without MSG
Lots of fresh ground pepper
Low-fat yogurt
Low-fat (part-skim) Mozzarella cheese
Low-fat cottage cheese

Salt-free sparkling water or seltzer
Variety of raw vegetables for crudités: carrots, celery, radishes, broccoli, cauliflower, etc.
Variety of steamed vegetables to munch on cold, topped with mustard, to reheat, or to turn into cold or hot soups
Variety of fresh fruits: apples, pears, oranges, tangerines, and bananas in winter; melons, nectarines, peaches, plums, berries, apricots, and grapes in summer

The First Night of the Diet

SERVES: 6
Hungarian Potted Chicken
Toasted Rice
Broccoli with Carrot and Lemon Garnish
Light Apple Mousse

There's nothing quite like the buddy system to help us get through the pitfalls of dieting unscathed. When we laugh together, trade suggestions, and give each other encouragement, we reinforce our chances for success. Throwing a party to start a diet makes it something desirable rather than an occasion to think of oneself as deprived.

Starting a diet can elicit some apprehension, so set the scene for fun and encouragement. Go for vibrant colors—blues, yellows, greens—even alternating different colored napkins for a definite party mood. That helps overcome the worry that dieting has to be dull.

But shedding pounds takes determination. Have a camera ready for instant pictures—some "before" shots (for those who are willing) to compare with the slim you later on. Then set a date and *promise* to get together again for a progress check and moral support.

For party favors, how about colorful pocket-sized spiral notebooks, each dressed up with a bow? They're handy for use as food and calorie diaries, recording weight progress, and collecting a list of weight-watching tips. In fact, why not ask each guest to share his or her favorite suggestions? Trade tips for the times you get the munchies, favorite low-calorie recipes, and exercises. Exchange phone numbers for emergency help during an attack of the hungries.

Looking for role models? Hang up posters of slim and trim people—Victoria Principal, Linda Evans, Tom Selleck, or any other favorites. If your nearest teenager doesn't already have a collection of these posters, he or she can tell you where to find some.

To really get folks inspired, try some lively, exercise-oriented tapes or records, like Jane Fonda's Workout music for background music and encouragement.

You can cut calories by serving sparkling water instead of wine with this dinner, or try serving ice water with a slice of lemon in each glass.

Be sure the food is served to look as good as it tastes. The flavors and textures here are varied and delicious, so you should hear no groans of "Yuck, diet food!" If dinner is delayed, cut up raw vegetables for an easy low-calorie hors d'oeuvre.

The Hungarian Potted Chicken comes with a flavorful sauce that's thick without starch. Serve it garnished with parsley, on a pretty platter or from the skillet set on a trivet. Save some parsley to color up the rice, served in a warmed bowl alongside the broccoli with its colorful garnish of carrot and lemon.

Wind down with a delicious Light Apple Mousse—a treat for all. It's a cooling and refreshing finish to this tasty but slimming start toward successful dieting.

Hungarian Potted Chicken

SERVES: 6
Preparation time: 10 minutes
Cooking time: 45–60 minutes

This recipe comes from my friend Mara O'Laughlin's grandmother. No extra liquid is added to the dish. The juices from the onions and chicken provide a flavorful and thick sauce.

The Ingredients:

1 3½–4 pound chicken, cut into serving pieces
2 medium onions, roughly chopped
1 16-ounce can tomatoes, drained and roughly chopped (use the no-salt/no-sugar brand if available)

2 tablespoons freshly chopped parsley
2 teaspoons sweet Hungarian paprika
Freshly ground pepper to taste
Garnish: Freshly chopped parsley

The Steps:

1. Place chicken in deep covered skillet.
2. Add remaining ingredients, bring to a boil, cover, and simmer slowly for 45–60 minutes or until tender.
3. Taste for seasonings, adjust as necessary, and serve hot, garnished with additional chopped parsley.

Variations:

1 large ripe fresh tomato, roughly chopped, may be substituted for the canned tomatoes.

Sliced mushrooms can be added in Step #2 if desired.

Make-It-Easy Tips:

√ Prepare a day in advance and refrigerate so that excess fat can be easily removed when chilled.

√ Sweet Hungarian paprika, sold in colorful cans, is a red powdered spice prepared from grinding chilis. The color of the powder should be bright red, not brownish, which indicates age.

Toasted Rice

SERVES: 6
Preparation time: 10–15 minutes
Cooking time: 30–40 minutes

Toasting rice in a hot oven adds nutty flavor and crunchy texture without adding any extra calories.

The Ingredients:

1½ cups raw rice
1 tablespoon unsalted butter
1 medium onion, finely chopped

3 cups chicken broth
Salt and freshly ground pepper to taste
Garnish: Chopped watercress leaves

The Steps:

1. Preheat oven to 400°.
2. Pour rice onto baking sheets in single layer and bake for 10–15 minutes, shaking the pan occasionally, or until golden brown. Allow to cool.
3. Melt butter in saucepan and sauté onion over medium heat until golden. Add rice and stir to coat with mixture.
4. Add broth, salt, and pepper; bring to a boil, cover, reduce heat, and simmer for 20–25 minutes, or until tender and liquid is absorbed.
5. Serve rice in heated bowl garnished with chopped watercress leaves.

Variation:

Substitute beef or vegetable broth for chicken.

Make-It-Easy Tips:

√ Make sure the cover of the pot fits snugly. If not, place a sheet of aluminum foil on top of pot, cover, and press down to seal tightly.
√ Rice is served in a heated bowl because if hot rice is placed in a cold dish, the part that touches the dish may develop a gummy consistency.

Broccoli with Carrot and Lemon Garnish

SERVES: 6
Preparation time: 10–15 minutes
Cooking time: 2–3 minutes

The Ingredients:

4 cups broccoli florets, about 2 pounds (reserve the stems for another use)
1 large carrot, peeled and grated

1 teaspoon grated lemon zest
1 tablespoon fresh lemon juice
Salt and freshly ground pepper to taste

The Steps:

1. Drop broccoli into large pot of boiling salted water; when water returns to a boil, cook uncovered for 2–3 minutes, or until just tender, but still crunchy. Drain in colander.
2. In the meantime, combine grated carrots with lemon zest and mix well.
3. Sprinkle lemon juice on drained hot broccoli, top with garnish of carrot and lemon zest, and serve immediately with salt and pepper to taste.

Variations:

Cauliflower can be substituted for broccoli.

Freshly minced garlic combined with freshly chopped parsley can be added to the garnish as desired.

Broccoli can be boiled in chicken or beef broth for added flavor.

Make-It-Easy Tip:

√ Select broccoli heads with firm, compact bud cluster, which should be green or purple-green. Avoid heads with open, yellow flowers or wilting leaves. Keep broccoli cold and humid and use as soon as possible.

Light Apple Mousse

SERVES: 4
Preparation time: 15 minutes
Chilling time: 1 hour

A refreshing and chilling treat that is only 60 calories per serving.

The Ingredients:

1½ cups unsweetened applesauce
1 teaspoon grated lemon rind

- ¼ teaspoon vanilla extract
- ¼ teaspoon cinnamon
- Pinch nutmeg
- Honey or other sweetener, in limited quantities, to taste
- 4 egg whites, at room temperature
- ¼ teaspoon cream of tartar
- Garnish: Thin slices of apple, dipped in lemon juice to prevent discoloration

The Steps:

1. In a large bowl, combine applesauce, lemon rind, vanilla, cinnamon, nutmeg, and sweetener to taste.
2. Whip egg whites until foamy; add cream of tartar and continue to whip until stiff peaks form. (Do not overbeat.)
3. Gently fold into applesauce mixture.
4. Chill and serve garnished with thin slices of apple.

Variation:

For a high-calorie version, a little heavy whipped cream folded into the dessert is super.

Make-It-Easy Tips:

√ Do not prepare this dessert more than a few hours in advance or it may separate slightly.

√ The egg whites are whipped to foamy before adding the cream of tartar. The cream of tartar acts to delay the foaming action, so the whites must already by foamy.

√ If a copper bowl is available, use it to whip egg whites. Copper helps to stabilize the beaten whites.

Midsummer Night's Supper

SERVES: 4
Iced Curried Zucchini Soup
Poached Halibut with Mustard Dill Sauce
Vegetables à la Grecque
Berry Whip

These are recipes to keep handy even when you're not watching your weight. They're perfect for any night when it's just too hot to eat indoors and a pleasant breeze is stirring outside.

They also get you out of the kitchen fast! None keeps the stove hot for more than 20 minutes. Prepare any of these recipes before the heat of the day if you like, then allow them to chill. Give the Vegetables à la Grecque extra chilling time by doing the cooking as early as the night before.

Since a variety of fresh herbs and spices enhance this menu, why not use them as a fragrant way to accent your table? Either in terra-cotta pots or as a bouquet, fresh dill, mint, parsley, basil, and watercress sprigs (or whatever herbs are in season) make a fitting table decoration. Mix them with daisies if you like, or even float an assortment of seasonal brightly colored flowers by themselves in a glass bowl of water.

The abundant fresh fruit of summer can make an easy centerpiece that's wonderfully low-calorie, too. Mound a variety in a bowl or a basket, on a platter, or a bread board—you can't go wrong.

Citronella candles around the yard give a soft, flickery light while helping to fend off mosquitoes. Their scent is too subtle to compete with dinner.

Whether you use a picnic, patio, or bridge table, you can experiment with an outdoor motif. It's a great time to choose a tablecloth and napkins in cool shades—green, blue, violet—or flowery pastels. Napkins can be rolled into a swirl shape, bent in the middle, and placed in a glass.

Or a rustic look with burlap is attractive outdoors. This inexpensive fabric is also very easy to fringe, for an attractive finish to the table.

A wooden platter for the salmon harmonizes with the rustic mood. Dress up the fish with the greenest curly lettuce leaves, sprigs of dill, and lemon slices. If time permits, tie up lemon halves in cheesecloth with a green ribbon for color. Guests can use the covered lemons without worrying about the seeds. You might slice up extra sticks of zucchini to accent the soup. Save a few whole berries to make the dessert sparkle.

For one more way to break the heat, chill your dishes and flatware, zipping them from refrigerator to table just before supper time. And get an extra measure of cool by popping soup bowls or mugs as well as dessert dishes into the freezer.

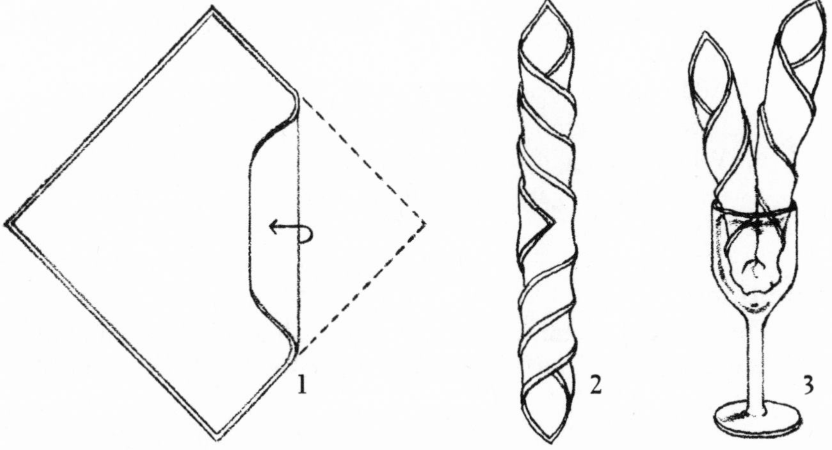

The Swirl
1. Lay the napkin out flat. 2. Starting with one of the corners, roll the napkin up. 3. Bend the napkin in the middle and place it in a glass.

Iced Curried Zucchini Soup

SERVES: 4–6
Preparation time: 15 minutes
Cooking time: 20 minutes

This cooling soup is refreshingly low in calories.

The Ingredients:

4 medium zucchini, roughly chopped
4 large scallions, roughly chopped (green and white parts included)
1 10½-ounce can undiluted chicken broth
¾ cup water
1 tablespoon freshly chopped chives
1 tablespoon freshly chopped parsley
1 teaspoon strong curry powder, or to taste
Salt and freshly ground pepper to taste
1 cup buttermilk
Garnish: Freshly chopped chives or parsley

The Steps:

1. Place zucchini, scallions, broth, and water in covered saucepan. Bring to boil, cover, and simmer slowly for 20 minutes. Cool slightly.
2. Puree vegetables with liquid in food processor or blender, until smooth.
3. Add chives, parsley, curry powder, and salt and pepper to taste; process and chill.
4. When thoroughly chilled, add buttermilk and adjust seasonings; serve chilled, garnished with additional freshly chopped chives or parsley.

Variations:

For a higher-calorie version, substitute half and half for buttermilk. A dollop of yogurt in each soup bowl makes an attractive garnish.

Make-It-Easy Tips:

√ Keep canned broth in the refrigerator. When ready to use, open with a can opener, remove congealed fat, and use fat-free.

√ Spices such as curry powder should be replaced annually. Store in a cool, dry place away from the light.

Poached Halibut with Mustard Dill Sauce

SERVES: 4
Preparation time: 15 minutes
Cooking time: 15 minutes

Poached Halibut is a wonderful entrée on hot summer nights or any time of the year as a light supper. Select halibut or other seasonally available fish steaks which are low in calories when poached in a court-bouillon (a seasoned stock for poaching fish).

The Ingredients:

2½ cups dry white wine
2½ cups water (chicken broth may be used)
1 lemon, very thinly sliced
2 tablespoons lemon juice
1 small onion, very thinly sliced
6 peppercorns
1 teaspoon freshly snipped dill or ¼ teaspoon dried dillweed
½ bay leaf
4 halibut steaks, cut 1″ thick
Garnish: Lemon wedges, dill sprigs
Accompaniment: Mustard Dill Sauce (recipe follows)

The Steps:

1. In covered skillet large enough to hold fish in single layer, heat wine, water, lemon, lemon juice, onion, peppercorns, dill, and bay leaf until boiling; allow to boil 2 minutes.
2. Place fish in liquid, return to boil, cover and simmer slowly for 8–10 minutes, or until tender and flaky. (Do not overcook.)
3. Uncover, allow fish to cool in liquid for 5 minutes, and remove to platter; cover and chill.

4. Serve fish cold, garnished with lemon wedges and dill sprigs, accompanied by Mustard Dill Sauce

Variation:

Other thick, firm, fleshy fish and fish steaks, like haddock or salmon, may be used for poaching.

Make-It-Easy Tips:

√ The amount of liquid for the court bouillon (seasoned stock) should be about 1″ deep in the skillet. The remaining court bouillon should be frozen and used again and again, getting better and better with each usage.

√ For poaching, try to get the center-cut steaks or even the fillet from the tail end.

Mustard Dill Sauce

YIELD: 1⅓ cups
Preparation time: 10 minutes

The Ingredients:

1 tablespoon freshly snipped dill or 1 teaspoon dried dill weed
2 teaspoons chopped parsley
½ teaspoon capers
1 scallion (green and white parts included)
1 cup plain low-fat yogurt
2 tablespoons mayonnaise
1 egg yolk
1 teaspoon Dijon mustard
1 teaspoon lemon juice
Pinch of paprika
Salt and freshly ground pepper to taste

The Steps:

1. In food processor or blender, process dill, parsley, capers, and scallion.
2. Add remaining ingredients and continue to puree until smooth.
3. Serve immediately or chill until ready to use.

Variation:

½ cup peeled, seeded, and finely chopped cucumber can be folded into sauce.

Make-It-Easy Tip:

√ Yogurt is perishable and must be stored in the refrigerator. Plain yogurt will keep 3–4 weeks. Blot or pour off accumulated liquid that naturally separates from the solid yogurt after it is cut or spooned to keep yogurt thicker and less runny in consistency.

Vegetables à la Grecque

SERVES: 4
Preparation time: 15–20 minutes
Cooking time: 20 minutes
Chilling time: 4 hours or overnight

Any seasonal vegetables can be prepared in this Greek style, with a fragrant lemon and oil marinade. It's very low in calories if shared among four people.

The Ingredients:

Marinating Mixture:

2 cups chicken broth
2 tablespoons lemon juice
4 teaspoons olive oil
1 small piece lemon peel
1 clove garlic, crushed with knife, peeled but still intact
1 bay leaf
¼ teaspoon dried leaf thyme, crumbled
¼ teaspoon dried tarragon, crumbled
Salt and freshly ground pepper to taste

The Vegetables:

½ head cauliflower, broken into florets
½ head broccoli, broken into florets
Garnish: Freshly chopped parsley

The Steps:

1. In deep stainless steel or enameled saucepan, combine marinating ingredients, bring to boil, cover, reduce heat, and simmer for 10 minutes.
2. Add cauliflower and broccoli florets; return to boil, cover, and simmer for 6–8 minutes, or until *al dente*, just tender. Allow vegetables to cool for 15 minutes in liquid.
3. With slotted spoon, remove vegetables from pan, reserving stock in saucepan. Discard garlic and bay leaf.
4. Reduce stock by boiling until half its original volume. Pour over vegetables and chill for 4 hours or overnight.
5. Serve vegetables chilled or at room temperature, garnished with parsley.

Variation:

Artichoke hearts, asparagus, celery hearts, fennel, green beans, leeks, mushrooms, summer squash, or any vegetable desired can be prepared à la Grecque.

Make-It-Easy Tips:

√ Vegetables will keep in a covered container in the refrigerator for 7–10 days.

√ Select cauliflower with white, firm heads. Avoid ones with yellowing or blemishes. Do not cook cauliflower in an aluminum pan, which darkens the vegetables unless the cookware is the new anodized aluminum.

√ Select broccoli heads that are dark green, or purplish-dark green with tightly closed buds. Avoid open heads with yellowish coloring or little flowers.

Berry Whip

SERVES: 4
Preparation time: 5–10 minutes

The Ingredients:

1 cup fresh strawberries (about 6–8), sliced
1 tablespoon lemon juice

2 teaspoons honey (or equivalent sweetener)
1 cup plain low-fat yogurt

The Steps:

1. In food processor or blender, puree berries with lemon juice and honey until smooth.
2. Pour into bowl, fold in yogurt, and serve immediately or chill until ready to use.

Variations:

Substitute raspberries, blueberries, or any seasonal fresh berry, or use equivalent amount unsweetened frozen berries, thawed and drained.

Yogurt can be pureed with berries, resulting in a berry sauce to drizzle over sliced berries.

Make-It-Easy Tip:

√ If you don't have a huller, use a beer can opener to easily remove stem from strawberries.

Cocktail Party for the Calorie Conscious

SERVES: 10–12

Warm Bloody Bull Shot
Creamy Herb Dip
*** Vegetable Basket**
Light Liver Pâté
Romanian Eggplant "Caviar"
Chinese Marinated Bay Shrimp

A cocktail party can easily be a dieter's downfall—but not this one. With all these low-calorie treats, the party becomes a great way to entertain without later pangs of guilt. Your dieting friends will also be appreciative.

This assortment of food fills a buffet table beautifully, although you can simply place the dishes around the room on coffee tables, end tables,

* Not a recipe

or even bridge tables. For an elegant touch, accent the room with flowers in slender bud vases.

The Vegetable Basket and Creamy Herb Dip play double-duty—as low-calorie munchables and as a fresh and pretty centerpiece. The colorful vegetables look twice as lush and vibrant on a thick bed of curly lettuce leaves or deep green parsley. Arrange them on a tray or stand them in a basket, where they'll look as cheerful as a bouquet of flowers.

The yogurt-based dip rescues you from fattening sour cream. Serve it in an attractive dish or crock, and save a scallion or sprig of parsley for a garnish, either "planted" in the dip itself or dressing up a saucer underneath the dish. Another suggestion is to serve the dip in a glass bowl placed inside a hollowed-out red or green cabbage. It makes a particularly attractive presentation perfect for any dip or sauce.

The usual pâté de foie gras is just what its name means—"*fat* liver paste." But this Light Liver Pâté takes its place in a slim and trim way, without sacrificing flavor. And with its shiny glaze, it looks as fancy as it tastes. Unmold it onto a pretty plate and accent it with a spray of watercress.

Caviar and calories go hand in hand—but this Romanian Eggplant "Caviar" makes a super substitute. Surround it with crunchy crackers or melba toast in a variety of shapes and flavors.

Tiny bay shrimp are low in calories and less expensive than most seafood. Marinated in this Chinese dressing, they are a refreshing part of the hors d'oeuvres table, served on little plates with cocktail or salad forks alongside.

Alcohol is a fast way to waste calories, so guests will appreciate these zesty, unspiked, warm Bloody Bull Shots. Or serve sparkling mineral water and lime as a light, refreshing hot-weather alternative. And offer wine or wine spritzers to those who aren't counting their calories.

For a smaller party, pick and choose just a few of these goodies. But no matter how many or how few guests you have, remember that low-calorie food should look every bit as dressy as any party fare, if not more so. So get out the fancy plates and dishes, spread a lace tablecloth, runners or doilies, and choose pretty cocktail napkins. Then have yourself an elegant, guilt-free good time.

Warm Bloody Bull Shot

SERVES: 10–12
Preparation time: 5–10 minutes
Cooking time: 5 minutes

The Ingredients:

2 quarts vegetable juice cocktail (I use V-8, S&W, or a local brand)
2 cups strong undiluted beef bouillon
¼ cup fresh lemon juice
1 tablespoon Worcestershire sauce
1 teaspoon white horseradish, or more, to taste
Tabasco to taste
Salt and freshly ground pepper to taste
Garnish: Lemon slices

The Steps:

1. Heat all ingredients until hot.
2. Pour into mugs and serve with a slice of lemon floating on top.

Variations:

Substitute lime juice for lemon juice.

Spicy V-8 juice can be substituted for plain V-8, adjusting other ingredients to get the degree of spiciness you prefer.

Make-It-Easy Tip:

√ Serrated knives with narrow blades are the best tools for slicing lemons. Carbon steel knives and occasionally aluminum utensils may permanently discolor from the lemon acid.

Creamy Herb Dip

YIELD: 3 cups
Preparation time: 15 minutes

The Ingredients:

¼ cup minced scallions (green and white parts included)
2 tablespoons freshly chopped parsley
2 teaspoons freshly snipped dill or ½ teaspoon dried dill weed, crumbled
2 teaspoons freshly chopped basil or ½ teaspoon dried basil, crumbled
2 teaspoons freshly chopped tarragon or ½ teaspoon dried tarragon, crumbled
1 teaspoon finely minced garlic
2 cups plain low-fat yogurt
3 tablespoons mayonnaise
Salt and freshly ground pepper to taste
Accompaniments:

Raw vegetables:
- 2 boxes cherry tomatoes
- 1 bunch celery cut up
- 1 pound carrots cut up
- 3 medium zucchini, cut up
- ½ pound mushrooms, sliced
- 1 bunch radishes
- 1 bunch scallions, trimmed

The Steps:

1. In food processor, blender, or by hand, chop scallions, parsley, dill, basil, tarragon, and garlic.
2. Place in bowl, fold in yogurt and mayonnaise; season with salt and pepper to taste and chill until ready to use.
3. Serve chilled accompanied by raw vegetables.

Variations:

Any seasonal chopped herbs can be used as desired.
Dip can be also used as a salad dressing.

Make-It-Easy Tips:

√ The herbs and seasonings are chopped in a food processor or blender and then folded into the yogurt to keep the texture of the yogurt thick and creamy. Once processed, the yogurt will become thinner and often watery.

√ Crumble dried herbs between fingers before adding to recipes to release essential flavors.

Light Liver Pâté

YIELD: 9″ x 5″ x 3″ loaf
Preparation time: 15 minutes
Cooking time: 25 minutes
Chilling time: 1–2 hours for gelatin
4–6 hours or overnight for pâté

Serve this elegant but low-calorie chicken liver pâté attractively garnished with a layer of gelatin. Or, for a quicker version, omit the gelatin and serve packed into a crock or bowl.

The Ingredients:

Gelatin Topping:

¾ cup undiluted beef broth
1 package (1 tablespoon) unflavored gelatin

Pâté:

1 tablespoon unsalted butter
1 medium onion, roughly chopped
1 pound chicken livers, roughly diced
2 tablespoons Marsala, Madeira, port, or red wine
2 tablespoons undiluted beef broth
Pinch of ground allspice
Pinch of ground cloves
Pinch of ground nutmeg
Pinch of thyme, crumbled
Pinch of cayenne pepper
Salt to taste

Garnish: Watercress sprigs
Accompaniment: Melba toast

The Steps:

1. Pour broth into small saucepan, sprinkle with gelatin, and cook over high heat, stirring until gelatin is dissolved. Do not boil. Pour into large loaf pan or similar-sized mold or dish. Chill for 1–2 hours or overnight.
2. In large nonstick skillet, heat butter and sauté onion over medium heat until just soft, about 5 minutes.
3. Add livers, sauté for 1–2 minutes, stirring constantly; add wine, broth, and remaining seasonings, cover and simmer slowly for 15–20 minutes. Cool slightly.
4. Place mixture in food processor or blender and process until smooth, or put through food mill. Cool for 30 minutes. Season to taste, place over gelatin layer, and chill for 4–6 hours or overnight.
5. Unmold pâté and serve on platter garnished with watercress sprigs, accompanied by Melba toast or other low calorie crackers.

Variations:

Calves' or beef livers can be substituted for chicken livers.

Add a tablespoon of Marsala, Madeira, port, or red wine to the gelatin mixture.

Make-It-Easy Tips:

√ Whenever you buy a chicken, freeze the livers together and soon there will be enough for a pâté.

√ Remove any yellowish skin attached to the livers before using. This skin is part of the gall sac and will give a bitter taste to the pâté.

√ To easily unmold pâté, carefully run a paring knife around the edge of the pâté, place in a basin filled with 1–2 inches of hot water, and count to ten. Place platter on top of mold, invert, and pâté will easily fall onto plate.

√ It is best to use a nonstick skillet since the amount of butter is only one tablespoon.

√ The pâté must be cooled slightly before placing atop gelatin or it will melt the gelatin.

Romanian Eggplant "Caviar"

SERVES: 10–12
Preparation time: 10–15 minutes
Cooking time: 40–45 minutes
Chilling time: 1–2 hours

The Ingredients:

2 medium eggplants
½ cup finely minced onion
2 tablespoons olive oil
2 tablespoons lemon juice
2 tablespoons freshly chopped parsley
Salt and freshly ground pepper to taste
Accompaniments: Melba toast or thin crackers

The Steps:

1. Preheat oven to 400°.
2. Wash eggplants, discard green end, place in baking pan. Pierce randomly with knife and bake for 40–45 minutes, or until soft to the touch. Cool for 15 minutes or until easy to handle.
3. Peel eggplant with sharp paring knife or vegetable peeler and mash pulp in food processor, blender, or by hand until smooth.
4. Add onion, oil, lemon juice, parsley, salt, and pepper, stir until well blended, and chill for 1–2 hours or until ready to use.
5. Serve chilled or at room temperature accompanied by melba toast or other thin crackers.

Variation:

Traditionally, the eggplant for this spread is pierced with a long fork and held over an open gas flame until scorched and browned. This method gives a smoky flavor to the spread. To achieve this without lengthy chores, place eggplant on grill over barbecue and bake until scorched on the outside and soft to the touch. Remove peel and mash.

Make-It-Easy Tip:

√ Eggplant is pierced to keep it from bursting and exploding in the oven.

Chinese Marinated Bay Shrimp

SERVES: 10–12
Preparation time: 10–15 minutes
Chilling time: 2–4 hours

The Ingredients:

1½ pounds (3 cups) bay shrimp
12 large mushrooms, finely chopped
4 scallions, finely chopped (green and white parts included)
4 stalks celery, finely chopped

Dressing:

6 tablespoons rice wine vinegar
2 tablespoons soy sauce
4–5 teaspoons toasted sesame oil
1 teaspoon freshly grated ginger or ¼ teaspoon ground ginger
Pinch of sweetener
Salt and freshly ground pepper to taste
Garnish: Coriander or watercress sprigs

The Steps:

1. In large bowl, combine shrimp with mushrooms, scallions, and celery.
2. In separate bowl, whisk dressing ingredients together until smooth.
3. Pour dressing over shrimp and vegetables, toss, and allow to marinate for 2–4 hours in refrigerator.
4. Serve chilled or at room temperature, garnished wtih sprigs of coriander or watercress.

Variations:

Crabmeat can be substituted for shrimp.
½ teaspoon hot sauce, or to taste can be added as desired.

Make-It-Easy Tip:

√ Store peeled ginger in a jar, covered with dry sherry, in the refrigerator. Ginger can also be tightly wrapped and stored in the freezer indefinitely.

Dinner from the Famous Spas

SERVES: 4
Toasted Potato Shells (*La Costa*)
Game Hens à l'Orange (*The Canyon Ranch*)
Skinny Spinach Salad (*The Oaks* and *The Palms*)
Mango-Lime Paradise (*The Golden Door*)

Pampering is what spas are all about—and pampering is the mood of this dinner. Reminders of all the creams, oils, and assorted treatments should be present as the centerpiece—but in a new form. Take old cold cream jars or other low-shaped containers, wash them thoroughly, and fill them with radishes. On a new gummed label use colored marker pens to write—NO LIMITS! A large mayonnaise jar used as a container for stalks of celery and carrots can have a label reading—NO TOXINS! On a jar filled with cucumbers and zucchini spears make a label saying—ENERGY BOOSTERS! And as the perfect beverage, a large pitcher of mineral water labeled—ALL YOU WANT!

To complete the spa mood, set up a basket of four towels, each filled with cutlery and rolled and tied with new pairs of sneaker laces. Fresh herbs or greens can be added to the basket, which is capped off with a label reading—HERBAL TOWELS.

The menu is easily organized. The potatoes can be baked in advance, scooped and readied for last-minute baking. They can be served as a first course or as a side dish along with the main course.

The game hens can be totally cooked beforehand, reheated, and served attractively garnished with orange slices and parsley sprigs. The salad can be crisped and the dressing readied but tossed just before serving.

The wonderfully cooling dessert is best prepared ahead of time and allowed to chill. Top each portion with colorful slices of kiwi mixed with seasonal berries.

Toasted Potato Shells (La Costa) *

SERVES: 4
Preparation time: 5–10 minutes
Cooking time: 1 hour

La Costa Health and Beauty Spa—located in Carlsbad, California, 30 miles from San Diego—is both a hotel and spa combined. With golf courses, tennis courts, and exercise rooms, it offers all the amenities of a country club. The separate men's and women's spas provide personalized programs and diets upon request. They suggest a sound, sensible 800-calorie daily intake in a beautifully presented weight-loss routine that teaches portion control.

The Ingredients:

2 medium baking potatoes, washed and pierced with fork
1 tablespoon chopped chives
1 teaspoon Parmesan cheese
½ teaspoon caraway seeds

The Steps:

1. Preheat oven to 500°.
2. Bake potatoes for 45–60 minutes or until skins are crisp and centers are done.

*Recipe courtesy of *The La Costa Diet and Exercise Book* by R. Phillip Smith, M.D. (New York: Grosset and Dunlap, 1977).

3. Cut potato in half horizontally, scoop out flesh, leaving ⅓″ nearest the skin. (Reserve potato flesh for another use.)
4. Reduce oven to 350°, return shells, and continue to bake for an additional 10 minutes, or until fairly crisp.
5. Combine remaining ingredients; sprinkle a little of mixture in each shell, return to oven, and continue to bake 5 minutes or until cheese melts. Serve immediately.

Variations:

Caraway seeds can be omitted.

Leftover potato flesh can be mashed with a small amount of yogurt and pepper for a low-calorie mashed potato.

Make-It-Easy Tip:

√ Store potatoes in cool, dry, dark, ventilated place. Do not refrigerate or an overly sweet taste will result from the conversion of starch to sugar at cold temperatures.

Game Hens à l'Orange (The Canyon Ranch)

SERVES: 4
Preparation time: 10 minutes
Cooking time: 1 hour

The Canyon Ranch, located in Tucson, Arizona, is one of the new-style spas—no "fat farm" here! It is the perfect place for singles, or especially couples, to retreat to an unstructured atmosphere of exercise classes and walking and hiking in the Arizona desert. The dieting plan is basically low in fats, high in fiber, and contains no refined sugar. Their creative recipes are from food consultant Jeanne Jones.

The Ingredients:

2 game hens, split in half
Corn oil
Freshly ground white pepper
1 large onion, quartered
3 ounces frozen unsweetened concentrated orange juice, thawed
1 cup dry white wine or dry vermouth
Garnish: Orange slices, parsley sprigs

The Steps:

1. Preheat oven to 350°.
2. Lightly rub game hen halves with oil and sprinkle all sides with pepper.
3. Place 4 onion quarters in roasting pan. Place hen halves, cut side down, atop each onion quarter and bake for 15 minutes.
4. Combine remaining ingredients, stir, pour over hens, and continue to cook for 45 minutes longer, basting occasionally.
5. Remove from oven, place hens and onion quarters on platter, spoon sauce over all, and serve hot, garnished with orange slices and parsley sprigs.

Variation:

Chicken breasts can be substituted for hens, but cooked only 30–40 minutes or until just tender.

Make-It-Easy Tips:

√ Game hens can be cooked in advance and reheated just before serving in a 400° oven until golden brown.

√ Rock Cornish game hens are now available fresh or frozen in the supermarkets. Select the smallest and lightest ones, which are the most tender.

Skinny Spinach Salad (The Oaks at Ojai and The Palms at Palm Springs)

SERVES: 4–6
Preparation time: 10–15 minutes

Under the ownership of Sheila Cluff, both The Oaks at Ojai and The Palms at Palm Springs have become well-priced retreats for singles or couples in a casual atmosphere. The diet is a sound and sensible 750-calorie regimen utilizing natural foods without additives, salt, sugar, or white flour.

The Ingredients:

6 cups spinach, washed, stems removed, torn into pieces
6–8 medium mushrooms, cleaned and sliced

1 hard-cooked egg, grated
2 tablespoons minced scallions (green and white parts included)

Dressing:

⅓ cup white wine vinegar
⅓ cup water
2 tablespoons safflower oil
2 tablespoons minced scallions (green and white parts included)
2 tablespoons freshly chopped parsley
2 tablespoons freshly grated Parmesan cheese
1 clove garlic, finely minced

The Steps:

1. Place spinach in bowl; top with mushrooms, egg, and scallions.
2. Combine dressing ingredients in food processor or blender until smooth.
3. Pour dressing over salad, toss, and serve immediately.

Make-It-Easy Tips:

✓ If possible, prepare dressing several hours in advance and chill until ready to use.

✓ To easily clean mushrooms, dip a paper towel into lemon juice and quickly rub mushrooms clean.

Mango-Lime Paradise (The Golden Door)*

SERVES: 4
Preparation time: 10 minutes

The Golden Door—located in Escondido, California, 40 miles northeast of San Diego—is among the most exclusive of spas (limited to 34 guests per week). Under the leadership of Deborah Szekely, the spa specializes in individual attention coupled with rigorous workouts, yoga, and other exercise routines. The diet prescribed is designed to maintain a high energy level while still achieving a significant weight loss.

*Recipe courtesy of *The Golden Door Cookbook* by Deborah Szekely, with Chef Michel Stroot (Foreman Publishing, 1982).

The Ingredients:

2 cups mango pulp (2–3 mangoes)
½ cup fresh orange juice
1 tablespoon fresh lime or lemon juice
1 tablespoon honey (omit if mango is very sweet)
Garnish: Kiwi slices, raspberries, or strawberry halves

The Steps:

1. In food processor or blender, puree mango pulp with orange juice, lime juice, and honey until smooth.
2. Pour into 4 individual dessert dishes and serve immediately, or chill until ready to serve, garnished with kiwi slices, raspberries, or strawberry halves.

Make-It-Easy Tips:

√ Always slice mangoes over paper towels to avoid staining.
√ Select smooth-skinned mangoes that have started to color up. Green ones may never ripen properly. A ready-to-eat mango should yield to mild pressure.

Gourmet Vegetarian

SERVES: 4
Individually Baked Vegetable Terrines au Gratin
Bulgur Pilaf
Coleslaw with Buttermilk Dressing
Marinated Oranges and Strawberries

Here's a dinner that truly does double-duty. Serve it to your weight-watching or vegetarian friends—you're bound to delight both.

The vegetables themselves set the theme, giving you all sorts of options for a centerpiece. Round up your houseplants to "green" up the dining area for a garden look. Let multicolored vegetables cascade from a cornucopia basket. Fill a basket with nuts and grains. Many seed packets are even country-pretty. They can fill a parsley-lined basket by themselves, or accent other arrangements. They also make fun favors or place cards for friends who garden.

Table linens can be white to contrast with all the plants and vegetables. Or earth tones can be used for natural harmony. Add another earthy touch with sprigs of ivy or other greens slipped through the napkin rings.

One great way to get people's minds off their calorie cutbacks is to satisfy them with a wide variety of tastes and textures. The vegetable terrines (yes, an easy-on-the-calories casserole) bring a savory, herbal flavor—not to mention lots of color. Bulgur Pilaf lends its satisfying nutty taste and crunchy texture. Crunch is also evident in the coleslaw, which also has a zing with its buttermilk dressing—spiked with mustard and Worcestershire sauce. Then refresh everyone with Marinated Oranges and Strawberries—a naturally bright and luscious combination made twice as elegant with a hint of Marsala wine.

Both the coleslaw and the dessert save you fuss as well as calories since you can prepare them the night before. Make the coleslaw a day or two earlier, if you prefer.

This menu will look lovely served on fancy dishes for a sophisticated approach, or on earthenware and wooden dishes for a natural look. Either way, choose serving dishes that can be filled to capacity with the amounts of food you cook. This gives the illusion of larger quantities, while big, partially empty dishes always look skimpy, unless painstakingly and artistically garnished.

For a dressy dessert presentation, frost goblets or glass dessert dishes by moistening them and putting them in the freezer. Mound them with the marinated fruit and set them on saucers lined with paper doilies.

Individually Baked Vegetable Terrines au Gratin

SERVES: 4
Preparation time: 20 minutes
Cooking time: 35 minutes

This recipe is a Make-It-Easy version of one taught to me by Chef Michel Stroot of The Golden Door spa in Escondido, California. The vegetables can be baked in one large casserole, but the individual casseroles make a particularly attractive presentation.

The Ingredients:

1 tablespoon olive oil
1 medium onion, finely minced
1 28-ounce can tomatoes, drained and roughly chopped (I use the no-salt no-sugar brand)
1 teaspoon finely minced garlic
1 teaspoon freshly chopped basil (or ⅓ teaspoon dried basil, crumbled)
Salt and freshly ground pepper to taste
1 small eggplant (about 1 pound), roughly diced
¼ pound (10–12 medium) mushrooms, sliced
1 pound (about 3 medium) zucchini, cut into ½″ slices
2 green peppers, roughly diced
¼ cup diced and drained pimientoes
1 tablespoon freshly chopped parsley
1 tablespoon freshly chopped basil, chives, or other fresh herbs, to taste (or 1 teaspoon dried herbs)
2 teaspoons freshly grated Parmesan cheese
8 very thin slices part-skim Mozzarella cheese

The Steps:

1. In large, heavy, nonstick skillet, heat oil and sauté onions over medium heat until lightly golden.
2. Add tomatoes, garlic, basil, oregano, salt, and pepper; simmer uncovered very slowly for 10 minutes.
3. Add eggplant, stir to coat, cover, and simmer for 10 minutes, or until tender.
4. Preheat oven to 375°.
5. Stir in mushrooms, zucchini, and peppers, season to taste, and cover for an additional 10 minutes.
6. Stir in pimientos, parsley, fresh herbs; spoon into 4 individual casseroles, sprinkle each with ½ teaspoon Parmesan cheese, and top each with 2 slices Mozzarella cheese. Bake for 15 minutes, or until hot and bubbly.

Variation:

Diagonally cut-up asparagus or broccoli or cauliflower florets can be added with the zucchini. Any seasonal vegetable desired can be used, adhering to necessary cooking times.

Make-It-Easy Tip:

√ Select small or medium eggplants, which generally have fewer seeds and better texture than larger ones. Avoid ones that have dark brown spots or ones that do not have green end intact.

Bulgur Pilaf

SERVES: 4
Preparation time: 10–15 minutes
Cooking time: 25–30 minutes

Bulgur, the Middle Eastern staple, is cracked wheat that is golden in color with a nutty taste and texture. The vegetable broth I use in this recipe is saved from cooked vegetables; or if I'm out, I use the reconstituted powdered vegetable broth or cubes available in supermarkets and health food stores.

The Ingredients:

2 teaspoons vegetable oil
¼ cup minced onion
1 cup bulgur
2 cups vegetable broth
¼ teaspoon oregano, crumbled
⅛ teaspoon thyme, crumbled
Salt and freshly ground pepper to taste
Garnish: Freshly chopped parsley

The Steps:

1. In large skillet, heat oil and sauté onions over medium heat for 2 minutes; add bulgur and continue to sauté until golden.
2. Add broth, oregano, thyme, salt, and pepper; bring to a boil, reduce heat, cover, and simmer slowly for 20–25 minutes, or until tender and liquid is absorbed.
3. Serve hot, garnished with freshly chopped parsley.

Variations:

Any type of broth can be used for the pilaf.
Oil can be reduced to barely 1 teaspoon if using a nonstick skillet.

Or, to avoid any fats at all, heat 2–3 tablespoons vegetable broth or dry white wine in a skillet and soften the onions in the hot liquid over high heat.

Make-It-Easy Tip:

√ Bulgur is always cooked in the proportion of 1 cup grain to 2 cups liquid. When cooked, it increases to four times its volume.

Coleslaw with Buttermilk Dressing

SERVES: 4
Preparation time: 15 minutes
Chilling time: 2–3 hours or overnight

The Ingredients:

1 head green cabbage, shredded (about 4 cups)
3 scallions, minced (green and white parts included)

Dressing:

1 cup buttermilk
2 tablespoons mayonnaise
1 tablespoon lemon juice
1 teaspoon Worcestershire sauce
½ teaspoon minced garlic
½ teaspoon Dijon mustard
Salt and freshly ground pepper to taste
Pinch of cayenne pepper

The Steps:

1. Place shredded cabbage in bowl and top with minced scallions.
2. Combine dressing ingredients in separate bowl and whisk until smooth, or prepare in food processor or blender.
3. Toss cabbage with dressing and allow to marinate 2–3 hours or overnight.

Variations:

The dressing can top any type of greens for a low-calorie salad. Prepare it in large amounts with scallions added and keep it on hand.

Red cabbage or a combination of green and red cabbage can be used.

Marinated Oranges and Strawberries

SERVES: 4
Preparation time: 10 minutes
Chilling time: 2–3 hours or overnight

The Ingredients:

3 large navel oranges
1 pint strawberries, washed and hulled
2 tablespoons sweet Marsala wine
Sweetener (honey or sweetening substitute equivalent to 2 tablespoons sugar)
Garnish: Sprigs of fresh mint leaves

The Steps:

1. Peel oranges with sharp knife, removing all white pith around orange; divide into sections.
2. Slice berries in half or, if too large, into quarters.
3. Gently combine fruits together, add Marsala and sweetener, toss, and chill for 2–3 hours or overnight.
4. Serve fruit well chilled, garnished with sprigs of fresh mint.

Variation:

Kiwis, bananas, or other fruits can be added if desired. (Do not add bananas or apples until just before serving.)

Make-It-Easy Tips:

√ The fruit can be cut and marinated overnight.

√ A strawberry huller, a gadget shaped like a fat tweezer, makes hulling strawberries a breeze.

√ Select thick-skinned oranges for easy peeling.

√ An easy method of peeling oranges without the white pith clinging is to cover the unpeeled fruit with boiling water, allow to stand 5 minutes, drain, and easily peel.

√ When selecting strawberries, pick bright red ones; strawberries do not ripen after being picked.

√ Never buy berries more than a day or two in advance of serving. Keep refrigerated and do not wash until a few hours before using. Do not remove caps before washing the berries. The caps prevent water from soaking into the berries, thus diluting the flavor and changing the texture.

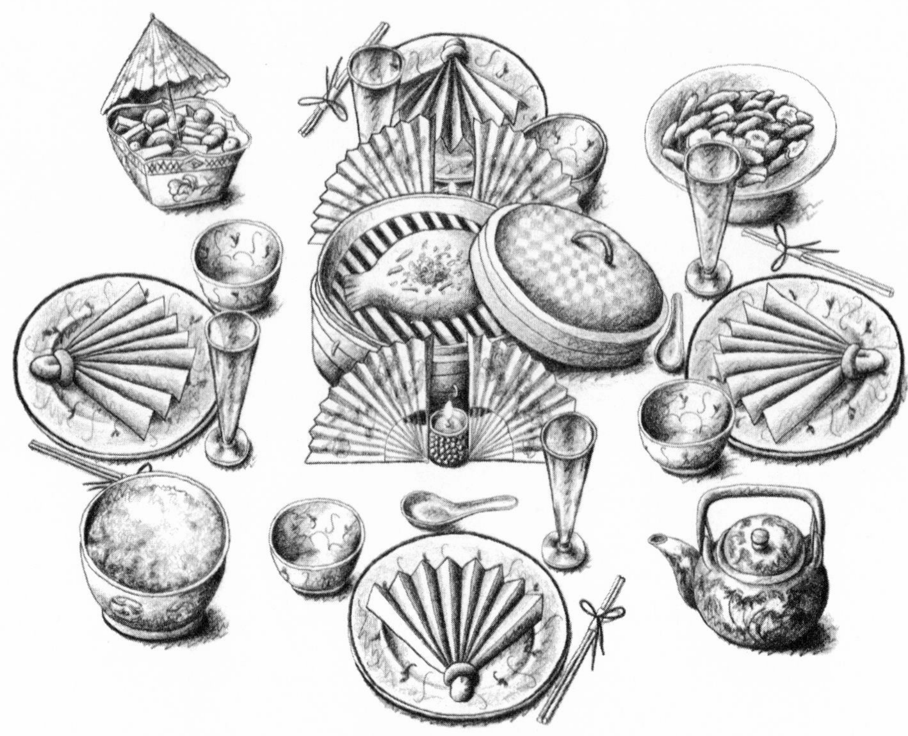

Dinner from the Orient

SERVES: 4
Chinese Steamed Fish
***White Rice**
Stir-Fried Snow Peas, Mushrooms, and Water Chestnuts
Frozen Fruits

Chinese cooking works wonders with slimming foods. It also gives us a chance to experiment with decor—some genuinely Far Eastern, some simply exotic.

Soft light, filtered and reflected, sets a mystical mood. A glass bowl of water can hold floating candles, while blossoms float among them like water lilies. Or take your cue from the steamed fish and cluster seashells on a tray or in a bowl. Use them to prop an arrangement of Chinese or Japanese fans, cloth flowers, or even chopsticks. A small candle can be very effective at the center of such an arrangement, but take care to keep flammable fans and flowers protected. A glass container for the candle shields the flame elegantly. If no one in your house has a seashell collection, don't despair. Substitute pebbles, uncooked rice, or beans.

* Not a recipe

A red tablecloth—it needn't be expensive—accentuates the Chinese mood and sets a striking backdrop for any Far Eastern utensils and accessories. Serve the fish directly from a bamboo steamer, garnished with coriander or watercress. Give the teapot a prominent place on the table. Chopsticks and graceful Chinese soup spoons are inexpensive table enhancers, and well worth acquiring when you enjoy Chinese cooking. Chopstick sets wrapped with small squares of aluminum foil and tied up with red yarn create a colorful effect for the center of the table.

Vivid napkins folded like fans take the Chinese theme a step further. Pleat them accordion-style, then fold them in half. Next, slip the folded end through a napkin ring, or tie a colorful ribbon an inch or so from the end. Lay each napkin on a plate, and open the pleats for a dramatic splash of color. (See illustration.)

To keep this meal as easy as it is elegant, both traditional Chinese steaming and stir-frying are used. The Frozen Fruits are prepared in advance, and the ingredients for the fish and vegetables should be organized and ready to assemble. While the rice cooks, the fish steams to a flaky texture. The vegetables are cooked just before serving. But don't worry; prepared in advance, this only takes about three minutes.

After a hot, steamy dinner the Frozen Fruits, served as finger food instead of the traditional fortune or almond cookies, deliver cool refreshment. It's a novel way to enjoy the natural sweetness of fruit without a drop of added sweetener—or a single added calorie.

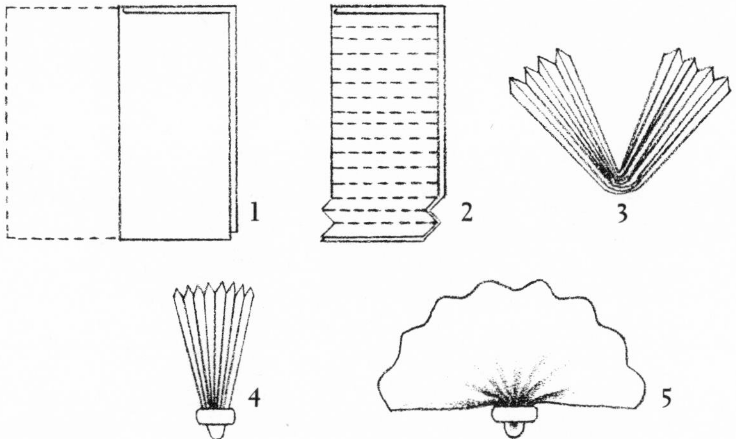

Fan in a Ring
1. Fold the napkin in half. 2. Pleat in 1″ accordion pleats all the way to the top. 3. Fold in half. 4. Slip folded napkin through a napkin ring, or tie with a ribbon an inch from the end. 5. Lay each napkin on a plate and open up pleats like a fan.

Chinese Steamed Fish

SERVES: 4
Preparation time: 20 minutes
Cooking time: 12–15 minutes

The ingredients in this steamed fish are simliar to the Chinese Baked Fish in *Make It Easy in Your Kitchen*, but the fish is lower in calories when steamed whole and just as tasty. White fish such as sea bass, whitefish, pike, trout, snapper, or rock cod are preferable for delicate steaming. Oily fish such as mackerel or bluefish are not suitable.

The Ingredients:

1 whole fish, about 2½–3 pounds, cleaned and scaled but with head and tail still on
3 tablespoons soy sauce
3 tablespoons dry sherry
½ teaspoon sugar
1 clove garlic, chopped
2 tablespoons fermented, mashed, and drained black beans (available at Far Eastern grocery stores or by mail order)
1 tablespoon finely shredded fresh ginger
2 scallions, split and cut in 2″ lengths (green part only)
2 teaspoons toasted sesame oil
Garnish: Coriander leaves (cilantro) or watercress

The Steps:

1. Pat fish dry with paper towels and make 3 diagonal slashes on each side of fish. Lightly spray a heat-proof platter or shallow dish that will fit into steamer with nonaerosol vegetable spray.
2. Mix soy sauce, sherry, and sugar together and pour over fish.
3. Sprinkle garlic/bean mixture over fish along with shredded ginger and scallions.
4. Place fish in steamer and steam over boiling water, for 12–15 minutes or until fish is flaky. (The timing depends on the size of the fish.)
5. Carefully remove hot platter from steamer, top with sesame oil, and serve immediately from this same dish, garnished with coriander leaves or watercress.

Variations:

For a French version of Steamed Fish, substitute lemon juice, fresh herbs, capers, and a topping of melted butter for the final step.

If black bean sauce is unavailable, it may be omitted.

Make-It-Easy Tips:

√ Ginger can easily be shredded with the fine end of a grater.

√ In general, the rule of thumb for cooking fish is 10 mnutes per inch, judging from thickest part of fish.

√ To improvise a steamer: place platter of fish on a trivet to act as a rack in a large roasting pan. Pour enough boiling water in pan to cover bottom by 1″–2″ but not to touch the platter. Cover the top with heavy-duty aluminum foil and seal tightly. Place it either over low heat so that water keeps to a slow boil or in a 375° oven to bake. (Note: Inverted 2″ muffin tin can also be used as a rack.)

Stir-Fried Snow Peas, Mushrooms, and Water Chestnuts

SERVES: 4
Preparation time: 15 minutes
Cooking time: 4–5 minutes

If available, the new sugar-snap peas, a cross between a Chinese snow pea pod and a green pea, can be substituted for snow peas. Sugar peas are totally edible, shell and all, and the crunchy texture is excellent in stir-fried dishes and salads.

The Ingredients:

1 tablespoon soy sauce
½ teaspoon sweetener (optional)
Salt and freshly ground pepper to taste
2 teaspoons peanut oil
¼ teaspoon finely minced garlic
½ pound snow peas, strings removed
6 mushrooms, cleaned and sliced

½ cup sliced water chestnuts, drained
2 teaspoons sesame seeds, toasted
1 teaspoon toasted sesame seed oil

The Steps:

1. In small bowl, combine soy sauce, sugar, salt, and pepper; stir and place near cooking area.
2. Heat wok or large skillet and add oil; when hot, stir-fry garlic for 30 seconds.
3. Add peas, mushrooms, and water chestnuts; continue to stir-fry for 2–3 minutes longer.
4. Add soy sauce mixture, stir to combine; add sesame seeds and oil. Toss thoroughly and serve immediately.

Variation:

Japanese or Chinese dried mushrooms, soaked in water and julienned (cut in matchstick strips) can be substituted for regular mushrooms.

Make-It-Easy Tip:

√ As in all Chinese stir-fry quick cooking, all ingredients must be assembled in advance and placed near the cooking area.

Frozen Fruits

SERVES: 4
Preparation time: 5 minutes
Freezing time: 3 hours

This mixture of cooling frozen fruits is the perfect treat to satisfy a dessert craving without lots of calories.

The Ingredients:

2 ripe bananas
2 slices watermelon
1 bunch grapes, washed

The Steps:

1. Peel bananas and immediately wrap tightly in plastic wrap or aluminum foil; freeze for 3 hours, or until ready to serve.
2. Cut away rind from watermelon, slice into spears, and wrap in plastic wrap or aluminum foil; freeze for 3 hours, or until ready to serve.
3. Wrap grapes in plastic wrap or aluminum foil and freeze for 3 hours, or until ready to serve.
4. Unwrap bananas, cut into slices, and serve immediately on platter with frozen watermelon and grapes.

Variation:

All of one fruit may be substituted for combination.

Make-It-Easy Tips:

√ Fruits will keep for 5–7 days in the freezer

√ Keep a supply of frozen fruits on hand for nutritious children's snacks or satisfying dieters' desserts.

Elegantly Light Dinner

SERVES: 6
***Chilled White Wine**
Seviche
Poulet Citron
Parsleyed Brown Rice
Poireaux Braisés
Minted Melon

This dinner is for that special occasion when you want to entertain in fine style without destroying your weight-watching progress—or that of your guests. It uses those low-calorie standbys—chicken and fish—in a flavorful and international style.

For a dressy dinner, your prettiest candlesticks, best china, and finest table linens add atmosphere—and no calories! All white linens lend a classic elegance to your table. The colors blue and white together denote French atmosphere, and deep reds, like crimson and burgundy, add drama. Runners add an out-of-the-ordinary look that fits the occasion. On a round table, three crisscross runners make a striking starlike pattern.

* Not a recipe

Flowers definitely belong on this table. Place one large arrangement in the center of the table—just keep it low enough so that people can see each other! Or set individual bud vases at each place to accentuate the slender look. Baby's breath adds delicacy to any arrangement and dries well for later use. And for an extra added touch, try the bottle wrap around the white wine or even a bottle of sparkling mineral water. Fold a napkin or bandana in half diagonally, then fold the bottom edge up by one-quarter two times, and tie the napkin around the bottle as an attractive table decoration. (See illustration.) It also helps to catch extra drips.

Start your dinner with Seviche served on salad plates. This colorful Peruvian version of sushi transforms fish or scallops into a delicacy—all with no added oil, gooey sauces, or even any cooking. To avoid extra steps and dishes, Seviche can be served as an hors d'oeuvre on crackers at cocktail time.

Poulet Citron is a classic French combination of chicken freshly seasoned with garlic, lemon, and parsley. Only the white meat is used, without the skin; therefore a good portion of the calories is removed. This dish is cooked quickly and served immediately. Save yourself steps at dinnertime by readying the chicken for the pan ahead of time. Give it a fresh and colorful presentation with lemon slices and sprigs of watercress.

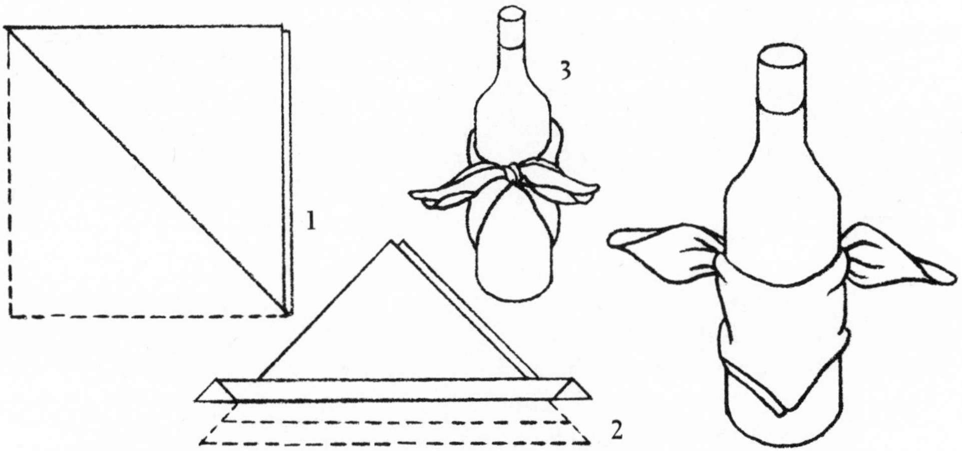

The Bottle Wrap
1. Fold the napkin in half diagonally. **2.** Fold the bottom edge up by one quarter twice. **3.** Tie the napkin around the bottle and fold the points to the base.

Note: If you want to catch condensation from a chilled wine bottle, turn back one of the points over the band formed after step 2, set the bottle on the other flap and then wrap the band around the bottle. Be sure to catch the rear flap securely as you tie the napkin in a knot.

An embellished version of brown rice and a flavorful European serving of leeks—Poireaux Braisés—accompany the chicken. Both add satisfying flavors and textures. Mound the rice in a round bowl, and show off the green and white leeks on a flat plate.

Finish with a wonderfully slimming dessert of Minted Melon. It's hard to believe how melons can taste so incredibly sweet with so few calories. It's a dessert that merits as much attention as any mousse—so serve it in goblets or dessert dishes on doily-lined saucers, adorned with sprigs of mint.

Seviche

SERVES: 6
Preparation time: 20 minutes
Marinating time: 6–8 hours or overnight

This traditional Peruvian seviche is prepared less expensively with fish but can also be made with scallops. The fish must be very fresh, since it is not cooked but marinated and eaten raw. So ask at the fish market for the freshest and best fish to use for Seviche.

The Ingredients:

2 pounds very fresh fillets of fish (snapper, sole) cut into 2″–3″ strips
½ cup lime juice
1 pimiento, finely chopped
½ cup finely chopped onion
½ cup finely chopped green pepper
½ cup finely chopped tomato
1 clove garlic, finely minced
2 tablespoons freshly chopped parsley
1 teaspoon sugar
¼ teaspoon chili powder
Salt and freshly ground pepper to taste
Garnish: Freshly chopped coriander (cilantro) or parsley

The Steps:

1. Lay fish strips in shallow dish, pour lime juice over, and toss to coat. Cover and marinate in refrigerator for 6–8 hours or overnight.
2. Drain off juice, add remaining ingredients, toss well, and chill for 2 hours.
3. Serve Seviche chilled, garnished with freshly chopped coriander or parsley.

Variations:

The recipe may be prepared with bay or sea scallops if available.
Lemon juice may be used as a marinade but lime juice is traditional.

Make-It-Easy Tips:

√ Even though older limes turn from dark green to yellow, the quality of the juice remains good. Limes kept refrigerated will keep for 6–8 weeks.

√ Roll room-temperature limes between the palm of your hand and the counter, pressing down firmly; this loosens the pulp, in turn releasing the juice.

Poulet Citron

SERVES: 6
Preparation time: 15 minutes
Cooking time: 10 minutes

This low-calorie chicken utilizes fresh garlic and lemon juice as flavor enhancers.

The Ingredients:

6 6-ounce chicken breasts, skinned and boned and dried with paper towels
4 teaspoons whole wheat flour mixed with ½ teaspoon freshly ground pepper
1 tablespoon unsalted butter
1 tablespoon vegetable oil
3 tablespoons minced scallions (green and white parts included)

¼ cup fresh lemon juice
¼ cup freshly chopped parsley
3–4 tablespoons chicken broth
2 teaspoons freshly minced garlic
1½ teaspoons freshly grated lemon peel
Garnish: Watercress, lemon slices, and cherry tomatoes

The Steps:

1. Flatten chicken breasts, lightly dust with flour mixed with pepper, and shake off excess.
2. In large nonstick skillet, heat butter and oil and sauté scallions for 1 minute; add chicken and sauté over high heat for 2–3 minutes a side, or until tender; remove to platter.
3. Add remaining ingredients; allow to heat through for 1 minute, pour over chicken, and serve immediately, garnished with watercress, lemon slices, and cherry tomatoes.

Variation:

Veal Scaloppine can be substituted for the chicken, but cook only 1–2 minutes per side.

Make-It-Easy Tips:

√ A powdered sugar shaker makes an excellent flour shaker for dusting meats or cake pans.

√ The chicken breasts must be flattened to facilitate quick cooking. Use a mallet, hammer, or side of a large knife.

√ A nonstick skillet reduces the amount of fats necessary and thereby reduces the amount of calories.

Parsleyed Brown Rice

SERVES: 6
Preparation time: 10 minutes
Cooking time: 35–40 minutes

The Ingredients:

2 cups chicken broth
1 cup water

1½ cups raw brown rice
Salt and freshly ground pepper to taste
2 tablespoons freshly chopped parsley
1 teaspoon freshly grated lemon peel

The Steps:

1. In deep saucepan, bring broth and water to a boil; add rice but do not stir.
2. Sprinkle with salt and pepper, cover; reduce heat and simmer slowly for 35–40 minutes, or until liquid is absorbed and grains are tender.
3. Fluff rice with fork, stir in parsley and lemon, and serve immediately.

Variations:

Rice can be cooked with all broth and no water.

Leftover rice can be chilled, tossed with vinaigrette, and served as a rice salad.

Make-It-Easy Tip:

√ Brown rice is nutritionally superior to white rice. It is closest to its natural state, with only the hull and some of the bran removed. As with any whole grain cereal, brown rice requires a slightly longer cooking time and a little more liquid than white rice.

Poireaux Braisés (Braised Leeks)

SERVES: 6
Preparation time: 10–15 minutes
Cooking time: 35 minutes

Leeks are an extremely popular vegetable in Europe, often called the "poor man's asparagus." In the United States, they have previously been relegated to exotic status, although they are currently gaining in popularity as a vegetable rather than a seasoning.

The Ingredients:

12 medium leeks
1½ tablespoons unsalted butter
¾ cup white wine or dry vermouth
1 tablespoon lemon juice
½ teaspoon Worcestershire sauce
Salt and freshly ground pepper to taste

The Steps:

1. Trim off leeks' root ends; cut off green part, leaving only 1" of the green section. Thoroughly and carefully wash leeks under cold running water, fanning out leaves to remove all sand and grit.
2. In large skillet, heat butter and sauté leeks over medium heat, turning often, for 2–3 minutes or until barely colored.
3. Add remaining ingredients; bring to a boil, cover, reduce heat, and simmer slowly for 25–30 minutes, depending on size, or until leeks are tender.
4. With slotted spatula or tongs, transfer leeks to platter. Thicken pan juices by boiling over high heat until reduced and syrupy. Pour juices over leeks and serve.

Variation:

Leeks can also be baked in a 350° oven for 45–50 minutes, or until tender.

Make-It-Easy Tips:

√ Leeks must be carefully scrubbed under cold running water to remove sand lodged between the leaves.
√ Select leeks with tightly rolled leaves and brightly colored green tops.

Minted Melon

SERVES: 6
Preparation time: 10–15 minutes
Chilling time: 2–4 hours

Minted melon is imbued with the sweet flavor of Marsala wine.

The Ingredients:

2 ripe cantaloupes, sliced in half, with seed and strings removed
2 tablespoons Marsala wine
1 tablespoon lemon juice
Garnish: Mint sprigs

The Steps:

1. Using melon-ball scoop, prepare 3–4 cups melon balls and place in large bowl.
2. Sprinkle with wine and lemon juice; toss gently, cover with plastic wrap, and allow to chill for 2–4 hours.
3. Serve in large goblets or dessert dishes garnished with mint sprigs.

Variations:

Honeydew, Crenshaw, or any combination of melons can be used. Marsala can be omitted if desired.

Make-It-Easy Tip:

√ Cut melons absorb refrigerator odors easily, so make sure to cover tightly with plastic wrap or aluminum foil.

Outdoor Barbecue on Skewers

SERVES: 4
Oriental Grilled Shrimp
Lamb Shish Kebab in Mustard Marinade
Skewered Vegetables
Iced Pineapple Sherbet

Barbecues are wonderful for dieters because much of the poultry or meat fat easily drips off.

This skewered rendition gives the barbecue a sophisticated touch by serving the skewered Oriental Grilled Shrimp as a first course. Many dieters find that eating a light snack just before a meal helps them eat less altogether by taking the edge off their appetites. So the shrimp have a practical side to their elegance.

Lamb is often thought of as a fatty meat, but here the leaner leg of lamb is used. Barbecuing or broiling also helps the fat melt away—which will hopefully help the fat on our hips to do the same.

The long, slender shape of skewered foods adds some artistic ideas to serving options. Lay the skewers out in circles or fans on parsley-lined platters or trays. Or go vertical and "plant" the skewers in an eggplant, cut in half, flat side down.

You might even carry over the long and lean look to a floral arrangement. Try tall, spiky blooms like statice, gladiolus, or tulips. Since the statice dries without wilting, it stays pretty when slipped through napkin rings, where it doubles as a take-home favor.

For evening, I use candles to create a romantic mood. Tall tapers echo the lean motif; they can be "planted" like the skewers in halved, hollowed-out eggplants for a surprisingly dramatic effect. But during mosquito season it's best to go with citronella candles—in whatever shape you can find.

Last-minute rushes are avoided with this menu, since the shrimp, lamb, vegetables, and fruit are all prepared in advance and wait in the refrigerator until they're ready. That leaves only the barbecuing itself for last.

Wind down with Iced Pineapple Sherbet—a treat for any "ice cream freaks" in the group. Contrast its sunny yellow color with mint leaves, or mandarin orange slices with the syrup rinsed off. It's a delightful, refreshing finish to this outdoor barbecue.

Chinese Grilled Shrimp

SERVES: 4
Preparation time: 10–15 minutes
Marinating time: 1–2 hours
Cooking time: 6 minutes

The shrimp can be cooked outdoors on a grill or indoors in the broiler.

The Ingredients:

2 dozen large raw shrimp, cleaned and deveined

Marinade:

1–2 tablespoons peanut oil
3 tablespoons soy sauce

3 tablespoons dry sherry
2 tablespoons lemon juice
1 tablespoon Dijon mustard
1 teaspoon freshly minced garlic
1 teaspoon freshly minced ginger (or ¼ teaspoon powdered ginger)
Garnish: Sprigs of fresh coriander (cilantro) or parsley

The Steps:

1. In shallow dish, combine marinade ingredients and stir.
2. Coat shrimp with marinade, cover, and allow to marinate at room temperature for 1–2 hours (or in refrigerator for 3–4 hours).
3. Preheat outdoor grill or broiler to high.
4. Thread marinated shrimp on 2–4 skewers and grill on broil for 3 minutes a side, basting often with marinade.
5. Serve immediately, garnished with sprigs of coriander leaf or parsley.

Variation:

2 tablespoons minced scallions can be added to marinade.

Make-It-Easy Tip:

√ If fishmonger will not devein shrimp for you, use a shrimp deveiner or arc-shaped tool that removes the shell and the black vein in one motion.

Shish Kebab in Mustard Marinade

SERVES: 4
Preparation time: 10 minutes
Marinating time: 3 hours or overnight
Cooking time: 8 minutes

The Ingredients:

Marinade:

¼ cup Dijon mustard (smooth or the new grainy style)
2 tablespoons white wine vinegar

2 tablespoons olive oil
2 tablespoons soy sauce
2 garlic cloves (¼ teaspoon), finely minced
¼ teaspoon ground rosemary
Freshly ground pepper to taste

1½ pound lean leg of lamb, cut in 1″ cubes

The Steps:

1. Combine marinade ingredients in mixing bowl and whisk until smooth; add lamb, stir to coat, and marinate for 3 hours at room temperature or overnight in refrigerator.
2. Allow meat to come to room temperature before broiling; preheat outdoor grill or broiler.
3. Place lamb cubes on skewers and grill or broil until golden on the outside and rare on the inside, about 4 minutes per side, basting occasionally with marinade.

Variation:

Minced shallots can be substituted for the garlic.

Make-It-Easy Tips:

√ The meat is broiled on separate skewers from the vegetables to keep the meat rare and the vegetables from getting overcooked.

√ The best way to grind rosemary is with a mortar and pestle. It can also be ground in large amounts in a coffee grinder and stored in a covered jar for several months.

Skewered Vegetables

SERVES: 4
Preparation time: 10 minutes
Cooking time: 6–7 minutes

When cooking vegetable kebabs, the skewers should be threaded with similar sizes and shapes of vegetables to promote even cooking. Alternate colors and shapes for variety.

The Ingredients:

2 green or red peppers, seeded and cut into 2″ chunks
2 medium zucchini, cut into 1″-wide slices
8 large mushroom caps, stems cut off
2 tomatoes, cut into wedges

Basting Sauce:
3 tablespoons lemon juice
2 tablespoons vegetable oil
2 teaspoons soy sauce

The Steps:

1. Preheat outdoor grill.
2. On first skewer, alternate slices of pepper and zucchini. On second skewer, alternate mushrooms with tomatoes.
3. Combine basting sauce ingredients together in bowl; whisk until smooth.
4. Grill pepper-zucchini skewer for 6–7 minutes per side and mushroom-tomato skewer for 2–3 minutes per side, basting often.
5. Remove from skewer, gently toss vegetables together, and serve immediately.

Variations:

- Small peeled onions, parboiled for 4 minutes, can be added to pepper-zucchini skewer and cooked.
- Yellow crookneck squash can be substituted for zucchini.

Make-It-Easy Tips:

√ Vegetables can be marinated in sauce earlier in the day and skewered and grilled just before serving.

√ Select well-shaped, firm, and glossy red or green pepper. They are perishable, so do not purchase more than 1–2 days in advance of cooking.

√ To avoid bursting onions, make a crisscross incision in the root end before parboiling; the onion will hold together when skewered.

Iced Pineapple Sherbet

SERVES: 6
Preparation time: 10 minutes
Freezing time: 3 hours

The cooling and refreshing taste of this dessert helps you start out on your diet without feeling deprived.

The Ingredients:

1½ cups canned crushed juice-packed pineapple, drained
1½ cups buttermilk
Sweetener (honey or sweetening substitute equivalent to ¼ cup sugar)
½ teaspoon vanilla extract
Garnish: Mandarin orange segments

The Steps:

1. Place ingredients in food processor or blender and puree well.
2. Pour into refrigerator tray or similar freeze-proof container and freeze for 2–3 hours, stirring from time to time to keep the dessert from becoming too firm.
3. Serve immediately in sherbet glasses or bowls, garnished with Mandarin orange segments.

Make-It-Easy Tip:

√ If sherbet gets too hard, process again until soft and chill again until desired firmness is achieved.

Holiday Celebrations

1. **New Year's Eve Celebration**
   Caviar Torte
   Steak Tartare
   Julienne of Carrot Salad
   Plum-Glazed Chicken Breasts
   Noodles Florentine
   Crème Brûlée

2. **Valentine's Dinner for Lovers**
   *Champagne
   Mushroom Soup for Two
   Steak au Poivre
   "Hearts" Salad
   *Baked Potatoes
   Lemon Champagne Sherbet
   *Chocolate Candies

3. **Mother's or Father's Day Family Dinner**
   Artichokes Vinaigrette
   Marinated Potted Beef
   Pasta Souffle
   Celery with Almonds
   Peach Melba

4. **Fourth of July Barbecue**
   "Parsley, Sage, Rosemary, and Thyme" Grilled Lamb
   Tomato and Mozzarella Salad
   *Sourdough Rolls
   Grilled Roasted Corn on the Cob
   Watermelon Bombe

5. **Labor Day Picnic**
   Picnic Chicken
   Red Potato Salad
   Colorful Coleslaw
   Blueberry Lattice Pie
   *Fresh Fruit

6. **Trick-or-Treat Party**
   Grape-Orange Punch
   Make-Your-Own French Bread Pizzas
   Black-and-White Cupcakes
   Pumpkin Spice Bars
   Incredibly Easy Chocolate Fudge
   Butterscotch Brownies
   *Candy

7. **Traditional Thanksgiving Feast**
   Hot Spiced Cider
   Perfect Roast Turkey
   Sourdough-Pecan Stuffing
   Glazed Sweet Potatoes
   Marmalade-Spiked Cranberry Sauce
   Spinach Flans on Tomato Rings
   Pumpkin Ice Cream Pie

8. **Merry Christmas Dinner**
   Christmas Glögg (Mulled Wine)
   Roast Beef
   Horseradish Cream Sauce
   Pan-Roasted Potatoes
   Cherry Tomato Salad in Parsley Wreath
   Quick-and-Easy Pecan Pie
   Hard Sauce
   Bourbon Balls

* Not a recipe

ALL YEAR LONG we gear up for holiday celebrations—from New Year's Eve to Christmas. We have high expectations, brimming with childhood memories of family gatherings. This section is designed to simplify holiday preparations while keeping them very special and indulging the child in all of us.

The recipes that are handed down through generations are always cherished, but the hours and hours of preparations they may require no longer are possible, given our busy lives and the demands on our time.

Normally when I entertain, I prepare light hors d'oeuvres so that guests are not full before dinner. The *New Year's Eve Celebration* menu offers an exception to this rule, since it is laden with heavy hors d'oeuvres. Dinner is often late and the champagne or wine flows freely. Therefore guests appreciate having more than light finger food available.

Valentine's Day is for couples, and the *Valentine's Dinner for Lovers* can be served on this special occasion or any night when love is the major topic of conversation.

A *Mother's or Father's Day Family Dinner* is a nice way to say thank you. Involve children in every aspect of the day, from preparing the food to setting the table to buying or even making gifts. I offer a complete menu, but if there is a food that is a special favorite of Mom's or Dad's, obviously this is the day to make that substitution.

The *Fourth of July Barbecue* and *Labor Day Picnic* are a salute to summer, so I offer Make-It-Easy recipes for a totally informal setting. The food is delicious, but it's typically only half the pleasure, since these are also occasions for out-of-door fun and games.

A *Trick-or-Treat Party* is designed to keep children safe, happy, and at home on Halloween night. They can make their own pizzas or even homemade fudge, along with playing the other traditional games.

The *Traditional Thanksgiving Feast* I've presented uses my favorite brown-bag turkey baking tip. Once in the bag, I don't have to baste or fuss. In addition, I always involve my family and friends in Thanksgiving food preparation. This is a time of sharing, and I am definitely not shy about asking for assistance with a long menu for a large group. That way I have additional time to make the table and the house look very festive.

The menu for the *Merry Christmas Dinner* is also traditional but, prepared with Make-It-Easy recipes, it is a pleasure to cook. Actually, this combination of roast beef and potatoes can be a wonderful menu any cool night of the year.

Both Thanksgiving and Christmas often require more than one meal. Guests usually finish the main meal early in the afternoon, relax for a while, and then are ready for a light supper. So, when preparing holiday feasts, I always buy a few interesting breads for late evening supper snacks.

New Year's Eve Celebration

SERVES 10–12
Caviar Torte
Steak Tartare
Julienne of Carrot Salad
Plum-Glazed Chicken Breasts
Noodles Florentine
Crème Brûlée

This great last bash of the holiday season gives us one more chance to celebrate during the chilliest, darkest days of the year. A variety of themes—last year's memories, the new year's resolutions, the finale of the holiday season—make planning and decorating enjoyable. And going buffet-style guarantees a Make-It-Easy way to serve.

Red, white, and black set a smashing color scheme. The red and white carry over from Christmas, and black adds a sophisticated touch. I use runners of red cloth to accent the table. Red and white candles carry the colors throughout the room. The Caviar Torte brings the color scheme right to the menu itself.

If you're feeling very clever or there's an artist in the family, try a clock-shaped centerpiece. Start with a styrofoam disk outlined in shiny black electric tape. Stick on black adhesive numbers and pin on black or red paper hands poised at midnight. Then mount your creation on a stick—a dowel or chopstick will do—standing in a base of styrofoam, a mound of pebbles, or even a bowl of dried beans.

If you're feeling less ambitious, fill a basket with small clocks, watches, and timers. Slip a few pages of the past year's calendar into the basket. Or line the pages end to end like a runner across the table. Leftover Christmas trimmings leave you with lots of decorating options. For starters, evergreen boughs and pinecones add color and life to any centerpiece.

Especially when the guests are family and close friends, it can be a warm experience to recall the year's events. Put out pictures and mementos of the year's milestones and good times—graduations, weddings, births, holidays, and trips. Or mark them in red on the calendar pages and ask guests to add others they can think of. An amusing party game idea is to suggest that each guest write his or her New Year's resolution anonymously and place them all in a hat. On or around midnight, the host or hostess can read them aloud and everyone can attempt to match the resolution to the guests.

It's easy to get carried away with ideas, but don't forget the practical side that also makes your party special. This menu is designed for a long, late-night party. It's really an extended cocktail hour, with lots of satisfying appetizers to last the evening.

The Steak Tartare must be prepared shortly before party time, but the torte is best done ahead and chilled. Only the topping goes on just before serving. These two dishes are placed at one end of the table, with a basket of toasted bread rounds or crackers nearby. The carrot salad can be served as part of the hors d'oeuvres or as a salad alongside the main course.

Next comes the more substantial foods: the Plum-Glazed Chicken, attractively garnished with orange wedges, and Noodles Florentine, as a side dish or for those who prefer a meatless alternative. Save yourself some kitchen hassles by having the chicken ingredients ready and the Noodles Florentine assembled in advance, ready for baking. I use a basket holder for the casserole to help protect the table and avoid burned fingers.

Forks are the only flatware needed until dessert. They may be wrapped in red and white napkins, tied with bits of Christmas ribbon, and placed in a basket or large candy jar.

Crème Brûlée, a rich and creamy make-ahead treat, is a fit ending for this feast. Individual ramekins or custard cups simplify serving, and may be carried on a tray in one trip from the kitchen.

Whatever beverages you choose, lots of glasses are a must. Plastic cups are handy, but can react with certain acidic spirits to form an unpleasant taste. And of course, include plenty of nonalcoholic choices for those who prefer it—and for those driving home.

Caviar Torte

SERVES: 10–12
Preparation time: 15–20 minutes

This is a variation on a traditional recipe that makes an especially attractive addition to the table.

The Ingredients:

8 hard-cooked eggs, chopped
3 tablespoons mayonnaise
Salt and freshly ground pepper to taste
2 bunches (1¼ cups) minced scallions (green and white parts included)
8 ounces cream cheese, softened
⅔ cup dairy sour cream
1 3½-ounce jar Danish or Icelandic Lumpfish Black Caviar
1 3½-ounce jar red caviar
Garnish: Lemon wedges and parsley sprigs
Accompaniments: Toasted bread crumbs or crackers

The Steps:

1. Generously oil or butter 9″ springform pan or pie plate.
2. Combine eggs with mayonnaise, salt, and pepper; spread over bottom of prepared pan and top with scallions.
3. Combine cream cheese with sour cream in blender, food processor, electric mixer, or by hand until smooth; spread over scallions, cover, and chill 3 hours or overnight.
4. Just before serving, using black and red caviar alternately, make 6 triangle shapes so pie wedges make a red-and-black color scheme.
5. Run knife around springform pan sides, loosen, lift off, and serve pie garnished with lemon wedges and parsley sprigs. (If using pie plate, serve torte directly from pan.) Accompany with toasted bread rounds or crackers.

Variation:

All-black or all-red caviar can be spread on top in place of the alternating colors.

Make-It-Easy Tips:

√ A wet spatula helps to spread cream layer easily over scallions.
√ Drain caviar in small strainer before spreading on top, to remove excess oil.

Steak Tartare

SERVES: 10–12
Preparation time: 15 minutes

You need the very best meat available for Steak Tartare. Ask the butcher for the leanest beef and have him grind it 2 or 3 times for you.

The Ingredients:

1 pound very lean top round steak, ground
¼ cup finely minced onion
1 tablespoon chopped fresh parsley
1 egg, lightly beaten
1 teaspoon Dijon mustard
1 teaspoon tomato paste
½ teaspoon Worcestershire sauce
½ teaspoon paprika
Dash of Tabasco sauce
Pinch of cayenne pepper
Salt and freshly ground pepper to taste
Garnish: Cornichons (sour pickles), cherry tomatoes, and parsley sprigs
Accompaniment: Pumpernickel bread rounds

The Steps:

1. Combine all ingredients, form log or mound shape, chill until ready to serve. (Do not do this earlier than 2 hours before serving.)

2. Garnish with cornichons, cherry tomatoes, and parsley sprigs and accompany with pumpernickel bread rounds.

Variations:

Fresh ground meat does not keep for a long time. Fry any leftover meat until crumbly in a skillet, add tomato sauce, and cook for a few minutes for a spicy meat sauce.

Steak Tartare may also be served as a part of a luncheon or brunch buffet.

Make-It-Easy Tip:

√ The entire recipe can be prepared in the food processor at one time but pulsated in an on-and-off rhythm just until chopped. In this case, begin with small pieces of meat and chop them yourself.

Julienne of Carrot Salad

SERVES: 8
Preparation time: 10–15 minutes

This recipe is an adaptation of a dish served at Leon Lionides's restaurant, The Coach House in New York City.

The Ingredients:

6 cups shredded carrots (about 1½ pounds)
⅓ cup capers, drained

Vinaigrette Dressing:

½ cup olive oil
3 tablespoons red wine vinegar
2 teaspoons Dijon Mustard
Salt and freshly ground pepper
Pinch of sugar
Garnish: Freshly chopped parsley

The Steps:

1. Combine carrots and capers together and chill until ready to use.
2. Combine vinaigrette ingredients together in a screw-top jar and shake until smooth.

3. Toss carrots with vinaigrette and serve immediately, or chill and serve later; garnish with freshly chopped parsley.

Variations:

If serving as hors d'oeuvre, accompany with crackers or small plates and forks.

Substitute ½ cup chopped scallion greens for capers.

Make-It-Easy Tips:

√ The food processor makes a perfect tool for shredding carrots easily.

√ Carrots with their leafy green tops remaining are more likely to be fresher than those wrapped in plastic bags.

Plum-Glazed Chicken Breasts

SERVES: 10–12
Preparation time: 10–15 minutes
Cooking time: 40–45 minutes

The Ingredients:

1 cup plum jam or preserves
6 tablespoons red wine vinegar
¼ cup finely chopped scallions
¼ cup soy sauce
2 tablespoons freshly grated ginger or 1½ teaspoons dried ground ginger
1 teaspoon dry mustard
Pinch of ground cloves
Pinch of cayenne
10 chicken breasts, split in half
Garnish: Orange slices

The Steps:

1. Preheat oven to 375°. Select a baking dish that can hold the chicken in a single layer and cover it with aluminum foil to save on messy cleanups.
2. In small saucepan, combine plum jam with vinegar, scallions,

soy sauce, ginger, mustard, cloves, and cayenne. Heat, stirring constantly until smooth.
3. Arrange chicken pieces in single layer, skin side down, in baking dish.
4. Brush half of sauce over chicken and bake for 20 minutes, basting occasionally.
5. Turn chicken and brush with remaining sauce; continue to bake for 20–25 minutes longer, or until tender and glazed.
6. Serve hot, garnished with orange slices.

Variations:

One whole chicken cut in 8 pieces can be substituted for the chicken breasts.

After baking, chicken can be placed under broiler for 2 minutes to further caramelize the color.

Make-It-Easy Tip:

√ Store peeled ginger in dry sherry in a covered jar in the refrigerator.

Noodles Florentine

SERVES: 12
Preparation time: 20 minutes
Cooking time: 45 minutes

This extra rich casserole is hearty, filling, and best of all can be assembled in advance.

The Ingredients:

20 ounces medium-wide noodles
6 tablespoons unsalted butter, at room temperature
2 pints dairy sour cream
4 10-ounce packages frozen chopped spinach, thawed and squeezed dry
6 eggs
1½ cups freshly grated Parmesan cheese
½ teaspoon Worcestershire sauce

Pinch of nutmeg
Salt and freshly ground pepper to taste
1–2 tablespoons unsalted butter

The Steps:

1. Preheat oven to 350°. Generously butter 9″ x 13″ x 2″ pan or similar-sized baking dish.
2. Drop noodles into boiling salted water and cook until just done; drain and place in large bowl. Immediately toss with butter, coating noodles well. Add sour cream and continue to toss.
3. Squeeze any excess moisture out of spinach and set aside.
4. Beat eggs with squeezed spinach until smooth. (This can be done in blender, food processor, with electric beater, or by hand.)
5. Toss noodles with spinach-egg mixture to combine. Add 1 cup of cheese and continue to stir. Season with Worcestershire sauce, nutmeg, salt, and pepper and pour into prepared pan.
6. Top with remaining cheese and a few tablespoons butter cut into tiny bits; bake for 45 minutes, or until hot and bubbling.

Variation:

Four 10-ounce packages frozen chopped broccoli, thawed, can be substituted for spinach.

Make-It-Easy Tips:

√ If casserole is not being used immediately, it can be refrigerated after assembly and baked when ready to use. If doing ahead, be sure to bring to room temperature before baking.
√ If using a glass baking dish, reduce heat by 25°.

Crème Brûlée

SERVES: 8–12
Preparation time: 20–25 minutes
Cooking time: 1 hour

Crème Brûlée sounds complicated, but in reality it only requires a few steps and can be made a day or two in advance. The best part of Crème Brûlée is that it is an instant winner. Forget the diets, however. It is best to make the dessert a day ahead. Chill it overnight, prepare the caramel topping the morning it is to be served, and allow to chill again.

The Ingredients:

1 quart heavy cream
6 tablespoons granulated sugar
8 egg yolks
2 teaspoons vanilla extract
1 cup light brown sugar, firmly packed

The Steps:

1. Preheat oven to 350°.
2. In large saucepan, scald cream by heating until bubbles just begin to form around edges of pan and steam escapes. Do not allow to boil or cream will scorch. Add sugar to cream and stir until sugar is completely dissolved.
3. In separate bowl, beat egg yolks until lemony in color. Add a little hot cream to eggs, stirring constantly and then gradually add remaining cream, whisking until smooth. Add vanilla and pour mixture into 8 ramekins, Pyrex custard cups, or a 10″ shallow baking dish.
4. Place dish or cups in roasting pan filled with 1″ of hot water and bake 35–40 minutes for ramekin dishes or custard cups, 50–60 minutes for 10″ baking dish, or until inserted knife comes out clean. Remove from oven, cool, cover with plastic wrap, and chill for 4–6 hours or overnight.
5. Preheat broiler to high.
6. With the back of a spoon, push brown sugar through a strainer and sprinkle on top of custards about ¼″ thick; broil 4″–6″ from broiler until sugar has caramelized, about 3 minutes, watching very carefully, and turning dish as necessary to avoid burning. Cool and chill again.
7. Serve Crème Brûlée chilled.

Variation:

A vanilla bean can be sliced open, added to the cream that is scalded for Step #2, and removed before proceeding with recipe. If using vanilla bean, omit extract.

Make-It-Easy Tips:

√ When cooking with egg yolks, it is important to introduce hot liquids gradually, to avoid curdling the eggs.

√ Cooking the custard in a hot-water bath prevents the custard from curdling or overcooking.

√ To keep very fresh, store brown sugar in a tightly closed plastic bag in freezer. Bring to room temperature before using.

Valentine's Dinner for Lovers

SERVES: 2
*** Champagne**
Mushroom Soup for Two
Steak au Poivre
*** Baked Potatoes**
"Hearts" Salad
Lemon Champagne Sherbet
*** Chocolate Candies**

It could be Valentine's Day, an anniversary, or just the fact that the kids are visiting Grandma and Grandpa. Lovers don't need an excuse to make their own private holiday. Here is a dinner you can prepare for your favorite person without getting too tired to enjoy the rest of the evening. You can even cook it together.

The table setting should be very simple—the emphasis is on the couple, not the decor. A white tablecloth with red napkins will set a Valentine mood. Napkins can easily be folded accordian-style and slipped into

* Not a recipe

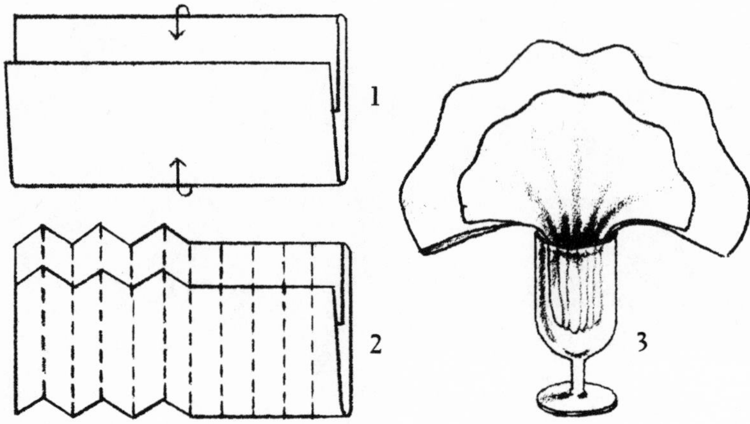

Napkin Fan
Begin with a crisp napkin 17–18″ square. **1.** Fold napkin as shown with some overlap. **2.** Accordion fold in sharp creases 1½″ wide starting from the left. **3.** Place napkin in glass and fan out.

champagne glasses, fanning out over the top. Three roses traditionally say, "I love you." And what romantic dinner is complete without soft candlelight? Either tall thin tapers or even lots of inexpensive small votive candles all around the house will set the mood for romance.

The soup can be prepared in advance and reheated at serving time. Bake the potatoes in a 375° oven, or even a toaster oven, for about 1 hour and 15 minutes. Don't worry if they overbake; the skins will get even crispier and the centers will become powdery-soft. The salad greens can be readied and chilled, and the dressing prepared and left at room temperature. This leaves plenty of time for setting the table—and making sure you look your best. Having your ingredients ready will make the steak especially easy to prepare.

The bottle of champagne looks extra-special wrapped in a white napkin (see illustration of bottle wrap on page 161) and set on a trivet. And speaking of champagne, be sure to leave a little for the Lemon Champagne Sherbet, which is made just minutes before serving. Spoon the sherbet into chilled goblets or dessert dishes, set them on doily-lined saucers, garnish with lemon slices, and perhaps a few Valentine's chocolates on the side. Then, back to the candlelight!

Mushroom Soup for Two

SERVES: 2
Preparation time: 15 minutes
Cooking time: 25 minutes

The Ingredients:

4 tablespoons (½ stick) unsalted butter
½ pound mushrooms, roughly chopped
1 small onion, roughly chopped
1½ tablespoons all-purpose flour
1½ cups chicken broth
Salt and freshly ground white pepper to taste
1 tablespoon dry sherry
½ cup half-and-half
Garnish: Freshly chopped parsley

The Steps:

1. Melt butter in a Dutch oven or large saucepan. Sauté mushrooms and onions until just golden.
2. Sprinkle flour over mushroom-onion mixture and stir well until absorbed.
3. Add broth, salt, and pepper, and taste for seasonings. Bring to a boil, lower heat, and simmer 20–25 minutes.
4. Add sherry and cream and heat until just warm.
5. Pour into blender or food processor and pulsate just until smooth. Taste, and adjust seasoning if necessary. Serve hot, garnished with parsley.

Variations:

Mushrooms may be sliced and sautéed and the soup served without pureeing.

Beef broth can be substituted for chicken broth.

Make-It-Easy Tips:

√ Raw mushrooms should be stored in a paper bag, which is porous, to keep them fresh.

√ The freshest mushrooms are closed around the stem by a thin veil, with no blemishes.

Steak au Poivre (Pepper Steak)

SERVES: 2
Preparation time: 10 minutes
Cooking time: 6–10 minutes

The Ingredients:

2 tablespoons black peppercorns, coarsely cracked
2 individual steaks, 1″–1½″ thick, completely trimmed (shell, club, or fillet)
1 tablespoon unsalted butter
1 tablespoon vegetable oil
Salt
3 tablespoons port wine
2 tablespoons strong beef broth
3 tablespoons heavy cream
Garnish: Freshly chopped parsley

The Steps:

1. Lay cracked pepper on sheet of waxed paper and press pepper into both sides of steaks.
2. Heat butter and oil in large skillet; when melted, sear steaks for 2–3 minutes on each side, seasoning with salt on each side.
3. Add wine and cook for an additional 2 minutes. With slotted spoon, remove steaks to warm platter.
4. Add broth and stir to scrape up browned particles; cook over high heat until liquid is slightly reduced.
5. Gradually add cream, stirring until sauce is smooth and thickened; pour sauce over steaks and serve hot, garnished with freshly chopped parsley.

Variations:

Steak au Poivre can be served traditionally over butter-fried slices of French bread.

Marsala or Madeira wine can be substituted for port wine.

Make-It-Easy Tips:

√ To crack peppercorns easily, place in plastic bag and pound with mallet, cleaver, or heavy object.

√ Both the club steak (also called Delmonico) or the shell steak (also called New York strip, Kansas City strip, or strip steak) are tender cuts of meat from the short loin of beef with the tenderloin parts removed. These cuts, as well as the fillet strip, which is the tenderloin itself, can be successfully used for Steak au Poivre.

✓ This recipe is for medium-rare steaks. If rarer steak is desired, sear only 1–2 minutes in Step #2; for medium to well done, sear for 3–4 minutes per side.

"Hearts" Salad

SERVES: 2
Preparation time: 10 minutes

Serve this mixture of "hearts" salad for Valentine's Day. It is an expensive mixture of vegetables that should be reserved for a special occasion.

The Ingredients:

4 canned artichoke hearts, drained
4 canned hearts of palm, drained
1 small bunch watercress

Vinaigrette Dressing:

7 tablespoons olive oil
2 tablespoons red wine vinegar
1 teaspoon Dijon mustard
¼ teaspoon curry powder
Pinch sugar
Pinch paprika
Salt and freshly ground white pepper to taste

The Steps:

1. Slice artichoke hearts in half and place 4 halves on each plate.
2. Slice hearts of palm and distribute evenly.
3. Break off watercress sprigs and place on plates decoratively; chill until ready to serve.
4. When ready to serve, combine vinaigrette ingredients together and mix well. Pour small amount of dressing on each salad and serve on chilled salad plates.

Variations:

The salad may be tossed with the dressing in a bowl and then distributed evenly between the two plates

Hearts of celery may be substituted for the more expensive hearts of palm.

Cooked frozen artichoke hearts may be substituted for the canned ones.

Make-It-Easy Tips:

√ Curry powder provides enough spiciness so that very little salt is necessary—a good tip for those on a salt-restricted diet.

√ Salad dressing can be prepared in advance and refrigerated until serving time.

Lemon Champagne Sherbet

SERVES: 2
Preparation time: 5 minutes

This cooling dessert must be served immediately. Enjoy champagne with dinner and save just ⅓ cup for this fabulous froth.

The Ingredients:

1½ cups lemon sherbet
⅓ cup champagne
½ teaspoon grated lemon peel
Garnish: Thin lemon slices

The Steps:

1. Place sherbet, champagne, and lemon peel in blender or food processor; process until smooth and ready.
2. Pour into stemmed goblets, wine glasses, or dessert dishes and serve immediately, garnished with lemon slices.

Variations:

Frozen lemon yogurt or lemon ice cream, if available, can be substituted for sherbet.

For a nonalcoholic version, substitute lemon-flavored soda or even ginger ale.

Make-It-Easy Tip:

✓ The froth can be prepared with white wine, but it is the bubbles that give the dessert its frothy effervescence.

Mother's or Father's Day Family Dinner

SERVES: 6–8
Artichokes Vinaigrette
Marinated Potted Beef
Pasta Soufflé
Celery with Almonds
Peach Melba

Long before Mother's Day and Father's Day were introduced in this country, the custom of Mothering Day arose in England. It was a time for children to visit Mother, bake her a soft "simnel cake" made of fine white flour, and in return receive her blessing. While simnel cakes have gone out of fashion, mothers and fathers alike are sure to appreciate a dinner served in their honor. It's a particularly thoughtful way to show your love when presents don't seem to say all you feel.

Here is a dinner with all the looks and tastes of a special meal, yet it can easily be served family-style. Enjoy it in the evening or as a midday Sunday dinner.

Fresh flowers are traditional, and an excellent selection certainly is available in May and June. Another creative centerpiece suggestion is a collection of toys—dolls, trains, miniatures, or whatever is available, clustered at the center of the table. Cards or a gift can be set at Mom's or Dad's place. And for extra family touches, include parents' baby pictures or family pictures from past years. It might be a fun time to show slides or home movies after dinner.

Like the flowers, fresh artichokes will be in season. Be sure to cut the stem straight across the bottom so that the artichokes will stand up, and provide large enough plates to accommodate the uneaten part of the leaves. Enjoy the artichokes while the beef simmers, the soufflé bakes, and the almonds sit chopped and ready for cooking. That way no one gets stuck alone in the kitchen.

With a little supervision, children can help prepare this meal. Junior cooks can be delegated to help mix the vinaigrette, toast the almonds, and, best of all, assemble the Peach Melba for dessert.

Artichokes Vinaigrette

SERVES: 6–8
Preparation time: 15 minutes
Cooking time: 30–45 minutes
Chilling time: 2–4 hours or overnight

Artichokes are at their peak in May, although you can find them in the markets year round. Even if your family is only 6, by all means boil enough artichokes to have extras cold for lunch the next day. Once cooked, artichokes will keep for several days covered in the refrigerator.

The Ingredients:

Water
1 teaspoon salt
8 medium to large artichokes
1 lemon, cut in half

Vinaigrette (yields 2 cups):
1 cup olive oil (or ⅓ cup olive oil and ⅔ cup corn, safflower, or soy oil)
6 tablespoons red wine vinegar (or lemon juice)
2 tablespoons minced parsley
1 tablespoon minced chives or scallion greens
1 teaspoon chopped capers (soft)
1 teaspoon Dijon mustard
½ teaspoon dry mustard
½ teaspoon freshly minced garlic
Pinch of sugar
Salt and freshly ground pepper to taste

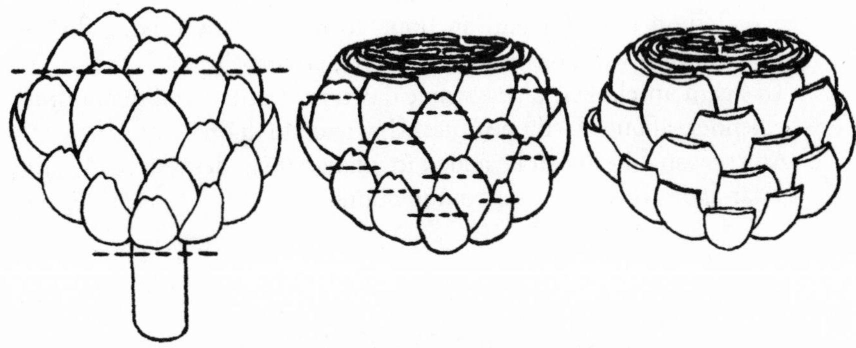

The Steps:

1. Wash artichokes. Slice off stems 1″ from base and remove small bottom leaves. Cut off about 1″ from top of artichoke. Trim tips of leaves easily with a kitchen scissors to avoid prickles. Rub cut side with cut lemon half.
2. Select deep kettle large enough to hold all artichokes standing upright (or use 2 large pots). Fill with enough water to cover artichokes, add salt, bring to a boil, and plunge artichokes into water. Cover and boil gently for 30–45 minutes (depending on size of artichokes), or until base can be pierced easily with fork.
3. Drain thoroughly upside down and chill for 4–6 hours or overnight.
4. Meanwhile, prepare vinaigrette by combining ingredients in food processor, blender, or small jar, blending or shaking until smooth. Chill until ready to use.
5. Serve each chilled artichoke on a large plate with a small cup containing about ¼ cup of salad dressing and enough room for the uneaten parts of the leaves.

Variation:

Artichokes can be served hot with melted butter plus a splash of brandy, or lemon-flavored butter if desired.

Make-It-Easy Tips:

√ If time permits, soak artichokes in cold water plus a pinch of vinegar or lemon juice for half an hour, to remove any lurking dirt or bugs. This will save time on washing chores.

√ To steam artichokes, place upside down in steamer, and steam until tender, about 45–60 minutes. (No need to drain.)

√ Any seasonal herb can be added to vinaigrette as desired: basil, dill, tarragon, oregano, or a combination.

Marinated Potted Beef

SERVES: 6–8
Preparation time: 15 minutes
Marinating time: 6 hours or overnight
Cooking time: 3–4 hours

It's easiest to marinate the roast a day in advance.

The Ingredients:

4 boneless chuck roast, brisket, tri-tip, or other beef for potting
3½ cups red wine (about 1 bottle)
¼ cup brandy
1 carrot, sliced
1 small onion, sliced
2 tablespoons freshly chopped parsley
1 teaspoon thyme, crumbled
¼ teaspoon ground allspice
Salt and freshly ground pepper to taste
1 tablespoon unsalted butter
Salt and freshly ground pepper to taste

The Steps:

1. Marinate beef in wine, brandy, carrot, onion, parsley, thyme, allspice, salt, and pepper in bowl or shallow dish so that meat is covered with marinade; cover and marinate 6 hours or overnight in refrigerator, turning once or twice.
2. Remove meat from marinade and pat dry on paper towels.

3. Heat butter in Dutch oven or deep skillet; when melted, sauté beef on all sides until brown.
4. Discard accumulated fat, add marinade, bring to a boil, cover, and simmer for 3–4 hours, or until meat is tender.
5. Remove meat from sauce and set aside on heated platter.
6. Continue to cook sauce in pan over medium-high heat, reducing until slightly thickened, about 20 minutes.
7. Defat gravy, season to taste with salt and pepper, and serve meat hot, sliced, with sauce spooned over.

Variation:

½–1 teaspoon minced garlic can be added to the marinade.

Make-It-Easy Tips:

√ It is best to prepare the beef a day ahead, remove any fat, slice, and reheat wrapped in foil with the sauce reheated and served on the side.

√ A quick method of defatting gravy is to chill in freezer for 30 minutes and easily remove the congealed fat with a spoon.

√ For a quick thickener, blend 2 teaspoons potato starch or cornstarch with 1 tablespoon cold water; add to sauce and stir until thickened. Gravy can also be pureed in a food processor or blender, or through a strainer.

√ When chopping parsley by hand or in a food processor, make sure it is thoroughly dry so that the pieces will separate easily and not adhere to each other.

Pasta Soufflé

SERVES: 6–8
Preparation time: 15 minutes
Cooking time: 1 hour

This is a variation of a recipe given to me by the famous caterer Milton Williams.

The Ingredients:

¼ pound unsalted butter, softened to room temperature
4 ounces whipped cream cheese
1 pint dairy sour cream
3 eggs
1 tablespoon lemon juice
1 teaspoon sugar
½ teaspoon Worcestershire sauce
Pinch of paprika
Salt and freshly ground pepper to taste
4 cups water
1 teaspoon powdered or 1 cube chicken stock base
8-ounce package fine noodles

The Steps:

1. Preheat oven to 350°. Generously butter 1½ quart soufflé dish.
2. In food processor or blender, combine butter, cream cheese, sour cream, eggs, lemon juice, sugar, Worcestershire sauce, paprika, salt, and pepper and process until smooth. Pour into large mixing bowl.
3. Bring water and chicken stock base to a boil, add noodles, and cook for 5 minutes; drain without rinsing.
4. Add noodles to butter mixture, toss to combine, pour into prepared baking dish, and bake for 1 hour. Serve immediately.

Variations:

To serve as a dessert, omit salt and paprika and add 2–3 tablespoons lemon juice, an additional egg plus ¼ cup sugar. Proceed as above and serve hot with fresh berries or other fruit and a sprinkling of powdered sugar.

Vegetable variations: add 2 tablespoons corn kernels, chopped zucchini, or other vegetables for a colorful variation.

Make-It-Easy Tip:

√ If timing is off and it is necessary to hold the soufflé, leave oven door shut and reduce heat to 300°; it will keep for an additional 45–60 minutes.

Celery with Almonds

SERVES: 6–8
Preparation time: 10–15 minutes
Cooking time: 4–5 minutes

The Ingredients:

- 3 tablespoons unsalted butter
- 4 cups celery, thinly sliced
- 1 8-ounce can water chestnuts, drained and sliced
- 3 scallions, finely minced (green and white parts included)
- ¼ teaspoon minced garlic
- ½ cup slivered almonds, toasted

The Steps:

1. In a large skillet, melt butter and, when hot, add celery; toss well, stirring constantly for 1 minute.
2. Add water chestnuts, scallions, and garlic and continue to cook, stirring constantly for 2–3 minutes, or until just cooked but still crunchy.
3. Add almonds, toss, and serve immediately.

Variations:

Shallots or onions can be substituted for the scallions.

Make-It-Easy Tips:

√ Celery can be easily sliced in a food processor.

√ Toast nuts easily in a toaster oven or under a broiler, watching carefully, until brown.

Peach Melba

SERVES: 6–8
Preparation time: 20 minutes
Chilling time: 1 hour

A traditional favorite, prepared Make-It-Easy style.

The Ingredients:

Sauce:
1 10-ounce package frozen raspberries in syrup, thawed
1 10-ounce jar currant jelly

4 fresh ripe peaches, about 1 pound
1 tablespoon lemon juice
2 pints vanilla ice cream
⅓ cup slivered almonds or pine nuts, lightly toasted

The Steps:

1. Prepare melba sauce by pureeing raspberries in food processor or blender until smooth. Mash puree through sieve to remove seeds. Place puree and currant jelly in small saucepan and heat, stirring constantly until jelly has melted. Chill for 1 hour or until ready to use.
2. Peel peaches easily by dropping into boiling water for 1 minute; then promptly remove peel. Slice peeled peaches thickly and sprinkle lightly with lemon juice to prevent discoloration.
3. Place scoop of vanilla ice cream in tall goblet or parfait glass, top with peach slices, spoon a little melba sauce over, and sprinkle tops with toasted almonds. Serve immediately.

Variation:

If fresh peaches are not in season, use thawed frozen unsweetened peaches.

Make-It-Easy Tips:

√ The sauce may be prepared several days in advance and kept in the refrigerator.

√ Select firm yellow or creamy-colored peaches that yield to slight pressure. Avoid green ones (which will not ripen) or those with bruises or spots indicating possible decay.

Fourth of July Barbecue

SERVES: 6–8

"Parsley, Sage, Rosemary, and Thyme" Grilled Lamb
Tomato, Basil and Mozzarella Salad
*** Sourdough Rolls**
Grilled Roasted Corn on the Cob
Watermelon Bombe

July 4th is both our country's birthday and our midsummer holiday. That gives our celebration the themes—one patriotic and one plain summer fun.

Red, white, and blue tablecloths and napkins, in solids or checks, reflect the day's theme. Small American flags can make a centerpiece, either bunched bouquet-style or even mingled with a vase or pitcher of fresh flowers. Napkins can be paper for a casual look, or cloth rolled up and tied with appropriately colored ribbons or heavy yarn. For an alternative, straw place mats give a rustic look, or crisscrossing cloth runners give an unusual touch to the table.

It's no wonder a barbecue has become so popular for this day—it al-

* Not a recipe

lows you to avoid a hot kitchen. The grilled lamb gives us both the traditional barbecue and a change from the usual hamburgers, hot dogs, and chicken. Sourdough rolls, or any variety of roll desired, can be warmed on the edge of the grill if you like, then served in a basket lined with colored napkins or a square of red gingham. The tomato salad will carry the color theme even further if served on a blue plate or set on a blue tablecloth.

It's hard to think of a more all-American treat than corn on the cob. Keep pot holders or oven mitts handy for easy husking. Little corncob holders are inexpensive, make corn neater to eat, and help prevent burned fingers.

The Watermelon Bombe is another variation on a tradition. Not everyone likes watermelon, but this one is made of ice cream. And who can turn down ice cream on the Fourth of July? But resist the urge to show it off too early. It should stay in the freezer until serving time.

Because of the summer sun, people will appreciate all the help they can get in keeping cool. If there are no trees, umbrellas will help. And folks of all ages will enjoy a plentiful variety of cold drinks.

"Parsley, Sage, Rosemary, and Thyme" Grilled Lamb

SERVES: 6–8
Preparation time: 20 minutes
Marinating time: 4–6 hours or overnight
Cooking time: 40 minutes

This recipe, courtesy of Myron Falk, requires a butterflied leg of lamb. Ask the butcher to bone the leg of lamb, leaving it open like a large jagged and lopsided piece of steak.

The Ingredients:

1 5–6 pound leg of lamb, butterflied with fell (tough outer skin) and any excess fat removed

Marinade:

1 cup olive oil
⅔ cup lemon juice

3 cloves garlic, crushed
2 bay leaves, crushed
6 sprigs parsley
1½ teaspoons ground sage
1½ teaspoons dried rosemary, crushed
1½ teaspoons dried thyme, crumbled
Salt and freshly ground pepper to taste

Sauce:

½ cup beef broth
¼ cup red wine
2 tablespoons chopped shallots (or white part of scallions)
1 teaspoon ground sage
1 teaspoon dried rosemary, crushed
1 teaspoon dried thyme, crumbled
3 tablespoons unsalted butter
3 tablespoons chopped parsley

The Steps:

1. Place lamb in flat dish; combine marinade ingredients and pour over meat; marinate 4–6 hours or overnight, covered, in refrigerator; bring lamb to room temperature before cooking.
2. Preheat broiler or outdoor grill to high.
3. Drain meat, reserving marinade, and sear over hot grill on both sides; lower heat to 450° or 500° (or if outside, raise grill slightly). Cook for 20 minutes a side, basting occasionally with marinade. (Lamb should be pink on the inside and crusty on the outside, with an internal temperature of 145°.)
4. In saucepan, combine beef broth, wine, shallots, sage, rosemary, and thyme, and ½ of reserved marinade; boil until reduced to ½ cup; add butter and parsley and stir until smooth.
5. Slice meat on the bias and serve with sauce on side.

Variations:

Lamb can also be served with mint jelly on the side.

Leftover lamb can be used cold for sandwiches the next day with mustard on dark rye bread.

Make-It-Easy Tips:

√ Crush rosemary easily in a mortar and pestle or place it between sheets of waxed paper and roll a rolling pin over.

√ Marinade can be prepared in advance and refrigerated overnight.

√ In Step #1, meat can be marinated in a jumbo plastic storage bag, securely tied, to facilitate turning without getting herbs and garlic on your hands.

√ Remember to ask the butcher for the lamb bone, which can be frozen and used for stock or soup making.

Tomato and Mozzarella Salad (Pomodori e Mozzarella)

SERVES: 6
Preparation time: 10 minutes

Serve this salad whenever tomatoes are at their peak and fresh basil is plentiful.

The Ingredients:

6 medium-sized ripe tomatoes
¾ pound Mozzarella cheese, as fresh as possible
4–5 tablespoons good olive oil (Italian is preferable)
6–8 fresh basil leaves, washed, dried, and coarsely chopped
Salt and freshly ground pepper to taste

The Steps:

1. Cut tomatoes in half horizontally and remove seeds by gently squeezing. Cut tomato halves in small cubes and place in bowl.
2. Cut Mozzarella in similar-size pieces and combine with tomatoes.
3. Toss with oil and basil, season with salt and pepper, and gently stir to combine.
4. Serve salad at room temperature or slightly chilled.

Variations:

If fresh basil is unavailable, do not substitute dried basil in its place. It is better to use freshly chopped parsley to bring out the flavor of ripe tomatoes.

Tomatoes and Mozzarella can be thinly sliced, presented in alternate slices, and garnished with basil leaves and a drizzle of olive oil.

An extraordinary variety of Mozzarella cheese, called Buffalo Mozzarella, has a wonderfully creamy texture and special flavor. Available only in Italian groceries or specialty cheese shops, it's very expensive; but if you're looking for an incredible treat, it's worth a try.

Make-It-Easy Tips:

√ A serrated-edged tomato or bread knife is an invaluable tool to use when cutting tomatoes.

√ To ripen tomatoes at home, store in a warm location away from direct sunlight, standing flat stem end down in a plastic bag with a few holes punched through. The natural ethylene gas of the tomatoes speeds up the ripening process.

Grilled Roasted Corn on the Cob

SERVES: 6–8
Preparation time: 10–15 minutes
Cooking time: 15–20 minutes

Use any seasonal fresh herb or combination of fresh herbs desired.

The Ingredients:

12 ears corn

Herb Butter:

6 ounces (1½ sticks) unsalted butter
⅓ cup freshly chopped herbs (chives, parsley, basil, etc.)
Salt and freshly ground pepper to taste

The Steps:

1. Light outdoor grill and allow coals to heat thoroughly.
2. Pull husks away from cob, leaving them attached at stalk end; remove silk with brush, and wrap husks back around corn. Soak in cold water for 10–15 minutes.
3. In food processor, blender, electric beater, or by hand, process butter and herbs until smooth and creamy.
4. Turn back husks of corn, place each ear on piece of heavy-duty

aluminum foil, spread corn with about one tablespoon butter, and wrap husks around corn again.

5. Wrap each foil packet securely and roast ears directly on hot coals, turning occasionally for 15–20 minutes or until tender. Unwrap and serve corn hot.

Variations:

Garlic, onion, or any flavor butter can be substituted for herb butter.

Corn can be husked, wrapped in strips of bacon, secured with skewers, and grilled on a rack until bacon is crisp and corn is golden and tender.

Corn can be cooked indoors in a preheated broiler.

Make-It-Easy Tips:

√ The corn is soaked to prevent burning or drying out.

√ Buy the freshest corn possible and it will be the sweetest. Once corn is picked, the sugar in the kernels starts converting to starch.

√ The tip-off for freshly picked corn is the stem. If damp and pale green, corn is freshly picked. After 24 hours, the stalk turns opaque; longer than that, it becomes brown.

√ Always refrigerate corn until use.

Watermelon Bombe

SERVES: 10–12
Preparation time: 10–15 minutes
Freezing time: 1–2 hours

This is the latest version of watermelon ice cream. It may not taste like the original—but it certainly looks like it and is sure to bring smiles. It's cool, refreshing, and amusing. Clear out enough space in the freezer to fit the bowl in comfortably.

The Ingredients:

1 quart (2 pints) green ice cream or ices (pistachio, mint, lime, etc.), softened for 10 minutes

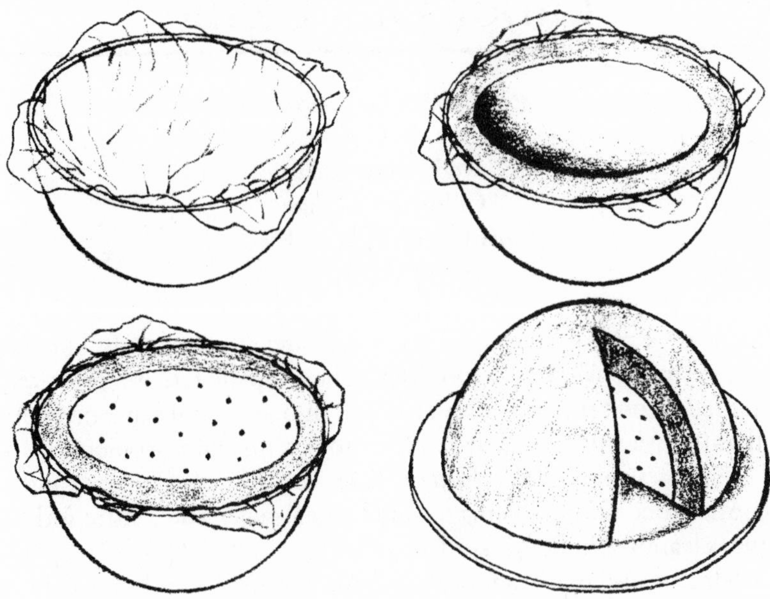

1 quart (2 pints) red or pink ice cream or ices (peppermint, strawberry, or raspberry), softened for 10 minutes
3 ounces chocolate chips

The Steps:

1. Line rounded 5- and 6-cup bowl (such as a metal mixing bowl) with plastic wrap, overlapping sides. Layer green ice cream 1″–2″ thick on bottom and up sides of bowl, and freeze until hard.
2. Fold chocolate chips into softened red or pink ice cream and fill cavity of mold with mixture; cover completely with plastic wrap and freeze until hard, 1–2 hours.
3. Open plastic wrap to expose top surface, place platter on top of bowl, and turn bowl and platter over. Remove remaining plastic wrap, slice in wedge-shaped pieces, and serve immediately.

Make-It-Easy Tips:

√ The bombe can be prepared up to four weeks in advance.
√ The plastic wrap lining in the bowl is essential if you wish to unmold the bombe easily.

Labor Day Picnic

SERVES: 6–8
Picnic Chicken
Red Potato Salad
Colorful Coleslaw
Blueberry Lattice Pie
*** Fresh Fruit**

Labor Day is almost everybody's day off, and it seems only fair that it should be the cook's day off too! Make-ahead picnic fare is a great way to guarantee a good time with a minimum of fuss. You'll have no more to do than transfer the finished product from refrigerator to picnic basket, with perhaps a simple tablecloth or sheet, napkins, plates, cups, and cutlery. And since no one seems to mind paper plates and plastic forks at a picnic, cleanup can be Make-It-Easy, too.

Labor Day also marks a transition from summer to fall, reflected in the contents of the picnic basket. Blueberry pie is generally a summer treat, while the Red Potato Salad shows a hint of fall color. A basket of fresh fruit makes a pretty and edible centerpiece, as well as a healthy alternative to potato chips and other "junk" foods found so often in a typical picnic lunch. Some summer fruits are still available in early September, and the first early apples may even be on the market. I also bring along a bunch of multicolored balloons to provide a splash of color and a feeling of festivity.

Plastic dishes with tight-fitting lids make packing secure and serving a snap. Many cities have restaurant supply stores, open to the public, which sell a wide variety of inexpensive, disposable containers. On the cleanup end, a large plastic bag keeps litter under control.

If picnic tables are unavailable and you prefer a smoother, more cushiony surface than a cloth spread directly on the grass, try a blanket or even exercise mats for padding. Wrap each napkin around a fork and a Wash'n Dri towelette—a handy addition since the chicken is messy finger food. A colored rubber band can hold each package together. Then pack along some extra napkins, just to be on the safe side. Once the cloth is laid out, a napkin package can be placed on each plate. Napkins and plates in contrasting outdoor colors add a casually pretty touch.

Of course, picnics are not just for food. They're for outdoor fun besides. Why not pack along a basket of games? Frisbees, a football, a soccerball, and potato sacks are great active fun, while board games like chess, checkers, or Scrabble are appreciated by others (especially if a little rain moves your outdoor picnic inside).

* Not a recipe

And while fall may be on the way, Labor Day can be a hot, sunny, thirsty day. Pack lots of cold drinks so your supply doesn't fall short. And remember the insect repellent—ants, mosquitoes, and bees don't take the day off.

Picnic Chicken

SERVES: 6–8
Preparation time: 15 minutes
Cooking time: 50 minutes–1 hour

The Ingredients:

2 whole chickens, split in quarters

Marinade:

¾ cup olive oil
¼ cup vegetable oil
6 tablespoons red wine vinegar
⅓ cup minced scallions (green and white parts included)
⅓ cup Dijon mustard
¼ cup freshly chopped parsley
1 tablespoon drained and chopped capers (optional)
½ teaspoon dried tarragon, crumbled
Salt and freshly ground pepper to taste

The Steps:

1. Pat chicken dry on paper towels and place in shallow dish.
2. Combine marinade ingredients in food processor, blender, or by hand; process until just smooth.
3. Pour mixture over chicken and marinate at room temperature for 1–2 hours. (Chicken can be marinated overnight in the refrigerator.)
4. Preheat broiler.
5. Remove chicken from marinade, place on rack, and broil 3″–4″ from heat, basting occasionally with marinade, for 15 minutes per side, or until tender and golden.
6. Cool, wrap securely in foil, and chill.
7. Serve chicken chilled or at room temperature.

Variations:

Chicken can be grilled outdoors over a charcoal fire.
Lemon juice can be substituted for vinegar.

Make-It-Easy Tip:

√ Longer shelf life increases the strength, saltiness, and dryness of mustard. But mustard will never "go bad." It may become dry or darken, but it will not mold or mildew. Once opened, refrigerate.

Red Potato Salad

SERVES: 8–10
Preparation time: 15 minutes
Cooking time: 20 minutes
Chilling time: 1–2 hours or overnight

No need to peel these potatoes. The bright color and nutritious peel add to this simply prepared salad.

The Ingredients:

20 tiny or 10 medium red potatoes, washed well
½ cup chopped scallions (green and white parts included)

Vinaigrette Dressing:

¾ cup olive oil
5 tablespoons lemon juice
2 tablespoons freshly chopped parsley
1 tablespoon Dijon mustard (smooth or grainy style)
1½ teaspoons freshly minced garlic
Salt and freshly ground pepper to taste

The Steps:

1. Place potatoes in pot of boiling, salted water; cover pot and cook potatoes until fork-tender, about 15–20 minutes for small size and 20–25 minutes for medium. (Do not overcook.) Drain, run under cold water, and allow to cool. Cut potatoes into small wedges and place in large bowl. Top with scallions.

2. Combine dressing ingredients in food processor, blender, or small jar and process or shake until smooth.
3. Pour dressing over potatoes and scallions, gently toss well, and chill for 1–2 hours or overnight. Serve cold or at room temperature.

Variations:

New potatoes can be substituted for red potatoes.

Sautéed, chopped, and drained bacon bits can be added if desired.

Make-It-Easy Tip:

√ Store potatoes in cool, dark, dry place but *not* in the refrigerator because the cold will cause the potato starch to convert to sugar and produce an undesirably sweet taste when cooked. Avoid potatoes with a greenish tint; they can be bitter and often toxic.

Colorful Coleslaw

SERVES: 6–8
Preparation time: 15 minutes
Chilling time: 2–4 hours or overnight

Serve this salad attractively arranged in a large bowl or on a deep platter.

The Ingredients:

½ large head green cabbage
½ large head red cabbage

Dressing:

1 cup mayonnaise
1 cup dairy sour cream
2 tablespoons lemon juice
1 tablespoon freshly snipped dill or 1 teaspoon dried dill weed
½ teaspoon capers (optional)
Salt and freshly ground pepper to taste
Garnish: Freshly snipped dill

The Steps:

1. Shred both cabbages separately, placing each in separate bowl.
2. Combine dressing ingredients in small bowl, whisk to combine, pour half over each kind of cabbage, and toss separately.
3. Arrange each half separately in large bowl or on lettuce-lined platter and chill for 2–4 hours or overnight.
4. Serve salad chilled, garnished with additional snipped dill.

Variation:

Chopped chives can be substituted for snipped dill.

Make-It-Easy Tips:

√ When selecting cabbage, avoid ones with separate leaves growing below the head from the main stems. These cabbages often have a stronger flavor and coarser texture.

√ When shredding cabbage in food processor, always use the slicing disc.

Blueberry Lattice Pie

SERVES: 8
Preparation time: 15 minutes
Cooking time: 45 minutes

The Ingredients:

- 1 package refrigerated folded pie crust or 1 package deep-dish frozen pie crust
- 3½ cups fresh blueberries
- ¾ cup light brown sugar, firmly packed
- 3 tablespoons all-purpose flour
- 1 tablespoon grated orange rind
- 1 tablespoon orange juice
- 2 tablespoons unsalted butter, diced
- Garnish: Whipped cream

The Steps:

1. Preheat oven to 400°.
2. Unfold pie crust and place in 9" pie pan (or use frozen pie crust, unthawed). Trim bottom crust even with edge of pan.
3. In large bowl, combine berries with brown sugar, flour, rind, and juice. Gently toss to combine. Spoon filling with prepared crust and top with butter bits.
4. On floured board, lay out remaining refrigerated pie crust. (If using frozen crust, thaw slightly, carefully remove from pie tin, and place on board.)
5. Cut 8 one-inch strips and lay 4 over filling, across pie, about 1" apart. Repeat with remaining 4 strips in opposite direction. Trim strips even with pie edge. Turn bottom crust up over ends of strips and press firmly all around to seal edges.
6. Place pie on cookie sheet and bake for 45 minutes or until golden brown on top.
7. Serve garnished with whipped cream.

Variations:

If fresh blueberries are unavailable, substitute two 16-ounce packages frozen unsweetened blueberries, thawed and drained.

Blackberries, strawberries, raspberries, peaches, and other seasonal fruits can be substituted for blueberries.

Lemon rind and juice can be substituted for orange rind and juice.

To bake as a two-crust pie, place second crust on top of filling, fold edges of top crust under bottom, press down, and flute with fork. Cut slits in top crust to allow steam to escape.

If picnic is indoors, serve pie warm, topped with vanilla ice cream.

Make-It-Easy Tips:

√ Remember to pack the pie in box or basket to keep it safe. Cut at picnic.

√ To avoid a soggy crust, do not prick bottom crust before filling.

√ To prevent excessive browning on edges of pie crust, cover edges with strips of aluminum foil.

√ Use kitchen scissors to easily trim edges of pie crust.

Trick-or-Treat Party

SERVES: 12–16
Grape-Orange Punch
Make-Your-Own French Bread Pizzas
Black-and-White Cupcakes
Pumpkin Spice Bars
Incredibly Easy Chocolate Fudge
Butterscotch Brownies
*** Candy**

Here is a Halloween party that satisfies the needs of both children and adults. First and foremost, it keeps children safe inside, which puts parents' minds at ease. At the same time, it lets children have their Halloween fun, while sneaking some real food in among the traditional Halloween sweets.

A brightly colored sheet will do for a table covering. Or use an inexpensive vinyl tablecloth and let the children draw on it with felt-tip pens.

* Not a recipe

No cutlery is necessary, but children will need plenty of napkins. A variety of colorful washcloths or inexpensive bandanas makes a handy napkin substitute. Spread out in a row of overlapping diamonds, the washcloths or napkins will make a bright and colorful border on the table.

A basket of apples makes a cheerful, seasonal, and healthy centerpiece. Children may have fun bobbing for apples in a large kettle of water—but be prepared for some mopping up afterwards.

Even your kitchen broom can moonlight as a witch's flying machine, dressed up with a black crepe paper bow and standing in a corner surrounded by pumpkins. Is she a bad witch or a good witch? The children will know for sure if they find her paper hat filled with candy for a Halloween cornucopia. The costume and decorating hats found in stores will work, with one side of the brim cut or folded straight to keep it from rolling.

As for the pumpkins, their usual Halloween dress-up includes a carved grin and a candle inside. But pumpkin carving is time-consuming, and candles are dangerous among all those flammable costumes. If you really want to carve your own pumpkin, consider lining it with plastic, then filling with goodies. If you compromise by painting a face with black markers, the pumpkin will stay fresh for later use in made-from-scratch pumpkin pies (*not* a Make-It-Easy recipe, but tasty!)

Besides the usual children's party games, youngsters will enjoy making their own pizzas. Top the bread with sauce and cheese, and put them on a tray or cookie sheet on the table. Next to the tray, place dishes of assorted toppings. Each child can choose his or her favorites, then set the finished creation on a cookie sheet for baking.

Grape-Orange Punch is a cold, colorful, even good-for-you treat. For extra color, ice cubes can be made from grape and orange juices. This also keeps the flavor from being diluted as the ice melts.

Baking will be simplified if the Pumpkin Spice Bars and Butterscotch Brownies are made in advance and frozen. And the fudge is so easy that your children can make it with very little help. They'll be proud to serve their friends a treat they made themselves.

Grape-Orange Punch

SERVES: 12–16
Preparation time: 5–10 minutes

Serve this punch in a large bowl with a ladle or in a large pitcher.

The Ingredients:

- 1½ quarts (48 ounces) grape juice, chilled
- 1½ quarts (48 ounces) orange juice, chilled
- 4–6 ice cubes
- 1 pint orange sherbet

The Steps:

1. Combine juices in bowl or pitcher and mix with ice cubes.
2. Just before serving, add sherbet in spoonfuls and serve immediately.

Variation:

Combine grape juice and apple juice for a Grapple Punch topped with orange or lemon sherbet.

For an added treat freeze orange juice in ice cube trays and use in place of ice cubes and sherbet.

Make-It-Easy Tip:

√ It is best to chill the jars of juice separately rather than find room in the refrigerator for a large and cumbersome punch bowl.

Make-Your-Own French Bread Pizzas

SERVES: 16
Preparation time: 10 minutes
Cooking time: 15 minutes

These pizzas are just as much fun at an adult party! Have each guest assemble a pizza of his or her choice.

The Ingredients:

4 sourdough, French, or Italian flutes (the smaller breads measuring 12″)
4 tablespoons (½ stick) unsalted butter
Pizza Sauce (recipe follows)
32 slices Muenster cheese
1 cup freshly grated Parmesan cheese

Toppings:

Crumbled sautéed sausages
Pepperoni slices
Sautéed sliced mushrooms
Sautéed strips of green pepper
Sautéed sliced onions
Sliced black olives

The Steps:

1. Preheat oven to 450°.
2. Slice bread in half horizontally, then cut each piece in half vertically, resulting in 4 open-faced pieces. Lightly butter each slice.
3. Place 1½–2 tablespoons pizza sauce on each piece, top with 2 slices Muenster cheese, and sprinkle with 2 teaspoons Parmesan cheese. Have each guest add topping desired.
4. Place assembled pizzas on cookie sheet and bake for 5 minutes.
5. Increase heat to broil and continue to broil pizzas until hot and bubbly.
6. Serve immediately, taking care they are not too hot for young children.

Variations:

English muffins, or even bagels, can be substituted for bread.
Bread can be slightly hollowed and sauce used as a filling.

Make-It-Easy Tip:

√ Despite the popularity of Mozzarella cheese for Italian food, I find the cheese that melts most evenly and quickly is Muenster; but Monterey Jack, Swiss, Cheddar, or even Mozzarella can be substituted.

Pizza Sauce

YIELD: 3¾ cups
Preparation time: 10–15 minutes
Cooking time: 30 minutes

The Ingredients:

2 tablespoons olive oil
½ cup finely minced onion
42 ounces (1½ large cans) crushed tomatoes packed in puree
1½ teaspoons finely minced garlic
1 teaspoon sugar
1 teaspoon dried oregano, crumbled
1 teaspoon dried basil, crumbled
Salt and freshly ground pepper to taste

The Steps:

1. Heat olive oil in deep, heavy saucepan and sauté onion over medium heat until just soft, about 3–4 minutes.
2. Add remaining ingredients, stir to combine, bring to boil, reduce heat, and simmer over low heat for 30 minutes, or until smooth and slightly thickened.
3. Puree in food processor or blender until smooth, and chill until ready to use.

Variations:

Sauce can be used without pureeing.

Use sauce as a topping for chicken or veal parmigiana, or as a basic marinara sauce for Italian cooking.

Tomatoes can be pureed before adding; Step #3 is then omitted.

If tomatoes packed in puree are unavailable, use regular whole juice-packed tomatoes; chop, drain off most of the liquid. Return tomatoes to can, and fill to the top with canned tomato puree.

Make-It-Easy Tips:

√ Sugar is added to cut the acidity in the canned tomatoes.

√ Garlic is added with the liquid for a more subtle flavor. If sautéed with onions, the garlic will brown and often take on an acrid and bitter flavor.

Black-and-White Cupcakes

YIELD: 24
Preparation time: 15 minutes
Cooking time: 20 minutes

The Ingredients:

8 ounces cream cheese
1 egg
1 tablespoon sugar
Pinch of salt
6 ounces semisweet chocolate bits
3 cups all-purpose flour
2 cups sugar
½ cup (2 ounces) cocoa
1 tablespoon baking soda
1 teaspoon salt
2 cups water
⅔ cup vegetable oil
2 tablespoons white vinegar
1½ teaspoons vanilla

The Steps:

1. Preheat oven to 350°. Generously butter muffin tins (24 cups) or line with paper or foil baking cups.
2. In food processor or electric mixer, process cream cheese with egg, sugar, and salt. Pour into bowl and fold in chips.
3. In separate bowl, sift flour with sugar, cocoa, soda, and salt. Add water, oil, vinegar, and vanilla and beat until smooth. (Use food processor or electric beater to achieve a smooth texture.)
4. Fill muffin cups ⅔–¾ full with cocoa mixture, then drop in 1 tablespoon cheese mixture on top of each. Bake for 20 minutes or until cake tester comes out clean.
5. Cool 10 minutes in pan, remove, and serve immediately; or freeze until ready to use.

Variation:

Chopped nuts can be added to cream cheese mixture.

Make-It-Easy Tip:

√ To save extra time and steps, prepare cream cheese mixture in food processor and pour out into bowl; then, without washing food processor bowl, blend cocoa mixture.

Pumpkin Spice Bars

YIELD: 20–24 bars
Preparation time: 20 minutes
Cooking time: 30–35 minutes

The Ingredients:

4 ounces (1 stick) unsalted butter, softened
1 cup dark brown sugar, firmly packed
¾ cup canned pumpkin
1 egg, lightly beaten
½ teaspoon vanilla extract
1 cup all-purpose flour
¾ teaspoon ground cinnamon
½ teaspoon baking powder
¼ teaspoon baking soda
¼ teaspoon ground ginger
¼ teaspoon ground nutmeg
¼ teaspoon ground allspice
Pinch of salt
Garnish: Sweetened whipped cream and chopped pecans

The Steps:

1. Preheat oven to 350°. Generously butter 9″-square baking pan and lightly dust with flour.
2. In large mixing bowl, cream butter and brown sugar together; add pumpkin, egg, and vanilla and continue to beat until smooth.
3. Sift dry ingredients together and add to batter.
4. Pour batter into prepared pan and bake for 30–35 minutes.
5. Cool for 5–10 minutes, cut into bars, and serve warm with sweetened whipped cream and a sprinkling of chopped pecans.

Make-It-Easy Tips:

✓ Batter may be easily blended with an electric mixer.

✓ To keep flour and other grains insect-free, add a bay leaf in each package and seal shut in airtight plastic bags.

Incredibly Easy Chocolate Fudge

YIELD: 16 bars
Preparation time: 10 minutes
Cooking time: 5 minutes
Chilling time: 2 hours

The Ingredients:

18 ounces (three 6-ounce packages) semisweet chocolate chips
1 14-ounce can sweetened condensed milk
½ cup finely chopped walnuts or pecans
1½ teaspoons vanilla
Pinch of salt

The Steps:

1. Line 8″-square pan with waxed paper.
2. In top of double boiler, or in heavy saucepan over very low heat, melt chocolate with milk.
3. Remove from heat and stir in remaining ingredients just until smooth. Pour into prepared pan, spread smooth, and refrigerate until firm, about 2 hours.
4. Place chilled fudge upside down on cutting board, peel paper off, and cut with sharp knife into small squares.
5. Serve immediately or store in airtight container.

Variations:

Nuts can be omitted if desired.

For Butterscotch Fudge, butterscotch chips can be substituted for chocolate chips.

Make-It-Easy Tip:

✓ Never cover a pot in which chocolate is melting. Any excess moisture or condensation will "stiffen" the chocolate and prevent it from combining easily with the rest of the ingredients.

Butterscotch Brownies

YIELD: 16 brownies
Preparation time: 15–20 minutes
Cooking time: 20–25 minutes

The Ingredients:

6 tablespoons unsalted butter, softened
1 cup dark brown sugar, firmly packed
1 egg, lightly beaten
½ teaspoon vanilla extract
¾ cup all-purpose flour
1 teaspoon baking powder
Pinch of salt
¾ cup chopped pecans

The Steps:

1. Preheat oven to 350°. Generously butter 8″-square baking pan and lightly dust with flour.
2. In large mixing bowl, beat butter with brown sugar with electric mixer or by hand until smooth and fluffy.
3. Add egg and vanilla; beat until smooth.
4. Sift flour with baking powder and salt into separate bowl; add dry ingredients and nuts to batter, and spread into prepared pan.
5. Bake for 20–25 minutes, or until golden.
6. Cool for 10–15 minutes in pan and cut into bars.

Make-It-Easy Tips:

√ Freeze the squares uncut; later slice into squares while semifrozen for easier cutting.

√ If you've forgotten to soften the butter, grate it and it will soften quickly.

Traditional Thanksgiving Feast

SERVES: 10
Hot Spiced Cider
Perfect Roast Turkey
Sourdough-Pecan Stuffing
Glazed Sweet Potatoes
Marmalade-Spiked Cranberry Sauce
Spinach Flans on Tomato Rings
Pumpkin Ice Cream Pie

Our Thanksgiving menu has come a long way since the Pilgrims roasted a meal of wild turkeys. Now it's rich with generations of tradition and regional favorites. Here's a real American menu—drawn from all corners of the country.

No colonial cook ever heard of roasting a turkey in a paper bag, but it's a sure and easy way to keep the bird moist and flavorful without bothersome basting. You save time (and a few calories, but on Thanksgiving who's counting?) by using the clear, seasoned liquids from the pan in place of thickened gravy.

The Pilgrims first enjoyed turkey in New England, but the stuffing in this menu combines sourdough from the West and pecans from the South for a great cross-country combination. Don't worry about having extra—you can bake it separately for later use.

At the first Thanksgiving, the Pilgrims had not learned how to turn cranberries into a tangy treat, although their native American neighbors knew how to sweeten them with maple syrup. Here the zingy Northern berries team up with oranges from Sunshine Country to add zest to your turkey—all without tedious chopping or grinding.

Two vegetables are included, and both add color to the table. The traditional cuisine of the Southeast inspires the glazed sweet potatoes, while the Spinach Flans reflect Southwestern tastes.

I serve steamy mugs of fragrant hot cider alongside. Here apples from the North Country's autumn are spiced in the New England style, while some sunny citrus flavors add a special touch.

Early Americans never enjoyed a pumpkin pie quite like this one—which is a pity, since we're told that George Washington, among others, dearly loved ice cream. Prepare this pie up to two weeks early and freeze it.

As for decor, a natural fall harvest mood is the prettiest and simplest without excess ornamentation. Table coverings of soft creamy or rich earthy tones warm up the harvest look. Fill a bowl or basket with nuts, gourds, squash, fruit, or any combination. Decorate the room with bouquets of dried flowers. But the best centerpiece will be the turkey itself—plump and roasted to a golden brown.

While these recipes minimize the kitchen fuss without undoing tradition, perhaps the best time-saver of all is very much a part of the traditional Thanksgiving spirit. Guests often ask what they can bring, or how they can help. Why not share some recipes with those who kindly offer?

Hot Spiced Cider

SERVES: 10
Preparation time: 5–10 minutes
Cooking time: 5 minutes

The Ingredients:

2 quarts apple cider or apple juice
1 cup orange juice
5 tablespoons lemon juice
2 tablespoons sugar
2 tablespoons allspice berries
2 teaspoons ground nutmeg
4 cinnamon sticks
4 cloves
Garnish: Thin orange slices; 1–2 tablespoons rum to taste (optional)

The Steps:

1. In large kettle or deep saucepan, combine ingredients; bring to a boil and stir until sugar is dissolved.
2. Strain cider into pitcher and serve in warm mugs with a thin slice of orange and maybe a splash of rum.

Variation:

Sugar can be omitted if desired.

Make-It-Easy Tips:

√ Traditionally "sweet cider" was fresh juice that had fermented only a brief time and therefore was only slightly alcoholic. Today, what we purchase as "sweet cider" is exactly the same as apple juice, pasteurized and totally nonalcoholic. By all means, substitute apple juice (filtered or nonfiltered) for cider in this recipe. Hard cider is juice that has finished the fermentation cycle and is higher in alcoholic content.

√ Spices can be wrapped and tied up in cheesecloth and boiled with remaining ingredients. No straining necessary: just remove bag of spices, squeeze out excess moisture, and discard.

Perfect Roast Turkey

SERVES: 12–16
Preparation time: 25–30 minutes
Cooking time: Approximately 5 hours, 15 minutes

Although my complete Thanksgiving menu serves 10–12, I've written a recipe for a larger bird, to ensure lots of delicious leftovers. Remember, for health reasons, always stuff a turkey at the last minute, just before placing in the oven. Bacteria can grow if a bird is stuffed and held for too long.

The Ingredients:

1 turkey (14–16 pounds) (hen is preferable)

Marinade:

1 cup oil
1 onion, thinly sliced
3 tablespoons lemon juice
2 tablespoons freshly chopped parsley
2 cloves garlic, minced
½ teaspoon oregano
Freshly ground pepper

3–4 tablespoons unsalted butter, softened
1 teaspoon paprika
Salt and freshly ground pepper to taste

1 large heavy brown paper bag (nonrecycled), available at the grocery store
2 13½-ounce cans chicken broth
2 onions, chopped
Accompaniment: Sourdough-Pecan Stuffing (recipe to follow)

The Steps:

1. Wash turkey well, clean out cavity, and pat dry with paper towels.
2. Prepare marinade by combining ingredients. Marinate turkey in marinade for 12–14 hours in refrigerator, making sure marinade goes under skin and into cavity.
3. Preheat oven to 325°.
4. Remove turkey from marinade, lightly pat dry with paper towels, and stuff cavity and neck area with prepared stuffing (see following recipe). Discard marinade. Truss with needle or skewer and tie securely. Massage bird with 1–2 tablespoons butter all over; sprinkle with paprika, salt, and pepper.
5. Place open brown paper bag on table, seam side up. Butter inside of bag with remaining butter and place turkey in bag, breast side down and with drumsticks at open end. Neatly fold over edge of bag, staple shut or clamp closed with metal clamp, and place on rack in roasting pan.
6. Place chicken broth and onions in bottom of roasting pan and roast for 4 hours.
7. Cut bag open, remove and discard; turn turkey and roast an additional 1 hour and 15 minutes.
8. Remove from oven and allow to rest 15 minutes at room temperature before carving or removing stuffing.
9. Strain liquids from pan. Remove fat with straining device, and serve clear liquids in a gravy boat alongside turkey and bowl of stuffing.

Variations:

For giblet gravy: For 1½–2 hours boil neck and giblets with 2–3 cups canned chicken broth, 1 roughly chopped carrot, 1 onion, and a few sprigs parsley. Remove vegetables, chop giblets, and shred neck meat into broth. Season with concentrated liquid or powdered poultry stock if desired; add salt and freshly ground pepper to taste and 1 teaspoon tomato paste for added sweetness and color. Add giblet gravy to defatted pan juices in a saucepan, thicken with 2–3 tablespoons instantized flour, and stir until smooth and slightly thickened.

Fresh turkeys are the most flavorful. Frozen turkeys can be substituted but avoid those that are "butter-basted." They are sometimes basted with saturated fats and additives. Read the label carefully.

Make-It-Easy Tips:

√ If turkey is frozen, the best and safest method of thawing is in the refrigerator 2–3 days, depending on size.

√ The bird can be marinated in a jumbo food storage bag and easily turned without messing your hands.

√ When stuffing a bird, do not pack the stuffing tightly. Stuffing expands as it cooks.

√ To test for doneness, place meat thermometer in hip joint. It should register between 180° and 185° and juices should run clear. If juices are red, bird needs more roasting.

Turkey Timetable (Stuffed)

(Reduce roasting times by 30 minutes for unstuffed birds)

Size of Bird	*Oven Temperature*	*Total Cooking Time*
4–8 lbs.	325°	2½–3½ hours
8–12 lbs.	325°	3½–4½ hours
12–16 lbs.	325°	4½–5½ hours
16–20 lbs.	300°	5½–6½ hours

Sourdough-Pecan Stuffing

YIELD: 2½–3 quarts
Preparation time: 15–20 minutes
Cooking time: 5 minutes

The Ingredients:

2 quarts (8 cups) cubed stale sourdough bread
4 ounces (1 stick) unsalted butter
1 cup minced onion

- 1 cup minced celery
- ¾ teaspoon powdered thyme
- ¾ teaspoon sage
- ¾ teaspoon marjoram or oregano
- 1½ cups coarsely chopped pecans or walnuts
- ¼ cup freshly chopped parsley
- ¼–⅓ cup chicken broth

The Steps:

1. Preheat oven to 300°.
2. Dry out bread cubes on cookie sheets for 10–15 minutes. Watch carefully to avoid burning.
3. In large deep skillet, heat butter and sauté onion and celery over moderate heat just until soft, about 5 minutes.
4. Add thyme, sage, marjoram or oregano, salt, and pepper and mix well.
5. Pour over bread cubes, add nuts and parsley, and stir until well mixed. Add enough chicken broth to barely moisten bread.
6. Place in bowl, cover, and chill until ready to stuff bird.

Variations:

Bread crumbs can be substituted for cubes.

For New England-style stuffing, add 1 cup diced peeled tart apple in Step #5.

To bind stuffing together, a beaten egg can be added to Step #5.

Make-It-Easy Tips:

√ It is easiest to prepare stuffing a day in advance and stuff chilled stuffing into bird just before roasting.

√ Any remaining stuffing can be placed in a buttered dish, covered with foil, and baked separately for 45 minutes to 1 hour.

√ Immediately remove cooked stuffing from leftover bird, wrap, and refrigerate separately to reduce risk of food poisoning.

Glazed Sweet Potatoes

SERVES: 10
Preparation time: 15 minutes
Cooking time: 45 minutes

What we buy under the label "yams" are actually sweet potatoes in two varieties: a dry-fleshed yellow one with a pale brown outer skin, and a moist-fleshed orange one with a reddish-colored outer skin. The latter variety is best suited for this recipe.

The Ingredients:

8 medium sweet potatoes
1½ cups dark brown sugar, firmly packed
¼ pound (1 stick) unsalted butter
½ cup orange juice
¼ cup golden raisins
3 tablespoons Grand Marnier or other orange-flavored liqueur
Garnish: Orange slices

The Steps:

1. Drop sweet potatoes in salted boiling water to cover, and cook covered for 15–20 minutes, until tender but still firm. Drain, cool, and peel. Cut lengthwise into ¼″-thick slices.
2. Preheat oven to 350°. Generously butter 1 large or 2 smaller-size baking dishes.
3. Lay potatoes in prepared baking dish, overlapping slightly.
4. In small saucepan, combine brown sugar, butter, and juice; bring to a boil, stirring until smooth. Add raisins and Grand Marnier and stir to combine.
5. Spoon over potatoes, bake for 30–35 minutes, basting occasionally, until golden and glazed.
6. Serve hot, garnishing each portion with orange slice.

Variations:

1–2 tablespoons grated orange rind can be added if desired.
1–2 tablespoons slivered crystallized ginger can be added if desired.

Make-It-Easy Tips:

√ To save time and easily peel potatoes, instead of waiting for potatoes to cool, wear heavy-duty gloves.

√ Recipe can be assembled a day in advance; bake just before serving.

√ Do not store raw sweet potatoes in refrigerator. They should be stored in a humid, well-ventilated area. Once cooked, of course, they should be refrigerated.

Marmalade-Spiked Cranberry Sauce

SERVES: 10
Preparation time: 15 minutes
Cooking time: 5 minutes
Chilling time: 4–6 hours

The Ingredients:

1 large juice orange
6 whole cloves
Fresh orange juice
1 pound fresh cranberries
1 cup granulated sugar
½ cup cold water
½ cup orange marmalade
1 tablespoon lemon juice

The Steps:

1. Remove a coin-size piece of peel from orange and stud it with cloves.
2. Grate remaining rind of orange and measure out 2 tablespoons.
3. Juice orange and add enough fresh orange juice to equal ⅓ cup liquid.
4. In large heavy saucepan, combine cranberries, sugar, water, studded peel, rind, and juice; bring to a boil and cook over moderate heat for several minutes, or until berries have stopped popping.
5. Remove from heat and discard studded peel; add marmalade and lemon juice, stir to combine, and cool; then chill in refrigerator.

Variation:

Thawed frozen cranberries can be used to enjoy this recipe all year long.

Make-It-Easy Tip:

√ The cranberries will explode as they pop, so stand back—and loosely tent the pot with foil for protection.

Spinach Flans on Tomato Rings

SERVES: 10
Preparation time: 15 minutes
Cooking time: 35–40 minutes

Spinach flans—vegetable custards called *timbales* in France—make a particularly attractive presentation especially when served on ripe red tomato slices.

The Ingredients:

3 tablespoons unsalted butter
1 large onion, finely chopped
2 10-ounce packages frozen chopped spinach, thawed and thoroughly squeezed dry
1¼ cup half-and-half
6 eggs
½ cup Gruyère or Monterey Jack cheese, grated
2 tablespoons freshly grated Parmesan cheese
Salt and freshly ground pepper to taste
Pinch of freshly ground nutmeg
10 tomato slices, cut ¼″ thick
Garnish: Watercress

The Steps:

1. Preheat oven to 350°. Generously butter ten 5-ounce custard cups, porcelain ramekin dishes, or timbale molds.
2. In large skillet, heat butter and sauté onion for 5 minutes over medium-heat, until soft. Add spinach and continue to cook for

2–3 minutes longer, until thoroughly combined; allow to cool slightly (about 5 minutes).

3. In large bowl, beat half-and-half, eggs, cheeses, salt, pepper, and nutmeg and stir until well mixed. Add spinach and stir to combine. Distribute mixture among cups, place cups in shallow roasting pan with 1" boiling water, and bake for 35–40 minutes, or until custard is set.
4. Loosen custard from sides of each mold with sharp knife. Lay tomato slices over tops of molds, invert, and set attractively on platter garnished with sprigs of watercress.

Variations:

If time permits, 3 pounds of fresh spinach can be used, cooked, covered for 4–5 minutes, drained thoroughly, and roughly chopped.

If molds are unavailable, bake in a large deep-dish pie shell, invert on a platter, and garnish top with slices of tomatoes.

Make-It-Easy Tips:

√ Molds can be brushed with oil or coated with nonaerosol vegetable cooking spray.

√ Fresh nutmeg is preferable to ground nutmeg, which loses its potency and flavor on the market shelves.

√ Custard is baked in a warm bath to keep an even temperature throughout.

√ To prepare in advance, bake flans in the morning and reheat by covering with foil and setting in hot water in a 350° oven for 10 minutes. Or cover the baking pan with foil and set on back of stove to keep warm until serving.

Pumpkin Ice Cream Pie

SERVES: 10
Preparation time: 15 minutes
Freezing time: 30–60 minutes

The Ingredients:

Gingersnap Crust:

25 gingersnaps (1½ cups) crushed

5 ounces (5 tablespoons) unsalted butter, softened
⅓ cup granulated sugar

Pie Filling:
1½ cups canned pumpkin
½ cup granulated sugar
½ teaspoon cinnamon
¼ teaspoon ground nutmeg
¼ teaspoon salt
⅛ teaspoon ground ginger
⅛ teaspoon ground allspice
1 quart vanilla ice cream, softened
½ cup chopped pecans (2¼-ounce package diced pecans)

The Steps:

1. Crust: Crush gingersnaps; reserve 2–3 tablespoons for topping; mix crumbs with butter and sugar in bowl and press into 9″ pie plate. Chill.
2. Pie Filling: In large bowl, combine pumpkin, sugar, cinnamon, nutmeg, salt, ginger, and allspice and mix well.
3. Fold pumpkin mixture into softened ice cream, stir in pecans, and spoon into pie shell; sprinkle with reserved crumbs.
4. Freeze uncovered for 30 minutes, or until set. Cover with plastic wrap or foil and keep frozen until ready to use.
5. Remove from freezer 10 minutes before serving, cut into wedges, and serve icy cold.

Variations:

Chopped walnuts can be substituted for pecans.
1 teaspoon pumpkin pie spice can be substituted for all the spices.
Vanilla wafers, zwieback crackers, or any type of plain cookie desired can be substituted for gingersnaps.

Make-It-Easy Tips:

√ Pie can be frozen for up to two weeks.
√ Filling can be easily combined in food processor or blender.

Merry Christmas Dinner

SERVES: 8–10
Christmas Glögg (Mulled Wine)
Roast Beef
Pan-Roasted Potatoes
Horseradish Cream Sauce
Cherry Tomato Salad in Parsley Wreath
Quick-and-Easy Pecan Pie
Hard Sauce
Bourbon Balls

Christmas is that special holiday when, no matter how busy we've become all year, we tend to gather at home. Add to this the chilly weather of December, and you have the perfect time to heat up the oven for traditional favorites—like roast beef and potatoes—that take a minimum of preparation and bake slowly to perfection.

An extra plus comes from all those Christmas trimmings. When the whole house is fully decked out for the season, your table will need little more to set the scene for a holiday dinner. It's easy to use what's at hand. Candles surrounded by pinecones or boughs make a quick and lovely centerpiece, and some Christmas tree ornaments provide a shiny accent. Or include some oranges—a traditional Christmas stocking-stuffer.

Red ribbons can tie your napkins, with perhaps a sprig of holly slipped under the bow. Holly leaves also make a festive garnish, especially for dessert. The berries can give food a bitter taste, however, so substitute some cranberries instead. Besides holly berries, it's wise to keep yew berries, poinsettia, and mistletoe away from the table. They may be pretty, but beware—they're poisonous!

Luckily, lots of very edible holiday color is available for the table. The Cherry Tomato salad proves that food can look Christmasy, yet be healthy and nonfattening, all at the same time. (We have to save some calories for the Pecan Pie!) Make it the night before to save steps on Christmas day.

The recipe for Christmas Glögg, the traditional Swedish holiday punch, adds cranberry juice, an American touch that adds zest and extra holiday color. The pronunciation stays Swedish, though—a sound somewhere between "gloog" and "glurg".

The Bourbon balls can be made weeks before the holiday season reaches its hectic climax, to sit quietly mellowing while you're busy shopping, wrapping, and mailing. Serve them after dinner with coffee, or wrap them up as special holiday house gifts direct from your own kitchen.

Christmas Glögg (Mulled Wine)

YIELD: 3 quarts
Preparation time: 10–15 minutes
Cooking time: 15 minutes

This traditional Swedish mulled wine is always a big hit with the addition of American cranberry juice. Prepare enough, but warn guests that because the wine is warmed, it's more powerful than it seems.

The Ingredients:

- 2 cups cranberry juice
- 2 cups water
- 1 cup sugar
- ½ lemon, sliced
- 6 allspice berries
- 4 whole cloves
- 2 cinnamon sticks
- ⅛ teaspoon ground cinnamon
- ⅛ teaspoon ground ginger
- Pinch of nutmeg
- 2 bottles red wine (I prefer claret)
- ½ lemon, sliced
- ½ orange, sliced
- ¼ cup raisins
- Accompaniment: Cinnamon sticks

The Steps:

1. In large saucepan, combine cranberry juice, water, sugar, ½ lemon, allspice, cloves, cinnamon sticks, cinnamon, ginger, and nutmeg; bring to a boil, stirring often, until sugar is dissolved. Boil over medium heat for 15 minutes. Strain through cheesecloth or very fine strainer and set aside.
2. When ready to serve, heat cranberry base, add wine, lemon slices, orange slices, and raisins; heat until warm but do not boil. Pour into punch bowl and serve warm with ladle, and accompanying cinnamon-stick stirrers.

Variation:

Lemon slices, orange slices, and raisins can be omitted for a clear punch.

Make-It-Easy Tips:

- √ To avoid straining, tie up spices in cheesecloth before adding to the base in Step #1. When boiled, discard cheesecloth and proceed.
- √ Base may be prepared 2 or 3 days in advance, through Step #1, and refrigerated until ready to use.
- √ If available, serve wine on a heated tray to keep at warm temperature.

Roast Beef

SERVES: 8–10
Preparation time: 10 minutes
Cooking time: 2–2½ hours

The roast suggested for this menu is the eye of the standing rib. It may be called by different names in your area, such as Spencer roast or rib-eye roast. Make sure to ask the butcher to leave a thin layer of fat around the roast to keep it tender and create a crusty exterior when roasted. The meat should be about 3″–4″ in diameter in the center section, and it is not rolled or tied.

The Ingredients:

6–8 pound eye of the rib roast, left at room temperature 2 hours
1 clove garlic, smashed and peeled
Salt and freshly ground pepper to taste
2–3 tablespoons all-purpose flour
1 cup beef broth
½ cup red wine
Accompaniment: Horseradish Cream Sauce (recipe follows)

The Steps:

1. Preheat oven to 450°.
2. Rub roast with garlic, sprinkle with salt and pepper, rub with flour, and place on rack in roasting pan, fat side up.

3. Roast meat for 20 minutes or until well seared. Reduce heat to 350°, insert meat thermometer in fleshiest part of meat, and continue to roast for 14–15 minutes per pound—or until thermometer registers 120° for rare, 130° for medium-rare, 140° for medium, and 150° for well-done.
4. Remove from oven and allow roast to rest for 20–30 minutes before carving.
5. Remove rack and skim off excess fat from pan. Place pan over heat, add broth and wine and cook, stirring to mix browned particles from bottom of pan into sauce. Boil until thickened, season with salt and pepper to taste, and serve alongside sliced meat, with horseradish sauce on side.

Variation:

Roast can be served cold in the summer, sliced on a platter with Mustard Sauce (see page 50)

Make-It-Easy Tips:

√ A meat thermometer is the only safe way to be sure of the correct degree of doneness. It is an inexpensive item that can ensure the success of an expensive cut of meat.

√ Remember that the roast continues to cook as it rests, so be sure to remove it from the oven at the correct internal temperature.

√ After searing, a 6-pound roast will take 1½ hours to cook while an 8-pound roast can take up to 2 hours.

Horseradish Cream Sauce

YIELD: 2 cups
Preparation time: 5 minutes
Chilling time: 1 hour

Prepare this sauce according to taste. Increase the amount of horseradish at your own risk!

The Ingredients:

1½ cups dairy sour cream
½ cup prepared white horseradish, drained

1 teaspoon Dijon mustard
Salt to taste

The Steps:

1. In medium-size bowl, combine ingredients together until smooth.
2. Cover and chill for at least 1 hour before serving.

Make-It-Easy Tip:

√ To prepare with fresh horseradish: Peel and cube horseradish root, chop in food processor until just grated. Add 2–3 tablespoons lemon juice or white vinegar, 1 teaspoon dry mustard, ½ teaspoon sugar, and proceed with recipe.

Pan-Roasted Potatoes

SERVES: 8–10
Preparation time: 5–10 minutes
Cooking time: 1 hour, 15 minutes

It is beneficial to oven-roast potatoes without peeling, since so many nutrients are in the skin. It also saves extra KP duties for the family.

The Ingredients:

6 large baking potatoes, well scrubbed and cut into 3 sections; or 12–16 new potatoes, well scrubbed.

The Steps:

1. Drop potatoes into boiling salted water and boil 10–15 minutes, or until barely tender; drain well.
2. About 1 hour before roast is done, add potatoes to pan, coat well with drippings, and roast until golden brown, basting occasionally with drippings.
3. Serve hot, alongside slices of roast beef.

Variation:

Parboiled, peeled onions can be added.

Make-It-Easy Tips:

√ If roast needs longer cooking time, it will not harm the potatoes to be overcooked.

√ When roast is removed from oven to rest and pan juices are boiled down, place glazed potatoes on separate pan in warm oven until ready to serve.

Cherry Tomato Salad in Parsley Wreath

SERVES: 8
Preparation time: 10–15 minutes
Chilling time: 2 hours or overnight

This attractive presentation makes this holiday dish worthy of serving all year long.

The Ingredients:

2–3 large bunches parsley, large stems removed
1 quart cherry tomatoes, stems removed, washed and dried

Vinaigrette Dressing:

½ cup olive oil
3 tablespoons red wine vinegar
2 teaspoons freshly minced parsley
½ teaspoon Dijon mustard
½ teaspoon freshly minced garlic
Pinch of sugar
Salt and freshly ground pepper to taste

The Steps:

1. In large ring mold, pack down parsley tightly, cover with foil, and refrigerate for 2 hours or overnight to firm into shape.
2. Slice tomatoes and place in medium bowl.
3. Combine vinaigrette dressing ingredients together in food processor or blender, or in small bowl with whisk. Pour dressing over tomatoes and gently toss.
4. Unmold chilled parsley onto a platter, tapping to release parsley onto plate. Place tomatoes in center and serve immediately, or chill until ready to use.

Variations:

Tomatoes can be served whole to save preparation time.

Substitute chopped fresh basil, dill, chives, or a combination of green herbs for parsley.

Make-It-Easy Tip:

√ Tomatoes can be marinated in vinaigrette for several hours in the refrigerator.

Quick-and-Easy Pecan Pie

SERVES: 8
Preparation time: 10 minutes
Cooking time: 45–50 minutes

Pecans are strictly an American nut. George Washington carried pecans in his pocket throughout the American Revolutionary War. They are traditionally raised in the Southern states but now grow in California too.

The Ingredients:

½ cup white sugar
½ cup dark brown sugar, firmly packed
½ cup light corn syrup
2 ounces (¼ cup) unsalted butter, melted
3 eggs, well beaten
1 cup pecan halves
1 9″ unbaked pie shell (if frozen, thawed)
Accompaniments: Vanilla ice cream, hard sauce (recipe follows), or whipped cream.

The Steps:

1. Preheat oven to 375°.
2. In large bowl, mix together sugars, syrup, and butter.
3. Add eggs and pecans, stir well, and pour into pie shell.
4. Bake for 45–50 minutes, or until set and golden.
5. Serve warm or at room temperature with accompanying hard sauce, vanilla ice cream, or whipped cream.

Make-It-Easy Tips:

- √ Pie can be prepared in advance and frozen successfully.
- √ Store nuts in freezer to keep fresh.
- √ Store brown sugar in a tightly sealed jar once box is opened.
- √ When measuring sticky liquids like corn syrup, rub the cup with oil and the syrup will pour out easily.

Hard Sauce

YIELD: 2 cups
Preparation time: 10 minutes
Chilling time: 2 hours

Hard Sauce is the traditional accompaniment to English plum pudding, but it can be served year round to flavor hot fruit puddings or pies or to give as an unusual house gift. It is easy to prepare in a food processor, blender, or electric mixer.

The Ingredients:

- ½ pound (2 sticks) unsalted butter, softened
- 2 cups powdered sugar
- 2 tablespoons brandy or rum
- 1 teaspoon vanilla extract
- Pinch of salt
- 1 teaspoon grated lemon rind (optional)

The Steps:

1. Cream butter and sugar together, adding sugar to butter gradually for softness.
2. Add brandy or rum, vanilla, salt, and optional lemon rind and process until light and creamy.
3. Pack hard sauce into crock and refrigerate until hard, about 2 hours.
4. Serve atop pie.

Make-It-Easy Tip:

- √ If you've forgotten to soften the butter, grate it and it will quickly soften.

Bourbon Balls

YIELD: 70
Preparation time: 20 minutes

These bourbon-laced candy/cookie combinations are a dessert and after-dinner drink in one. Prepare a large batch, wrap in an attractive container, and give as a gift with a copy of the recipe enclosed. Remember to prepare 2 weeks in advance to allow them to "ripen" and become really flavorful.

The Ingredients:

1½ cups confectioner's sugar
1 teaspoon unsweetened cocoa
Pinch of powdered instant coffee
⅓ cup light corn syrup
⅓ cup bourbon
1 teaspoon vanilla extract
1 12-ounce box vanilla wafers, crushed
1½ cups pecans, chopped
1 cup raisins, chopped
½ cup confectioner's sugar
1 teaspoon unsweetened cocoa

The Steps:

1. In food processor, blender, or by hand, combine 1½ cups confectioner's sugar, with 1 teaspoon cocoa and pinch of coffee; add corn syrup, bourbon, and vanilla and stir to combine.
2. Add crumbs, nuts, and raisins and continue to process until mixture holds together.
3. In separate bowl, combine ½ cup confectioner's sugar with 1 teaspoon cocoa and set onto a flat plate.
4. Shape pecan mixture into 1″ balls and roll them in the sugar-cocoa mixture.
5. Store in airtight container until ready to serve.

Variations:

Chopped walnuts can be substituted for pecans.
Chopped dates or apricots can be substituted for raisins.

Make-It-Easy Tips:

- √ Get the family involved in this fun holiday activity.
- √ Wrap the balls in small plastic bags tied up with ribbon in plastic jars attractively labeled, or even miniature cans or crocks.

Big Splashes

1. **Royal Tea Party**
   The Perfect Pot of Tea
   Sesame Seed and Egg Spread Sandwiches
   Five-Ingredient Tea Sandwiches
   Glazed Lemon Bread and Lemon Butter
   Chutney Bread and Orange-Honey Butter
   Chocolate Tea Loaf

2. **Carbo-Loading Pasta Party**
   Spaghetti all'Amatriciana
   Fusilli with Spinach and Cream
   Insalata di Mare con Farfalle
   *Toasted Sourdough Bread
   Biscuit Tortoni

3. **Open House Championship Chili Party**
   LBG's Salsa
   Easiest Championship Chili
   Sour Cream Corn Bread
   Spicy Tomato Salad
   Heavenly Caramel-Pecan Squares
   Cookie Crunch

4. **Surprise! Birthday Party**
   Chilled Julienne of Celery Root
   Seafood Stew Provençale
   Whole Baked Garlic With Crusty French Bread
   Leaf Lettuce Salad with Creamy Mustard Vinaigrette
   Fudge Layer Ice Cream Cake

5. **Demi-Dinner**
   Fish Salad Wrapped in Lettuce Leaves
   Baked Brie
   Laurie's Special Sliced Steak
   Frosted Chinese Chicken Pâté
   Apple-Oatmeal-Raisin Bars
   Apricot Shortbread Squares

6. **Academy Award Buffet**
   Beer with Lime
   Spicy Cheese Spread on Cocktail Rounds
   Carbonnade à la Flamande
   Steamed Potatoes
   Romaine Salad with Oranges
   Toasted Coconut Bread
   Toffee Cake

7. **Pitch-In Paella Dinner**
   White Sangria
   Sour Cream-Avocado Dip
   Paella
   Green Salad with Lime Dressing
   Make-It-Easy Flan

8. **Guess Who's Coming to Dinner**
   Tossed Salad with Pine Nuts and Mushrooms
   Scallops of Veal in Madeira Sauce
   Brown Rice Primavera
   Cheesecake Pie

*Not a recipe

I CONSIDER A BIG SPLASH to be any major occasion—that special time when I want to toss a party to celebrate a birthday, a bridal shower, an open house, the night before a big race, or even a wonderfully special intimate dinner for four. We all know that holidays are big splashes, but other events equally deserve special festivities. The last section of this book is devoted to these important and unique occasions.

Each of the Make-It-Easy menus in this chapter is presented with a combination of food, music, decor, and ambience—all tied together with a theme.

The *Royal Tea Party* makes a splendid bridal or baby shower. In cold weather, it can be a cozy event around the fireside; in hot weather, it is perfect as a garden party.

The *Carbo-Loading Pasta Party* stresses carbohydrates in an effort to fuel the runners for the upcoming race. It offers three pasta dishes—two hot and one cold. The pasta suggests an Italian motif; red, green, and white, the colors of the Italian flag, set the decor to create an evening that becomes a perfect excuse to gorge on pasta in a casual setting.

The *Academy Award Buffet*, whether it's for the Oscars, Emmys, or election night, is an informal affair; guests will typically be seated, crowded on the floor, holding plates on their laps.

The *Open House Championship Chili Party* is a splash prepared beforehand. When I expect a large group, I cook as much as possible in advance. Buffet-style is the easiest to handle, and I stick to one-fork recipes, chili, salad, and corn bread, so guests don't have to balance plates in their laps.

The *Demi-Dinner* is my favorite answer to easy important entertaining. I serve guests a wide assortment of hearty and filling hors d'oeuvres and tell them to eat with abandon because there is no main course following. The guests are happy since they can enjoy hors d'oeuvres freely, and I save on extra work and extra plates and cutlery. I follow these plentiful tidbits with a few desserts for a great splash.

The *Pitch-in Paella Dinner* is an "in-the-kitchen participation party." Guests are invited to work and eat. A number of dishes lend themselves to this kind of warm and special evening; I've chosen Paella for the book since many can help while sipping refreshing White Sangria and nibbling on a little avocado dip. Everyone feels satisfied with his or her contribution—and the results.

Whether your big splash is an all-out party for a crowd or an elegant dinner for four to impress the boss, it requires advance thought and careful planning. Prepare lists for shopping, preparation chores, and table settings. Accomplish as much as possible in advance. Once carefully planned, these Make-It-Easy splashes become celebrations to remember.

Royal Tea Party

SERVES: 8–10
The Perfect Pot of Tea
Sesame Seed and Egg Spread Sandwiches
Five-Ingredient Tea Sandwiches
Glazed Lemon Bread and Lemon Butter
Chutney Bread and Orange-Honey Butter
Chocolate Tea Loaf

The English have invented some wonderful customs since tea first reached their shores more than 300 years ago. There is high tea with hearty, savory fare—really a light dinner. Then there's the basic afternoon tea, which started as a pick-me-up during the long afternoon hours before dinner. It was a time for ladies to sample sweet treats—and the latest news.

It's the ladies' tea that inspires this party, although the modern version can just as well go coed. It makes a great bridal or baby shower and fits the garden, the kitchen, or the fireside all with equal ease. And the food is perfect for buffet serving.

A tea party lends itself to a cozy but light, garden look—even by the fireplace. Bring all your brightest houseplants to the party for lots of green. In winter, a bowl, jar, or tea canister full of potpourri carries garden fragrance right indoors. So do bouquets of fresh or dried flowers. In summer, let fans turn lazily in the background. In winter, drape afghans or lap robes over soft, comfy chairs.

Table linens should be set for the season; spring- or summer-like floral pastels, or vibrant fall or subdued winter colors. Choose napkins in a rainbow of colors. Roll up the teaspoons in the napkins and place them in a pretty basket. Or stand them up like a bouquet in a tea canister.

The teapot and tea accompaniments—milk, sugar, and lemon slices—make pretty table accents themselves. Precede them on the buffet table with a parade of teacups and saucers, handles turned neatly in one direction or in a geometrical pattern. It's thoughtful, too, to include a pot of coffee for those who prefer it, as well as hot water and a basket of assorted herbal teas for people avoiding caffeine.

To simplify the buffet, put similar foods together so that people can see the choices available. Varieties of sandwiches should sit side by side, as do the sweet cakes and breads. Make sure a matching bread and spread, like the Glazed Lemon Bread and Lemon Butter, are placed together.

Fancy—but easy—presentation of the dainty sandwiches and cakes adds to the cozy atmosphere. Instead of flat, spread-out arrangements, experiment with height to add eye appeal to the table. Show off sandwiches, sliced cakes, and breads on tiered plates or stacked in pretty, mounded arrangments. It's also the perfect time to line plates with doilies and accent cakes with a small blossom or two.

The Perfect Pot of Tea

YIELD: 1 pot of tea
Preparation time: 5–8 minutes

A few simple guidelines in tea preparation: Use a good quality leaf and allow 1–1½ teaspoons per person, plus one "for the pot." China teapots are preferable but well-cleaned silver or stainless will suffice.

The Ingredients:

1–1½ teaspoons tea leaves per person
Water
Accompaniments: Milk, sugar, and lemon

The Steps:

1. Pour boiling water into teapot and allow to sit and heat pot.
2. Bring fresh cold tap water to a boil in kettle. As kettle is about to boil, empty teapot and measure tea into it.
3. Pour boiling water over tea leaves, put lid on pot, and allow to steep 4–5 minutes.
4. Pour into cups and serve with milk, sugar, or lemon.

Variations:

To make stronger tea, increase the amount of tea leaves rather than lengthening the brewing time. Strength of tea is not judged by color.

If adding milk, make sure it is cold and poured into the cup before the tea. It mixes better this way.

For China teas, serve a thin slice of unsqueezed lemon. Do not squeeze fruit or it will affect the true tea taste.

Make-It-Easy Tips:

√ It is important to use the water as soon as it boils; the shorter the time it remains at the boil, the more oxygen is retained and therefore the fresher the taste of the tea.

√ The water used also affects the tea taste. Soft water produces a golden color tea; hard water makes a thick and soupy-looking version.

√ A tea cozy is pleasant to look at, but often prolongs the brewing and brings out the bitterness of the tea.

Sesame Seed and Egg Spread Sandwiches

SERVES: 8–10
Preparation time: 10 minutes

The Ingredients:

Spread:

6 hard-cooked eggs, chopped
¼ cup mayonnaise
3 tablespoons chopped chives or scallion greens
2 tablespoons toasted sesame seeds
1 teaspoon Dijon mustard
½ teaspoon Worcestershire sauce
¼ teaspoon paprika
Salt and freshly ground pepper to taste

16 rectangular slices hors d'oeuvre-size pumpernickel bread.
Garnish: Parsley sprigs

The Steps:

1. In large bowl, combine eggs with remaining spread ingredients until smooth, cover, and chill in refrigerator until ready to use.
2. Spread on 8 bread slices, top with remaining bread, cut into triangular wedges, and arrange attractively on platter, garnished with parsley sprigs.
3. Serve immediately, or cover tightly and chill in refrigerator for 1–2 hours prior to serving.

Variations:

Can be used as an appetizer served with pumpernickel bread.
½ cup finely minced ham can be added if desired.

Make-It-Easy Tips:

√ A pastry blender chops eggs easily.
√ If holding sandwiches longer than 2 hours, spread bread lightly with butter, which acts as a sealer to prevent sogginess.

Five-Ingredient Tea Sandwiches

SERVES: 8–10
Preparation time: 15 minutes

The Ingredients:

Spread:

1½ pounds cream cheese, softened
1½ cups chopped pimiento-stuffed green olives
½ cup chopped watercress
½ cup chopped pecans, lightly toasted

20 slices whole wheat or whole grain bread, crusts removed
2–3 large tomatoes, sliced
Garnish: Pimiento-stuffed green olives

The Steps:

1. Combine cream cheese with olives, watercress, and nuts; stir until smooth.
2. Spread mixture on 10 slices of bread; add tomato slice to each piece and top with remaining slices of bread.
3. Slice each sandwich in half, attractively arrange on platter, and serve garnished with olives.

Variations:

½ cup chopped walnuts can be substituted for pecans.
Sandwiches can be sliced into quarters, if desired.

Make-It-Easy Tips:

√ Slice tomatoes vertically. They will hold their moisture better.
√ Toast nuts quickly in a toaster-oven or broiler.
√ Use a sharp serrated bread or tomato knife to cut sandwiches easily and smoothly.

Glazed Lemon Bread

YIELD: 1 large loaf or 4 mini-loaves
Preparation time: 15 minutes
Cooking time: 45–50 minutes for mini-loaves
55–60 minutes for large loaf

This light bread can easily be served as a dessert.

The Ingredients:

- ¼ pound (1 stick) unsalted butter, softened
- 1 cup sugar
- 2 eggs
- 1 tablespoon lemon juice
- 2 teaspoons lemon rind
- ½ teaspoon vanilla
- 1½ cups all-purpose flour
- 1 teaspoon baking powder
- ½ teaspoon baking soda
- ½ teaspoon salt
- ½ cup buttermilk

Glaze:

- Juice of 1 lemon
- ¼ cup sugar
- Accompaniment: Lemon Butter (recipe follows)

The Steps:

1. Preheat oven to 350°. Generously butter and lightly flour one 9″ x 5″ x 3″ loaf pan or four 6″ x 3½″ x 2″ mini-loaf pans.
2. In electric beater or by hand, cream butter and sugar together. Add eggs, lemon juice, lemon rind, and vanilla and continue to beat until smooth.
3. In separate bowl, sift flour, baking powder, baking soda, and salt together and add to butter/sugar mixture alternately with buttermilk.
4. Pour into prepared pan and bake for 55–60 minutes for large loaf and 45–50 minutes for mini-loaves, or until inserted knife comes out clean.

5. Remove bread from oven; allow to cool before inverting on rack set over piece of aluminum foil. Pierce loaf on top with fork.
6. Combine glaze ingredients together and drizzle over hot bread; allow to cool thoroughly.

Variation:

Chopped walnuts can be added if desired.

Make-It-Easy Tips:

√ Lemons release more juice when squeezed at room temperature. If time does not permit this, warm lemon in a 300° oven for 5 minutes.

√ The mini-loaf pans make wonderful house gifts.

Lemon Butter

YIELD: 1¼ cups
Preparation time: 5–10 minutes

Keep lemon butter in the refrigerator, ready to use with bread or with vegetables, poultry, or fish.

The Ingredients:

½ pound unsalted butter, softened to room temperature
3 tablespoons lemon juice
1 tablespoon grated lemon rind

The Steps:

1. In food processor, blender, or by hand, combine softened butter with lemon juice and rind.
2. Pack into crock or jar, or shape into stick. Cover and chill for 2 hours or until ready to use.

Variations:

Orange juice and rind can be substituted for lemon.

For poultry, meat, or fish, or vegetable dishes, assorted chopped herbs and/or garlic can be added to taste.

Make-It-Easy Tip:

√ Select thin-skinned lemons that are unwrinkled and free of blemishes. They should yield to soft pressure, which indicates they are juicy.

Chutney Bread

YIELD: 1 large loaf
Preparation time: 5–10 minutes
Cooking time: 55–60 minutes

This recipe is a variation on a bread served at tea time at Trumps Restaurant in Beverly Hills.

The Ingredients:

1½ cups all-purpose flour
1 cup whole wheat flour
½ cup white granulated sugar
½ cup brown sugar, firmly packed
1 teaspoon baking powder
1 teaspoon salt
1¼ cups whole milk
3 tablespoons vegetable oil
1 egg, lightly beaten
1 tablespoon grated orange rind
1 9-ounce jar mild Mango chutney, chopped (I use Major Grey's brand)
1 cup chopped walnuts
Accompaniment: Orange-Honey Butter (recipe follows)

The Steps:

1. Preheat oven to 350°. Generously butter 9″ x 5″ x 3″ loaf pan.
2. In large bowl, mix flours, sugars, baking powder, and salt.
3. Add milk, oil, egg, and orange rind and stir to just moisten dry ingredients. Add chutney and nuts; stir to combine, pour into prepared pan, and bake for 55–60 minutes, or until inserted knife comes out clean and bread is golden brown on top.

Make-It-Easy Tips:

√ Whole wheat flour is made from the kernel of the wheat, which includes the germ and the bran.

√ If baking in a glass dish, increase heat by 25°.

Orange-Honey Butter

YIELD: ¾ cup
Preparation time: 5 minutes

The Ingredients:

½ cup unsalted butter, softened
2 tablespoons honey
1 tablespoon grated orange peel

The Steps:

1. In food processor or blender, process ingredients until smooth.
2. Chill until serving time.

Variations:

Chopped pecans can be added as desired.
If orange honey is available, it adds extra flavor.

Make-It-Easy Tip:

√ If honey crystallizes, place closed jar in a bowl of hot water and it will liquefy.

Chocolate Tea Loaf

YIELD: 1 large loaf or 5 mini-loaves
Preparation time: 15–20 minutes
Cooking time: 55–60 minutes for large pan
45 minutes for mini-loaves

The Ingredients:

2 cups sugar
¾ cup vegetable oil
3 eggs
1 cup dairy sour cream
1 teaspoon vanilla
2 cups cake flour
½ cup unsweetened cocoa
2 teaspoons baking powder
½ teaspoon baking soda
Pinch of salt
6 ounces semisweet chocolate chips
Accompaniments: Whipped cream, vanilla ice cream, or crème fraîche

The Steps:

1. Preheat oven to 350°. Lightly butter 9″ x 5″ x 3″ loaf pan or 5 mini-loaf pans (6″ x 3½″ x 2″).
2. In large bowl, beat together sugar, oil, and eggs until smooth. Add sour cream and vanilla and continue to stir until smooth.
3. Sift together flour, cocoa, baking powder, baking soda, and salt; add dry ingredients to egg mixture, stirring until smooth.
4. Add chips; pour into prepared pan and bake for 55–60 minutes for large loaf or 45 minutes for mini-loaves, or until inserted toothpick comes out clean.
5. Cool in pan on wire rack and serve warm topped with whipped cream, vanilla ice cream or crème fraîche.

Variations:

2 ounces chopped walnuts or pecans can be added with chips in Step #4.

Make-It-Easy Tips:

√ If cake flour is unavailable, substitute ¾ cup plus 2 tablespoons all-purpose flour plus 2 tablespoons cornstarch.

√ To easily prepare crème fraîche, combine 1 pint heavy cream with 2 tablespoons buttermilk in a screw-top jar. Stir, cover, and allow to sit at room temperature for 12–24 hours or until slightly thickened. Refrigerate and use within two weeks.

Carbo-Loading Pasta Party

SERVES: 6–8

Spaghetti all'Amatriciana
Fusilli with Spinach
Insalata di Mare con Farfalle (Pasta Seafood Salad)
***Toasted Sourdough Bread**
Biscuit Tortoni

A race soon to follow is a great excuse for a pasta party. Runners need lots of carbohydrates before any race, whether it's a marathon or only a run around the park. So here are three different pasta dishes and a sweet dessert. (A tossed green salad with vinaigrette dressing can be offered as well for nonrunners who don't need a high-carbohydrate meal.) Pasta and Italy go hand in hand; the Italian theme makes this an easy, enjoyable, and colorful send-off even for those who only plan to watch the race.

Echo the three colors of the Italian flag with an amusing centerpiece made of bundles of dried white or green spaghetti tied with red ribbons. Place the bundles in glass jars, bottles, canisters, vases, boxes, decorated

* Not a recipe

tomato cans, or any attractive containers. Arrange them in the center of the table bunched together, with a few of the bunches at different heights. For a variation, you might mix different-colored dried pastas, such as carrot, beet, pumpkin, tomato, or herb, in these "spaghetti bouquets," or tie them up with brand-new colored sneaker laces instead of ribbons.

Sneaker laces can also tie up your napkins in place of napkin rings. Or, to accent the Italian theme, roll up the napkins and slip them through manicotti shells (uncooked, of course!).

Continue the tricolor Italian theme by serving the red Spaghetti and the green Fusilli in white bowls. Pile the Sourdough Bread in a basket lined with a red or green napkin—or two napkins, one in each color. Or use any red and white checkered or patterned cloth, even a colorful clean dish towel.

Supportive handmade banners, running posters, racing T-shirts, or old racing numbers are great ways to liven up the walls. And if people already have their numbers for the race, why not use them on place cards, too? Energize the atmosphere with some upbeat background music, like the theme from *Rocky*, and organize a quick stretch class before dinner.

Serve the two hot pastas at the last minute. The sauces can be assembled easily in advance. Then all you have to do is boil the pasta, top with the steamy hot sauces, and serve alongside the chilled seafood-and-pasta salad.

Spaghetti all'Amatriciana

SERVES: 6–8
Preparation time: 10–15 minutes
Cooking time: 35–40 minutes

This Italian specialty takes it name from the town of Amatrice, in the Sabine Hills near Rome. It is traditionally prepared in Italy with *pancetta*, Italian bacon. My version uses regular bacon, but if the salt-cured pancetta found in Italian grocery stores is available, use it for an authentic Italian taste.

The Ingredients:

12 thin slices bacon, diced (or 8 thick slices bacon)
1 large onion, finely chopped

1 28-ounce can crushed tomatoes packed in puree (I use Progresso brand)
½–1 teaspoon red pepper flakes
Salt to taste
1½ pounds spaghetti
Garnish: Freshly grated Parmesan cheese

The Steps:

1. In large skillet, sauté bacon over medium-high heat until it just begins to brown; drain off all but 2 tablespoons fat.
2. Add onion, and continue to sauté until bacon and onion turn lightly golden, stirring occasionally.
3. Add tomatoes, red pepper flakes, and salt; cook uncovered over medium-low heat for 20–25 minutes, stirring often.
4. Meanwhile, bring large pot of salted water to a boil and cook pasta just until *al dente*; drain.
5. Place cooked pasta in large bowl and immediately toss with sauce; sprinkle with cheese and serve at once, with extra grated cheese on the side.

Variations:

Parmesan and Romano cheese can be used, as a garnish alone or in combination.

Fettucine or other thick long noodles can be substituted for spaghetti.

If tomatoes packed in puree are unavailable, use regular whole juice-packed tomatoes; chop, drain off most of the liquid. Return tomatoes to can, and fill to the top with canned tomato puree.

Make-It-Easy Tip:

√ To freeze bacon easily, lay strips flat, slice after slice, on waxed or freezer paper; roll up, place in a plastic bag, and store in freezer. When ready to use, unroll, peel off slices, and cut easily by making a pile of frozen bacon slices; then dice with sharp knife or even kitchen scissors.

Fusilli with Spinach and Cream

SERVES: 6–8
Preparation Time: 10 minutes
Cooking Time: 10–15 minutes

Any type of short tubular or twisted pasta such as *penne*, small shells, or even *ziti* can be used for this pasta dish.

The Ingredients:

4 tablespoons (½ stick) unsalted butter
½ cup finely chopped scallions (green and white parts included)
2 10-ounce packages frozen chopped spinach, thawed and thoroughly squeezed dry
1 cup whole-milk ricotta cheese
1¾ cups heavy cream
½ teaspoon nutmeg
Salt and freshly ground pepper to taste
1½ pounds fusilli or similarly shaped pasta
1 cup freshly grated Parmesan cheese
Garnish: Toasted pine nuts, freshly grated Parmesan cheese

The Steps:

1. Heat butter in large nonaluminum saucepan and sauté scallions over medium heat until just soft, but not brown.
2. Add spinach and toss well; add ricotta and stir to combine.
3. Add cream, nutmeg, salt, and pepper and continue to cook over medium heat until sauce thickens.
4. Meanwhile, cook pasta in salted boiling water until *al dente*; drain.
5. Toss hot pasta with sauce and cheese; serve immediately, garnished with pine nuts and extra cheese.

Variation:

1 cup chopped mushrooms can be added with scallions, but increase butter to 5–6 tablespoons since mushrooms will absorb the fat.

Make-It-Easy Tips:

√ The cheese is added at the end to avoid a stringy texture.

√ A nonaluminum saucepan is advised because when cooking spinach in aluminum pots, a chemical reaction occurs that results in a slightly metallic taste.

Insalata di Mare con Farfalle (Seafood Salad with Bow-Tie-Shaped Pasta)

SERVES: 6–8
Preparation time: 20 minutes
Cooking time: 8–10 minutes or until pasta is tender
Chilling time: 2–3 hours

This pasta salad should be served the same day it is prepared, or possibly the next day, since the cooked seafood will not keep long.

The Ingredients:

1 pound small spaghetti twists (*farfalle* or *farfallette*)
2 tablespoons olive oil
6–8 ounces fresh crabmeat or one 6-ounce package frozen crabmeat, thawed and flaked
1 pound tiny bay shrimp
6 scallions (green and white parts included), finely minced
4 stalks celery, finely chopped

Dressing:

1½ cups mayonnaise
¼ cup chili sauce
1 tablespoon fresh lemon juice
1 teaspoon celery seed
Salt and freshly ground white pepper to taste

Garnish: Freshly chopped chives or scallion stalks

The Steps:

1. Cook pasta in boiling salted water, drain, and toss with olive oil to prevent sticking.
2. Place seafood in large bowl; top with scallions and celery.
3. Combine dressing ingredients in small bowl; whisk until smooth and toss with seafood.
4. Add cooked pasta, continue to toss; cover and chill for 2–3 hours.
5. Taste for seasonings, adjust with salt and pepper, and garnish with chopped chives or scallions.

Variations:

Serve the salad as an appetizer or main course salad.

If fresh or frozen crabmeat is unavailable, substitute canned crabmeat soaked in very cold water to remove any trace of tinny taste.

Cold cooked fish, such as flounder, snapper, or even the new, popular orange roughy can be substituted for the more expensive crabmeat.

Make-It-Easy Tips:

√ Pasta salad must be tasted after chilling since cold diminishes the intensity of the seasoning.

√ Even if crabmeat is frozen or canned, always pick through to detect pieces of shell before serving.

Biscuit Tortoni

SERVES: 8
Preparation time: 10–15 minutes
Chilling time: 1 hour or until ready to use.

A cooling, refreshing finish to a pasta dinner.

The Ingredients:

1 cup crushed almond macaroons (I use the Italian Ameretti di Saronna)
⅓ cup chopped almonds, toasted
3 tablespoons unsalted butter, melted
1 teaspoon almond extract
3 pints vanilla ice cream, slightly softened
1 12-ounce jar apricot preserves.

The Steps:

1. Line an 8″-square pan with aluminum foil, with overlapping edges.
2. Mix together macaroons, almonds, butter, and extract. Reserve ¼ cup mixture for topping. Sprinkle half of remaining mixture on bottom of pan.
3. Spoon half of ice cream over crumbs; drizzle with half the preserves; sprinkle with remaining half of crumb mixture.
4. Repeat ice cream and preserve layers; top with reserved ¼ cup crumbs. Freeze 1 hour, or until ready to use.
5. When ready to serve, pull out foil, cut into squares, and serve immediately.

Make-It-Easy Tips:

√ To quickly toast almonds, brown in toaster-oven or broil 4″–6″ from heat source, watching carefully.

√ For longer storage, place the finished Tortoni in a large food storage bag, tie closed, and freeze.

Open House Championship Chili Party

SERVES: 20
LBG's Salsa
Easiest Championship Chili
Sour Cream Corn Bread
Spicy Tomato Salad
Heavenly Caramel-Pecan Squares
Cookie Crunch

Housewarmings, celebrations, or holidays of any kind can mean a day full of guests dropping in. Surprise them with this hearty buffet menu that has a Southwestern flair.

To decorate, create a centerpiece of colorful paper Mexican flowers, or even fresh flowers, in a bowl or on a tray surrounded by clusters of small clay or earthenware pots of cactus plants. Ceramic tiles used as trivets add a dash of the Spanish-mission look. For the cowboy connection, a multicolor assortment of bright bandanas makes unusual napkins.

First on the buffet come napkins and cutlery. Fold the bandanas into triangles and lay them overlapping in a circle, like a big pinwheel. Slip a fork into the fold of each. Or roll up the forks in the bandanas, securing them with twine or rope tied like miniature lariats. Better yet, combine both styles—with a basket or clay pot full of bandana-wrapped forks, and extra napkins in a circle around it.

Since this is a large party, invitations are necessary. Have them reflect the party theme by drawing brightly colored Mexican flowers with marker pens on heavy white card stock. Or, for a great idea for a housewarming party, take Polaroids of your house, attach them to white card stock, and send them as postcard invitations!

Start your party off with piquant spicy salsa. It keeps for weeks in the refrigerator, so don't worry about making too much. Served with chips or even raw, cut-up vegetables, it makes great, easy hors d'oeuvres.

The main dish is thick, red chili. Serve it from an electric crockery cooker (crock-pot) to keep it steamy, or use an earthenware bean pot or casserole to retain heat. Cups or mugs for the chili balance easily on a plate. Arrange them in a pretty, geometric pattern on the table next to the pot. This chili freezes well—either in advance for your party, or as leftovers when the party's over.

The Spicy Tomato Salad adds even more color. It's one of those salads that's made to marinate, so don't worry about it sitting for hours as guests come and go.

The smooth, subtle taste of the Sour Cream Corn Bread complements the spicy chili and salad. This is a rich variation on an all-American tradition, equally delicious whether baked in muffin tins or in baking pans and cut into chunky squares. A crock of whipped butter, served at room temperature for easy spreading, is the perfect accompaniment for the bread. Serve the Corn Bread squares in an easy-to-make napkin basket. Open two stiffly-starched large napkins and place one on top of the other. Fold into a triangle. Fold the two end corners in, tucking the second one securely into the folds envelope style. Fold back the top flaps and place the napkin basket inside a wicker basket. (See illustration.)

The Heavenly Caramel-Pecan Squares can be frozen in advance, and the Cookie Crunch can be prepared a day or two ahead and kept fresh in a sealed container or plastic bag. Dessert is strictly finger food, so make sure to have lots of extra napkins on hand.

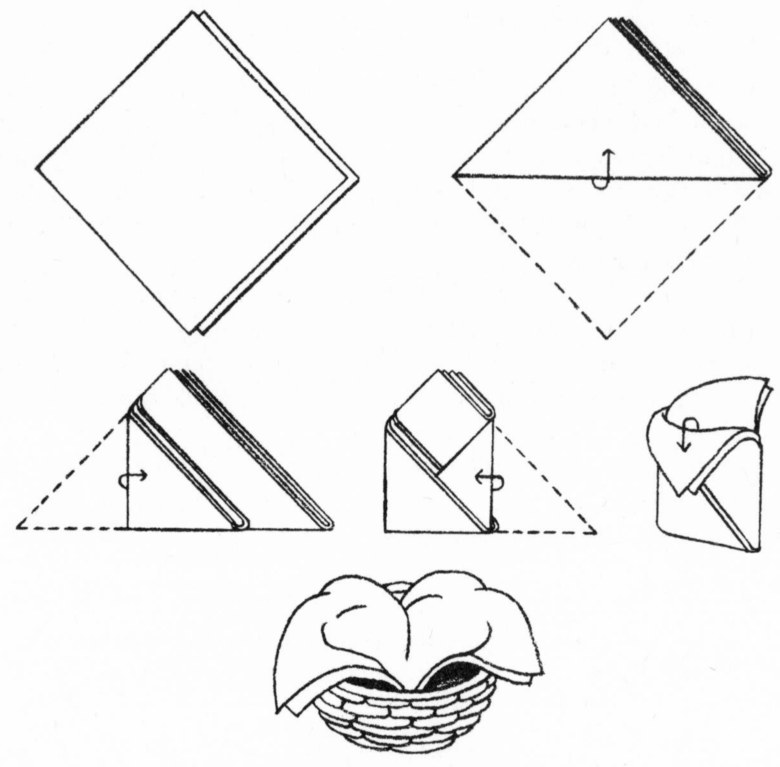

LBG's Salsa

YIELD: 3 cups
Preparation time: 10 minutes

This version of a spicy Mexican salsa is made easy with the use of canned tomatoes and tomato paste. Use the salsa with chips, on omelettes, or as a vegetable topping—wherever spiciness and flavor are needed.

The Ingredients:

3 tablespoons chopped onions
3 tablespoons chopped coriander (cilantro)
2 cloves garlic, minced
2 long green mild chili peppers, seeded
2 16-ounce cans whole tomatoes, drained and roughly chopped
3 tablespoons tomato paste

Salt and freshly ground pepper to taste
Accompaniments: Tortilla chips or raw cut-up vegetables (carrots, celery, or zucchini sticks)

The Steps:

1. In food processor or blender, chop onion, cilantro, garlic, and chili, pulsating on and off, until just chopped. (DO NOT OVERPROCESS.)
2. Add tomatoes, tomato paste, and salt and pepper to taste; continue to chop just until combined.
3. Serve immediately with chips or raw vegetables, or chill for future use.

Variation:

For hotter version, add spicy chili peppers to taste.

Make-It-Easy Tips:

√ Cilantro, occasionally called Chinese or Mexican parsley, is actually the leaf of the coriander plant. The parsley-like leaves, which have a zesty taste, should be used in moderation, or to taste.

√ Salsa will keep for several weeks in a jar in the refrigerator.

√ Tomato paste is now available in handy tube containers. Simply squeeze out what you need, cap the tube, and store it in the refrigerator for future use.

Easiest Championship Chili

SERVES: 20
Preparation time: 20–25 minutes
Cooking time: 2 hours

My favorite chili is Texas-style—without beans. It can be prepared way in advance and frozen until ready to use.

The Ingredients:

8 tablespoons (1 stick) unsalted butter
4 tablespoons olive oil

8 medium onions, finely chopped
4 large green peppers, finely chopped
8 pounds lean ground beef
2½ cups beer
2 28-ounce cans crushed tomatoes packed in puree
4 cups beef broth
8 cloves garlic, finely chopped
7 tablespoons chili powder
5 teaspoons ground cumin
1½ teaspoons paprika
1½ teaspoons dried oregano, crumbled
1½ teaspoons dried basil, crumbled
1½ teaspoons cayenne pepper, or to taste
1 teaspoon crushed red peppers, or to taste
Salt to taste
Garnish: Sour cream, grated cheddar, chopped onions

The Steps:

1. In large deep skillet or Dutch oven, heat butter and oil; when hot, sauté onion and green pepper over medium heat until golden. Add meat and brown over high heat, stirring until crumbly; drain off fat.
2. Add beer and allow to boil; add remaining ingredients and stir to combine.
3. Bring to a boil, reduce heat, cover, and simmer for 1½–2 hours.
4. Adjust seasonings to taste, adding more hot pepper if desired, and serve hot with garnishes.

Variation:

2–3 cans drained kidney or pinto beans can be added if desired.

If tomatoes packed in puree are unavailable, use regular whole juice-packed tomatoes; chop, drain off most of the liquid. Return tomatoes to can, and fill to the top with canned tomato puree.

Make-It-Easy Tips:

√ It may be necessary to sauté the meat in batches, draining off the excess fat as it accumulates. Once the beer is added, the chili can be transferred to a large stock pot or soup kettle for easy cooking.

√ Ask butcher to grind meat coarsely for chili.

√ The food processor speeds up the chopping process for chili. Just keep chopping the ingredients without cleaning the work bowl, since it all goes into the same pot.

√ Garlic can be crushed in large amounts with a food processor or blender, covered with a few tablespoons of oil, then stored for several weeks in the refrigerator in a small, tightly capped jar.

Sour Cream Corn Bread

SERVES: 20
Preparation time: 10–15 minutes
Cooking time: 25–30 minutes

The Ingredients:

3 cups yellow cornmeal
3 cups all-purpose flour
6 tablespoons sugar
3 tablespoons baking powder
1½ teaspoons salt
2¼ cups dairy sour cream
1½ cups whole milk
6 eggs
18 tablespoons (2¼ sticks) unsalted butter, melted
Accompaniment: Whipped sweet butter

The Steps:

1. Preheat oven to 350°. Butter one 9″ x 13″ x 2″ rectangular and one 9″-square baking pan.
2. In large mixing bowl, combine cornmeal, flour, sugar, baking powder, and salt.
3. In separate bowl, whisk together sour cream, milk, and eggs. Gradually add butter and continue to whisk until smooth.
4. Combine dry ingredients with sour cream mixture; pour into prepared pans and bake for 25–30 minutes, or until knife inserted comes out clean.
5. Remove from oven, cut into squares, and serve with whipped sweet butter.

Variation:

Bake batter in muffin tins for 20–25 minutes, or until done.

Make-It-Easy Tip:

√ Stone- or water-ground cornmeal is more nutritious than the processed granulated variety. Since stone-ground only remains fresh a short time, purchase in small quantities.

Spicy Tomato Salad

SERVES: 20
Preparation time: 10–15 minutes
Chilling time: 1–2 hours

The Ingredients:

12 large tomatoes, stems removed and sliced
4 medium onions, thinly sliced (sweet Bermuda or sweet red onions are best to use)
1 large can (6 ounces net weight) pitted black olives (about 40), drained
⅓ cup freshly chopped parsley

Dressing:

¾ cup olive oil
½ cup fresh lemon juice
2 teaspoons sugar
1½ teaspoons ground cumin
¼ teaspoon turmeric
Salt and freshly ground pepper to taste
Garnish: Parsley sprigs

The Steps:

1. Place sliced tomatoes on deep platter and intersperse slices of onions. Top with olives and sprinkling of parsley.
2. Combine dressing ingredients in screw-top jar and shake until smooth.
3. Pour dressing over vegetables, cover, and marinate for 1–2 hours in refrigerator.
4. Serve chilled, garnished with parsley sprigs.

Variation:

Pitted ripe green olives can be substituted for black olives, or a combination of both can be used.

Make-It-Easy Tips:

√ Slice raw tomatoes vertically so that the inner pulp holds its shape for salads.

√ Select firm and plump-looking tomatoes with good color. Most tomatoes require further ripening at home. Place away from direct sunlight in a plastic bag with a few holes to allow air to circulate. Once ripened, refrigerate and use within a few days.

Heavenly Caramel-Pecan Squares

YIELD: 48 squares
Preparation time: 20 minutes
Cooking time: 20 minutes

The Ingredients:

2 cups all-purpose flour
1 cup dark brown sugar, firmly packed
4 ounces (1 stick) unsalted butter, softened
1 cup pecan halves
6 ounces (1½ sticks) unsalted butter
⅔ cup dark brown sugar, firmly packed
6 ounces (1 package) semisweet chocolate bits

The Steps:

1. Preheat oven to 350°. Lightly butter a 9″ x 13″ x 2″ baking dish.
2. In food processor or in mixing bowl, combine flour with 1 cup brown sugar and 4 ounces butter; mix until well combined and place in prepared pan.
3. Pat firmly and evenly to form crust, and distribute pecan halves over it evenly.
4. In small saucepan, combine 6 ounces butter with ⅔ cup brown sugar. Cook over medium heat, stirring constantly until entire surface of mixture begins to boil; stir and boil for 1 minute.

5. Spoon hot mixture evenly over pecans and crust and bake for 20 minutes, or until top is bubbly and crust is golden brown.
6. In the meantime, melt chocolate in small saucepan. When cookie dough is baked, drizzle melted chocolate over it; then cool completely before cutting into 1½″ squares.

Variation:

Walnut halves can be substituted for pecan halves.

Make-It-Easy Tip:

√ When melting chocolate, never cover the pot; moisture makes the chocolate stiffen.

Cookie Crunch

YIELD: about 24 cookies
Preparation time: 10 minutes
Cooking time: 10–15 minutes

This recipe is bequeathed to me by a friend, Susan Grode. Although graham crackers are associated with children, this recipe changes a child food into wonderful, tasty, crunchy dessert treats.

The Ingredients:

2 packages graham crackers (22 whole crackers), broken up into various sizes
8 ounces (2 sticks) unsalted butter, melted
1 cup sugar mixed with 1 tablespoon cinnamon
1 cup (3¾-ounce package) sliced almonds

The Steps:

1. Preheat oven to 275°.
2. On large cookie sheet or jelly roll pan with sides, place cookie pieces, allowing cookies to touch but not overlap.
3. Drizzle half of melted butter over crackers and sprinkle with half of cinnamon-sugar mixture. Top with half of almonds.
4. Drizzle with remaining butter; then top with remaining cinnamon-sugar and finally almonds.

5. Bake for 10–15 minutes, just until crackers appear soft. Remove from oven; cool 10 minutes before removing from cookie sheet.
6. Break apart and serve.

Variation:

Crumble cookies and use as a topping for ice cream.

Make-It-Easy Tip:

√ Cookies are baked at a low temperature to avoid burning. If your oven temperature tends to be erratic, watch cookies carefully while baking.

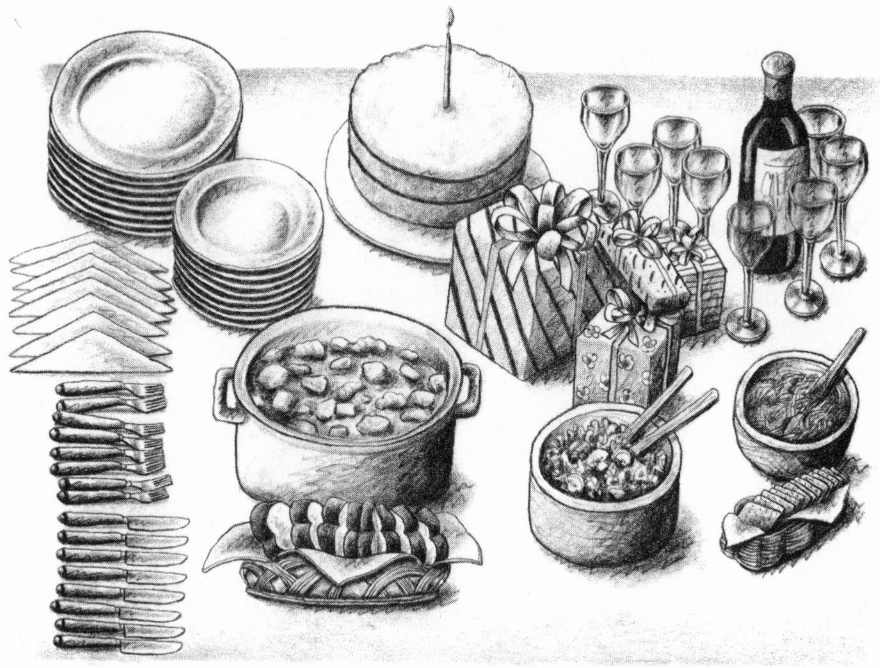

Surprise! Birthday Party

SERVES: 8
Chilled Julienne of Celery Root
Seafood Stew Provençale
Whole Baked Garlic with Crusty French Bread
Leaf Lettuce Salad with Creamy Mustard Vinaigrette
Fudge Layer Ice Cream Cake

Surprise birthday parties are not always easy to pull off. But, done correctly, they make the birthday person and all the guests feel special. This menu is a treat for all, including the host—flavorful, creative, with the ease and convenience of a complete one-pot dinner.

Baby pictures of the birthday guest can make a delightful centerpiece. It's also entertaining to round up old records from the birthday person's teen years for background music.

A white tablecloth sets off the evening's color—brightly wrapped packages, a meal full of reds and greens, and of course the birthday candles. (If the birthday person has reached the "sensitive" age, by all means, use one big candle to be tactful!)

Alternating napkins of two different colors accents the place settings. They can be folded or rolled up and tied with fancy bows like presents, then dressed up with a sprig of baby's breath. You might choose colors that reflect a bouquet of flowers on the table or the birthday candles.

The Seafood Stew Provençale is an easy variation of the more complex French bouillabaisse. Making the base in advance will simplify things even more. Only the seafood needs to be added a few minutes before the end of the cooking time. Never overcook fresh seafood; it will be dried out and tough.

The Julienne of Celery Root can be quickly prepared and allowed to chill for several hours in advance. Meanwhile, the garlic bakes for a butterless spread that calorie counters will appreciate.

Cake is naturally a must at a birthday party. But cake from scratch means lots of work, and cake from a mix tastes as if it came from a box. This unusual Ice Cream Cake delights the cook as well as the guests. It requires no baking and can be frozen weeks in advance. That leaves you with time for more important things—like standing guard at the light switch and shouting "Surprise!"

Chilled Julienne of Celery Root

SERVES: 8
Preparation time: 10–15 minutes
Chilling time: 1–2 hours

Celery root (also called celeriac or celery knob) makes an unusual appetizer when combined with prosciutto. Prepare it during the fall and winter months, when celery root is plentiful. If celery root is unavailable, grated carrots can be substituted.

The Ingredients:

2 pounds celery root, peeled and cut into julienne matchstick strips
2 teaspoons lemon juice
½ cup (about 2 ounces) finely shredded prosciutto

Dressing:

1 cup mayonnaise
2 tablespoons freshly minced parsley

2 tablespoons minced scallions (Green and white parts included)
4 teaspoons Dijon mustard
1 tablespoon drained and chopped capers (optional)
1 tablespoon drained and chopped sour pickles (cornichons) (optional)
1 teaspoon lemon juice
Salt and freshly ground pepper to taste
Garnish: Freshly chopped parsley
Accompaniment: Sesame crackers

The Steps:

1. Toss celery root with lemon juice to prevent discoloration; add prosciutto and toss to combine.
2. Combine dressing ingredients together, in food processor or blender, or whisk by hand until smooth.
3. Toss dressing with celery root mixture and allow to chill 1–2 hours before serving.
4. Adjust seasonings to taste and serve on lettuce-lined platter garnished with freshly chopped parsley and accompanied by sesame crackers.

Variations:

Serve as an appetizer, first course, or lunch dish.
Smoked ham may be substituted for the more expensive prosciutto.

Make-It-Easy Tips:

√ Shred the peeled celery root easily in the food processor.
√ Dressing may be assembled a day or two in advance. It can also be used by itself as a dip.

Seafood Stew Provençale

SERVES: 8
Preparation time: 20–25 minutes
Cooking time: 40 minutes

The Ingredients:

¼ cup olive oil
2 large onions, sliced
2 cloves garlic, minced
1 28-ounce can crushed tomatoes packed in puree (I use Progresso brand)
1 2¼-ounce can sliced black olives
1 teaspoon dried basil, crumbled
1 teaspoon dried oregano, crumbled
1 teaspoon freshly ground pepper
1⅓ cups dry white wine or vermouth
1 cup clam juice
1 pound fresh cleaned shrimp
2 pounds fleshy fish, cut into chunks (haddock, sea bass, or snapper)
½ pound sea scallops
Salt and freshly ground pepper to taste
Garnish: 16 slices toasted French, Italian, or sourdough bread, cut ½″ thick, and freshly chopped parsley

The Steps:

1. In 6–8-quart-deep casserole, heat olive oil; sauté onion and garlic over medium heat until soft, about 4–5 minutes.
2. Add tomatoes, olives, basil, oregano and pepper, stirring around to combine flavors.
3. Add wine and cook uncovered for 3 minutes; add clam juice and broth, bring to a boil, cover, and simmer for 10 minutes.
4. Stir in shrimps; cover and simmer for 2 minutes.
5. Add fish and scallops, increase to medium high heat and continue to cook covered for an additional 4–5 minutes or until fish is flaky. (Do not overcook.)
6. Taste for seasoning, adjust with salt and pepper if necessary. As main course, serve stew over bread in large soup bowls, garnished with freshly chopped parsley.

Variations:

Another interesting fish to use is monk fish (*lotte* in France) which has the texture of a scallop and is much less expensive.

Well-scrubbed clams, mussels, or just about any other kind of seafood can be used in the soup, depending on what is available at the fish store. The clams and mussels need 12 minutes of cooking time.

If tomatoes packed in puree are unavailable, use juice-packed canned tomatoes; chop and drain off most of the liquid, return tomatoes to can, and fill to the top with canned tomato puree.

Make-It-Easy Tips:

√ If more sauce is needed, add extra clam broth.

√ Prepare base for soup a day ahead (up through Step #4) and refrigerate, or freeze until ready to add fish.

√ If using fish heads and bones for extra flavor (ask the fishmonger for these), tie up in a cheesecloth bag and toss away after using. When cooked longer than half an hour, fish bones become softer and impart a bitter taste to the mixture.

√ An easy way to toast bread slowly is in a 325° oven for 20–25 minutes. The bread can be toasted several days in advance and kept in a sealed jar or plastic bag tied up until ready.

√ Use discretion when adding salt to the soup, since the clam broth, chicken broth, tomatoes, and seafood all contain high amounts of sodium. Add only in last step after tasting finished product.

Whole Baked Garlic with Crusty French Bread

YIELD: ½–1 cup
Preparation time: 5 minutes
Cooking time: 1–1½ hours

There are no messy peeling and chopping chores for this garlic puree; simply bake the garlic whole and unpeeled. When slow-cooked via this method, the garlic puree that results is delicate and nutlike in flavor. Squeeze the pulp out of the skin right onto pieces of fresh crusty French or Italian bread.

The Ingredients:

2 large heads garlic
Accompaniment: Crusty French or Italian bread

The Steps:

1. Preheat oven to 300°. Lightly oil baking pan.
2. Place garlic in prepared pan and bake for 1–1½ hours, or until garlic is tender when pierced with fork.
3. Allow to cool 5 minutes; squeeze out pulp onto slices of bread.

Variation:

Puree can be used as a wonderful topping for baked potatoes or steamed vegetables, combined with a little butter if desired.

Make-It-Easy Tips:

√ To remove the smell of garlic from hands, rub hands with cut lemon or salt.

√ To remove garlic odor from breath, chew a few sprigs of parsley, several juniper berries, or a coffee bean.

√ Garlic puree can be prepared in advance in large batches and refrigerated in a covered jar. To use, mash peeled cloves until smooth and spread on warm bread as you would any spread or jam.

Leaf Lettuce Salad with Creamy Mustard Vinaigrette

SERVES: 8
Preparation time: 10 minutes

The Ingredients:

2 heads red leaf lettuce, washed and dried
3 tablespoons lemon juice
12 mushrooms
2 hard-cooked eggs
½ cup sliced almonds, lightly toasted

Creamy Mustard Vinaigrette:

½ cup olive oil
3 tablespoons red wine vinegar
2 tablespoons heavy cream
2 teaspoons Dijon mustard
1 teaspoon sugar
Salt and freshly ground pepper

The Steps:

1. Break up pieces of lettuce and arrange in salad bowl. Dip paper towel in lemon juice, wipe mushrooms clean, and slice into salad bowl. Grate egg over all and sprinkle with almonds.
2. Combine salad dressing ingredients in blender or food processor, or put in small screw-top jar and shake until smooth.
3. Pour dressing over salad, toss, and serve immediately.

Variations:

Crumbled bacon bits or croutons can be added to salad as desired.

Romaine or Boston lettuce can be used, but the red leaf adds lots of color.

Make-It-Easy Tip:

√ Select plump, unblemished mushrooms with tightly closed caps. Store in brown paper, which is porous and will help keep them fresh.

Fudge Layer Ice Cream Cake

SERVES: 8–10
Preparation time: 20 minutes
Freezing time: 3 hours or overnight

The Ingredients:

4 almond or coconut macaroon cookies, crumbled
½ gallon (2 quarts) butter brickle ice cream (or coffee, caramel, or any combination that suits your whim), slightly softened
2 cups prepared chocolate fudge sauce topping or Hot Fudge Sauce (see page 90)

Garnish: ½ cup heavy cream, whipped (optional), toasted slivered almonds (optional), or crumbled Heath Bars

The Steps:

1. Lightly butter bottom of 9″ or 10″ springform pan.
2. Crumble macaroons (with the aid of food processor or blender or by hand, using hammer on cookies in plastic bag). Spread ⅓ of crumbs on bottom of prepared pan.
3. Spread 1 quart (½ of amount) of ice cream on top of crumbs; spoon ½ of chocolate sauce over ice cream and sprinkle on second ⅓ of macaroon crumbs.
4. Layer remaining ice cream, remaining sauce, and finally remaining crumbs; freeze for 2–3 hours, or until ready to serve.
5. Unmold and garnish with whipped cream if desired and some toasted slivered almonds or crumbled Heath Bars.

Variation:

Italian Amaretti di Saronna cookies may be used in place of the macaroons, but double the amount called for above.

Make-It-Easy Tips:

√ The cake may be prepared in advance, covered, and frozen for several weeks.

√ Ultra-pasteurized cream has a longer storage life but poorer whipping quality than regular cream. Look for the fresh cream available at supermarkets and health food stores.

Demi-Dinner

SERVES: 12–16
Fish Salad Wrapped in Lettuce Leaves
Baked Brie
Laurie's Special Sliced Steak
Frosted Chinese Chicken Pâté
Apple-Oatmeal-Raisin Bars
Apricot Shortbread Squares

So you're trying to plan a dinner for 16, but your table seats closer to 6? Don't despair—improvise elegantly, with this hearty, satisfying version of the cocktail party, the Demi-Dinner, served from 5 o'clock on.

Here's an unusual dinner menu that gives you the utmost in flexibility. It provides the beginnings, and endings, without the fuss of setting the table. Serve from a buffet, if buffet-style, or pass trays around the room. Everything comes in single-serving portions, so there's no bother with carving. And all these dishes are so easy to eat with just a fork that people will be equally comfortable sitting and chatting in a cozy corner or standing up and walking about. To keep the flow of a large party moving, you can even place the food in more than one location—on a cocktail table, side table, or the dining room table.

Set up a small bar in a convenient area of the room. I have noticed that guests are consuming less hard liquor lately and are requesting wine in its place. Therefore, I stock up on my favorite dry white wine, kept well chilled, plus a few bottles of a wonderful red wine. In addition, I provide lots of chilled sparkling water along with a variety of garnishes such as lemon and lime slices and orange twists.

The first step is to write up your invitations. Let people know that this is a "Demi-Dinner" with lots of appetizers and dessert. Remember to send an invitation to yourself, to make sure they go smoothly through the mail.

Since the whole room becomes your dining area, make each corner bright with an assortment of candlesticks and colorful candles. Add cheer with small, bright sprays of flowers around the room. Choose cocktail napkins in a variety of colors that echo your candles and flowers.

These recipes are almost 100 percent make-ahead delights. Bake the Apple-Oatmeal-Raisin Bars and Apricot Shortbread Squares in advance, then wrap them tightly for freshness. Also, prepare the Chicken Pâté and Fish Salad early—then let them chill while the Sliced Steak bakes. Meanwhile, relax, put your feet up, and save your energy for the party.

Fish Salad Wrapped in Lettuce Leaves

SERVES: 12–16
Preparation time: 20 minutes
Chilling time: 1–2 hours

This recipe comes from Los Angeles caterer Marcia McKeegan, who serves it as an appetizer or tossed together as a main-course salad.

The Ingredients:

Chicken or vegetable broth to cover:
3 slices onion
2 sprigs parsley
2 slices lemon
2 teaspoons freshly chopped tarragon (or ½ teaspoon dried tarragon, crumbled)
2 teaspoons freshly chopped basil (or ½ teaspoon dried basil, crumbled)
4 peppercorns
Salt to taste
5 pounds firm fleshy fish fillets (white fish, sea bass, cod, scrod, snapper, orange roughy, etc.)
2 bunches watercress, chopped
1 cucumber, peeled, seeded, and finely chopped
1 endive, thinly sliced (optional)
3 large heads butter lettuce

Dressing:

1 cup (½ pint) dairy sour cream
1 cup (½ pint) plain yogurt
2–3 tablespoons poppy seeds
2 tablespoons white wine vinegar
2 tablespoons toasted sesame oil
½ teaspoon sugar, or to taste
Pinch of nutmeg
Salt and freshly ground pepper to taste
Garnish: Cherry tomatoes, watercress

The Steps:

1. Fill deep skillet with enough broth to totally cover the fish; add onion, parsley, lemon, tarragon, basil, peppercorns, and salt. Bring to a boil, cover, and simmer for 10 minutes.
2. Add fish, lower heat, cover, and simmer *very* slowly for 5–10 minutes, depending on thickness of fillet, or until fish is flaky. Carefully remove fish from broth; allow to drain and cool. (Set broth aside for future use.)
3. In small bowl, combine dressing ingredients together; whisk until smooth.
4. Break fish into small pieces; place in bowl with watercress, cucumber, and optional endive, toss with dressing, and chill for 1–2 hours.
5. Separate lettuce leaves, and place leaves on large platters. Fill each with a dollop of fish salad and serve garnished with cherry tomatoes and additional watercress.

Variations:

For added flavor use a tarragon-flavored white wine vinegar.

Toasted sesame seeds can be substituted for poppy seeds.

Chopped cashews can be added to taste.

Make-It-Easy Tips:

√ If using frozen fish, poach frozen according to package directions.

√ Strain fish broth (called "court bouillon") and freeze in plastic containers for future use.

√ To remove lettuce leaves from head easily and intact, remove core with tip of paring knife and leaves will fall away.

Baked Brie

SERVES: 12–16
Preparation time: 5–10 minutes
Cooking time: 4–5 minutes

The Ingredients:

1 large wheel of Brie cheese (2 pounds)
1–1¼ cups sliced almonds

2 tablespoons unsalted butter, melted
Accompaniments: Warmed French bread or crisp crackers

The Steps:

1. Preheat oven to 450°.
2. Lightly scrape rind from top and sides of cheese and place in oven-proof serving dish; cover surface with almonds, pressing down to adhere.
3. Drizzle with butter, place in oven, and bake for 4–5 minutes, or until hot and runny.
4. Serve hot accompanied by French bread or crisp crackers.

Variations:

Crushed cereal crumbs can be substituted for almonds.
For smaller group, use just a large wedge of Brie.
Brie can also be baked in 300° oven for 20 minutes.

Make-It-Easy Tips:

√ This recipe can be assembled through Step #2 earlier in the day and heated just before serving.

√ The Brie for this recipe should not be ripe or runny since it softens when baked.

Laurie's Special Sliced Steak

SERVES: 12–16
Preparation time: 15–20 minutes
Cooking time: 60 minutes
Marinating time: 6 hours or overnight

This recipe is a variation on a baked steak from cooking authorities Rita Leinwand and Lois Peyser. This steak can be sliced and served on buttered, toasted bread with a little sauce on top of each helping. It can also be served as a main course, sliced, and served with the sauce on the side. For an even more flavorful dish, allow meat to marinate overnight.

The Ingredients:

4–5 pounds sirloin steak cut 2½″–3″ thick, well trimmed
2 teaspoons finely minced garlic
1 large onion, thinly sliced

Sauce:

1 28-ounce can crushed tomatoes, packed in puree
¾ cup dry red wine
¾ cup beef broth
3 tablespoons red wine vinegar
3 tablespoons dark brown sugar
Salt and freshly ground pepper to taste
Garnish: French, Italian, or sourdough bread—buttered, toasted, and sliced

The Steps:

1. Place steak in roasting pan, rub with garlic, and smother with onions.
2. In food processor or blender, combine sauce ingredients and process until smooth. Reserve ⅔ cup to serve as sauce on the side.
3. Spoon remaining sauce carefully over steak, covering totally. Allow to marinate in refrigerator for 6 hours or overnight.
4. Preheat oven to 425°. Remove steak from refrigerator 1 hour before cooking.
5. Bake for 60 minutes for medium-rare, or until cooked to desired degree of doneness.
6. Slice steak thinly on the bias and serve on thinly sliced, toasted buttered bread with reserved sauce on the side.

Variations:

Garlic- or onion-flavored bread can be substituted for plain bread.

If tomatoes packed in puree are unavailable, use regular whole juice-packed tomatoes; chop, drain off most of the liquid. Return tomatoes to can, and fill to the top with canned tomato puree.

Make-It-Easy Tips:

√ The tenderest and best-quality steaks are not lean. They are well marbled with fat, which keeps the meat moist, flavorful, and tender.

√ To easily toast bread, slice, butter, place on cookie sheet, and bake in a 325° oven for 10–15 minutes, or until golden.

Frosted Chinese Chicken Pâté

SERVES: 12–16
Preparation time: 20 minutes
Cooking time: 70 minutes
Chilling time: 4–6 hours or overnight

A food processor makes the preparation of this pâté incredibly easy. If using a blender, process in small batches.

The Ingredients:

1–2 tablespoons peanut oil
1½ pounds boneless chicken breasts, cut into 1″ pieces
3 eggs
2 scallions, cut into pieces (green and white parts included)
1 clove garlic
1 slice ginger (the size of a quarter)
2 tablespoons peanut oil
2 tablespoons toasted sesame oil
2 tablespoons soy sauce
2 tablespoons dry sherry
1 teaspoon sugar
Salt to taste
¾ cup Hoisin sauce (available at Chinese, Japanese, or specialty grocery stores)
1 cup scallion greens, cut with scissors into ¼″ pieces
Accompaniments: Thin rice crackers or toasted pita bread

The Steps:

1. Preheat oven to 325°. Rub inside of 8″ x 4″ x 2″ loaf pan with peanut oil.
2. In food processor or blender, process chicken with eggs to form a paste. (It may be necessary to process in two or three batches.) Remove and set aside.
3. Add scallions, garlic, and ginger to food processor bowl or blender container and chop finely. Add peanut oil, sesame oil, soy sauce, sherry, sugar, and salt and continue to pulsate until well combined.
4. Return chicken mixture and process until smooth. Pour chicken paste in prepared pan, seal tightly with aluminum foil, and place

loaf pan in larger pan filled with an inch of hot water. Bake for 70 minutes, or until inserted knife comes out clean.

5. Remove from oven and cool on rack. Loosen sides with sharp paring knife, cover, and chill for 4–6 hours, or overnight.
6. Unmold onto platter, frost with Hoisin sauce, garnish wtih scallion greens, and serve in thin slices on rice crackers toasted pita bread.

Make-It-Easy Tips:

√ Powdered ginger is not an adequate substitute for freshly grated. Store peeled fresh ginger in a jar covered with sherry in the refrigerator.

√ If Hoisin sauce is canned, transfer to covered jar and store in refrigerator indefinitely.

Apple-Oatmeal-Raisin Bars

YIELD: 24 cookies
Preparation time: 15–20 minutes
Cooking time: 30–35 minutes

The Ingredients:

1 cup apple juice
1 6-ounce package dried apples
1 cup seedless raisins
1⅓ cups brown sugar, firmly packed
1 teaspoon cinnamon
2 cups all-purpose flour
1 teaspoon baking powder
Pinch salt
1½ cups quick-cooking oats
2 sticks (1 cup) unsalted butter, softened
1 tablespoon unsalted butter, diced

The Steps:

1. Preheat oven to 325°. Generously grease 9″ x 13″ x 2″ baking pan.
2. Heat apple juice in saucepan. Remove from heat, add dried

apples, and soak for 15 minutes. Drain and chop coarsely in food processor or by hand. Set aside.

3. Coat raisins with ⅓ cup of the brown sugar and cinnamon and set aside.
4. Sift flour, baking powder, and salt together into mixing bowl. Add oats and stir together.
5. In another bowl, cream remaining cup brown sugar with softened butter and gradually add dry ingredients until mixture is crumbly.
6. Place half of crumbly mixture in prepared baking pan and press evenly into bottom. Over this place chopped apples in single layer and then coated raisins. Cover with remaining oat mixture and dot with butter. Bake for 30–35 minutes. Cut into bars while still warm.

Variation:

Substitute peach nectar for apple juice and dried peaches for apples.

Make-It-Easy Tip:

√ Dried apples are available all year long and require no messy peeling or chopping chores.

Apricot Shortbread Squares

YIELD: 36 squares
Preparation time: 15–20 minutes
Cooking time: 35–40 minutes

The Ingredients:

8 ounces (2 sticks) unsalted butter, softened
1 cup granulated sugar
2 eggs
2 cups all-purpose flour
Pinch of salt
1 12-ounce jar apricot preserves
½ cup sliced almonds
Garnish: Confectioner's sugar

The Steps:

1. Preheat oven to 350°. Lightly butter a 9″ x 13″ x 2″ pan.
2. With electric mixer or by hand, beat butter and sugar together. Add eggs and continue to beat well until combined. Add flour and salt and continue to mix until smooth.
3. Spread half the batter in prepared pan; spread preserves smoothly over and sprinkle with nuts. Distribute remaining batter over top.
4. Bake for 35–40 minutes or until lightly golden. Cool slightly, cut into squares, and sprinkle with confectioner's sugar.

Variations:

Raspberry, strawberry, blueberry, or other preserves desired can be substituted for apricot.

Chopped walnuts or pecans can be substituted for almonds.

Make-It-Easy Tip:

√ Store opened containers of shelled almonds in airtight containers in refrigerator or freezer.

Academy Award Buffet

SERVES: 8–10
Beer with Lime
Spicy Cheese Spread on Cocktail Rounds
Carbonnade à la Flamande (Beef and Beer)
Steamed Potatoes
Romaine Salad with Oranges
Toasted Coconut Bread
Toffee Cake

Whether it's the Oscars, the Emmys, the Miss America Pageant, or even an election night, parties geared to these national rituals provide wonderful excuses for friends to gather.

The television becomes the central focus of the evening, but don't let that stop you from adding to the mood. Pictures of movie or television stars, movie ads, or candidates' campaign posters can hang on the walls.

Get the group into action by setting up a ballot box on a table near the door, along with the ballots for everyone to fill out upon arrival. You may find sample ballots for entertainment awards in the newspaper or *TV Guide*. Or go for a not-so-secret ballot, with a prize for picking the winner.

Since people will be eating in front of the television, with dinner balanced on their laps, a buffet set-up is a must, with one-fork simplicity. There are no knives, no spoons—and no sloppy hard-to-handle foods.

As always, the key to a smooth buffet is good organization. Plan the steps logically, even doing a walk-through rehearsal. Plates go first—warmed in the dishwasher, if possible. Add a few extra plates for seconds. Next comes the salad, served with tongs for easy one-handed use. Follow with the hot Carbonnade and potatoes. If possible, serve them in thick, earthenware dishes to retain heat, or set serving dishes on a warming tray. Then come the forks and napkins. Rolling up the forks in the napkins and tying them in bundles with ribbon or thick yarn makes them easy to grab with one hand—or hold with one finger. Mugs of beer go last, so that they get carried the least distance possible. Don't forget to leave a few extra empty spaces on the table to allow guests to rest a plate while serving the stew or salad.

As for the Spicy Cheese Spread, team it up with crackers for do-it-yourself hors d'oeuvres before dinner. For a large crowd, serving the spread in two or three small batches instead of one large one keeps it within everyone's easy reach. And the crackers-and-dip approach saves you the bother of preassembling canapés, which tend to get soggy anyway.

The Carbonnade, a Belgian specialty, is one of those wonderfully easy stews that can be prepared several days ahead or even frozen for ease and convenience. You'll need to stock up on beer, since it goes into the Carbonnade as well as being served alongside. Purchase enough club soda and limes as well as a nonalcoholic beverage alternative. Potatoes are the traditional accompaniment to Carbonnade. Choose potatoes with smooth, unblemished skins, since these are fixed the easy way—without peeling them first.

Serve dessert after all the dinner dishes are cleared away. The Toffee Cake and Toasted Coconut Bread are delicious with ice cream, but served alone they make easy finger food—a big help when you're running short of forks.

Beer with Lime

YIELD: 1 drink

The Ingredients:

1 teaspoon Rose's lime juice
1 teaspoon fresh lime juice
8 ounces cold beer
Garnish: Slice of lime

The Steps:

1. In each chilled glass, place Rose's lime juice and fresh lime juice.
2. Pour in 8 ounces of cold beer, garnish with slice of lime, and serve immediately.

Make-It-Easy Tip:

√ Lime and dark beer don't combine as nicely as lime and regular or light beer.

Spicy Cheese Spread on Cocktail Rounds

SERVES: 8–10
Preparation time: 10–15 minutes
Chilling time: 2–4 hours

It's very easy and often less expensive to make your own equivalent of Boursin, Alouette, Rondele, or any other brand-name garlic-herb cheese spread.

The Ingredients:

2 ounces cream cheese
8 ounces farmer's cheese
2 tablespoons dairy sour cream
¼ cup finely chopped onion
¼ cup freshly chopped parsley

1 tablespoon freshly chopped basil (or 1 teaspoon dried basil, crumbled)
2 cloves garlic, finely minced
2 teaspoons freshly ground pepper
1 teaspoon freshly chopped tarragon (or pinch of dried tarragon, crumbled)
½ teaspoon fresh chopped thyme, (or a pinch of dried thyme, crumbled)
Dash Tabasco, or to taste
Salt to taste
Accompaniments: Pumpernickel or rye cocktail rounds

The Steps:

1. In food processor, blender, or by hand, mash cheeses and sour cream together. Add remaining ingredients and continue to process until smooth.
2. Place in crock and chill for 2–4 hours to make firm.
3. Serve with pumpernickel or rye cocktail rounds.

Variation:

Spread can be shaped into a log or ball and rolled in cracked pepper or chopped parsley.

Make-It-Easy Tip:

√ Chop garlic in food processor in large amounts, place in jar, cover with olive oil, and keep in refrigerator for 2–3 weeks.

Carbonnade à la Flamande

SERVES: 8–10
Preparation time: 20–25 minutes
Cooking time: 2 hours

Carbonnade, of French origin, was adapted by the Belgians so successfully that it is called Carbonnade de boeuf à la Flamande, or Flemish beef stew. A traditional Carbonnade Flamande, a wonderful mixture of beef, beer, and onions, usually calls for dark Belgian beer, but any good American brand will do.

The Ingredients:

4 slices bacon, diced
3–5 tablespoons unsalted butter
4½ pounds lean beef, cut into 2″ chunks (I use round steak)
⅓ cup all-purpose flour
4 large (2 pounds) onions, thinly sliced
2 cups (16 ounces) beer
1 cup beef broth
3 tablespoons brown sugar
3 tablespoons red wine vinegar
3 tablespoons freshly chopped parsley
2 teaspoons freshly minced garlic
1½ teaspoons dried thyme, crumbled
1 bay leaf
Salt and freshly ground pepper to taste
Garnish: Freshly grated lemon peel, freshly chopped parsley, bacon bits

The Steps:

1. Preheat oven to 325°.
2. In large skillet, sauté bacon until browned; remove browned bits and reserve. Add butter to pan and melt.
3. Toss beef cubes with flour, shake off excess, and brown in batches; place browned beef cubes in deep saucepan or Dutch oven.
4. If all fat has been absorbed, add an additional 2 tablespoons butter and sauté onions until golden; add to casserole with beef.
5. Pour off any excess fat remaining in skillet, add beer, and allow to boil for 1 minute. Then add broth, scraping up browned particles from bottom of pan. Pour over beef.
6. Add remaining ingredients to casserole, stir well, bring to a boil on top of range, and bake in oven for 1¾–2 hours, or until meat is tender.
7. Remove bay leaf and serve Carbonnade directly from casserole sprinkled with lemon peel, parsley, and reserved bacon bits.

Variations:

A whole piece of boneless chuck or similar potting beef can be used for Carbonnade and sliced as for pot roast after cooking.

Carbonnade can be cooked on top of range in a heavy pot over very low heat.

Onion can be finely chopped for a smoother sauce. Sauce can also be placed in a food processor or strainer after cooking.

Make-It-Easy Tips:

√ When browning beef cubes, do not crowd the pan. This drops the heat level so that the meat turns gray instead of searing and turning brown.

√ Leftover beer works just as successfully as freshly opened beer.

√ Flour can be placed in plastic or brown bag, beef cubes added, and shaken to coat evenly.

Steamed Potatoes

SERVES: 8–10
Preparation time: 5 minutes
Cooking time: 15–20 minutes

The Ingredients:

16–20 round, red, or other small potatoes
2–3 tablespoons unsalted butter, melted
1–2 tablespoons freshly chopped parsley
Salt and freshly ground pepper to taste

The Steps:

1. Scrub potatoes clean with stiff brush.
2. In large pot, place ½″–1″ boiling water. Add potatoes, cover tightly, and cook 15–20 minutes, or until fork tender.
3. Drain potatoes, toss in bowl with butter, parsley, salt, and pepper, and serve immediately.

Variation:

Butter and seasonings can be omitted if desired.

Make-It-Easy Tips:

√ If pot does not distribute steam uniformly, steam potatoes on a rack or in a steaming basket or strainer above water.

√ Avoid potatoes with a greenish hue. They are overexposed to light, have a bitter, unpleasant flavor, and are not good for you.

Romaine Salad with Oranges

SERVES: 8–10
Preparation time: 5 minutes

The Ingredients:

2 large heads romaine lettuce, washed and dried
1 11-ounce can mandarin oranges, drained

Dressing:

⅔ cup vegetable oil
3 tablespoons red wine vinegar
2 tablespoons lemon juice
2 tablespoons chopped chives or scallion greens
2 tablespoons freshly chopped parsley
1 tablespoon sugar
1 teaspoon Dijon mustard
Salt and freshly ground pepper to taste

The Steps:

1. Break up lettuce into small pieces, place in large salad bowl; distribute mandarin oranges over lettuce.
2. In screw-top jar, combine dressing ingredients. Shake well until smooth.
3. Pour dressing over salad, gently toss, and serve immediately.

Variation:

¾ cup tiny bay shrimp can be added to the salad.

Make-It-Easy Tips:

√ Dressing can be prepared in a food processor or blender for a creamier consistency.

√ Lettuce can be washed, dried, wrapped in paper towels, and sealed in a plastic bag for several hours to chill well.

Toasted Coconut Bread

YIELD: 1 large loaf
Preparation time: 15 minutes
Cooking time: 55–60 minutes

This recipe comes from the chef at the Caunterbury restaurant in Saratoga Springs, New York. It uses unsweetened coconut, which is readily available in packages at health food stores and in some supermarkets.

The Ingredients:

1 cup (about 2 ounces) grated, unsweetened coconut
2 cups all-purpose flour
¾ cup sugar
1 tablespoon baking powder
½ tablespoon salt
1 cup whole milk
¼ cup vegetable oil
1 egg, well-beaten
1 teaspoon vanilla

The Steps:

1. Preheat oven to 350°. Generously butter and flour a 9″ x 5″ x 3″ loaf pan.
2. Spread coconut on a baking sheet, place in oven, and toast for 3–4 minutes, shaking occasionally until lightly golden. Allow to cool slightly.
3. In large mixing bowl combine flour, sugar, baking powder, salt, and toasted coconut.
4. In separate bowl beat milk, oil, egg, and vanilla together. Add to flour mixture, stirring well until thoroughly combined.
5. Pour into prepared pan and bake for 50–55 minutes, or until golden brown. Invert onto rack, allow to cool slightly, and serve at room temperature.

Variation:

Sprinkle hot bread with confectioner's sugar and additional toasted coconut if desired.

Make-It-Easy Tips:

√ Watch the coconut carefully while toasting, to avoid burning.
√ Bread can be frozen successfully.

Toffee Cake

SERVES: 8–10
Preparation time: 15–20 minutes
Cooking time: 30–35 minutes

Serve the toffee cake cut in small squares like bar cookies for a buffet.

The Ingredients:

2 cups (1 pound) dark brown sugar, firmly packed
2 cups all-purpose flour
1 teaspoon baking soda
½ teaspoon salt
4 ounces (1 stick) unsalted butter, at room temperature
1 egg
1 cup whole milk
1 teaspoon vanilla extract
1 cup chopped pecans
1 cup chocolate chips
6 ounces toffee candy (Heath Bars) crushed (or 1 package Bits o'Brickle Almond Brickle Chips)
Accompaniment: Vanilla ice cream

The Steps:

1. Preheat oven to 350°. Generously butter and flour a 9″ x 13″ x 2″ pan.
2. In food processor or in bowl with pastry blender, combine brown sugar, flour, baking soda, and salt. Add butter and blend until crumbly coarse meal is formed. (Or pulsate food processor until texture is correct.) Reserve 1 cup of mixture in separate bowl.
3. Add egg, milk, and vanilla, blend well, and pour into prepared pan.
4. To reserved brown sugar mixture, add nuts, chips, and crushed toffee candy, stir well, and distribute evenly over cake.

5. Bake for 30–35 minutes, or until cake tests done. Do not overbake.
6. Cool slightly and serve warm or at room temperature with vanilla ice cream.

Variation:

Chopped walnuts can be substituted for pecans.

Make-It-Easy Tips:

√ Freeze shelled nuts for optimum freshness.
√ It is easiest to crush candy after chilling. Use food processor or place in thick plastic bag and bang with hammer until crushed.

Pitch-In Paella Dinner

SERVES: 8
White Sangria
Sour Cream–Avocado Dip
Paella
Green Salad with Lime Dressing
Make-It-Easy Flan

One of the easiest and most enjoyable ways to toss a big splash is to get everyone into the act. This informal dinner takes place right in the kitchen, where the guests play a role in the preparation of the meal.

Everyone has a good time and feels a great sense of accomplishment. The idea is to provide a very relaxed atmosphere for everyone.

An informally set table is ideal for this casual splash. Decorate with brightly colored paper flowers, or assorted fruits or vegetables such as avocados, oranges, and lemons, or even a wreath of red chili peppers to emphasize the Spanish theme. A cream-colored or white cloth can also be used, accented with colorful napkins laid out in a diamond pattern. In the summer, move the Paella party outdoors on a casually set picnic table.

A large pitcher fitted with a long-handled wooden spoon is perfect for the White Sangria. Prepare this and the Sour Cream-Avocado Dip in advance, ready to take the edge off the thirst and appetites of your helpful guests.

Paella is the perfect dish for participatory cooking because the chopping and "prepping" chores can be divided up and then the final assembly completed at the last minute. The chicken should be started first while another group can be dicing the ham. Still another few can be cleaning the seafood and vegetables. The Paella can be served in a traditional Paella pan, a large deep skillet, or even a wok.

The Green Salad can be prepared in a glass or ceramic bowl and tossed at the last minute. Place the salad, bowl and all, in a large glazed terra-cotta plant saucer for a Latin presentation. Little terra-cotta saucers can also be used as ashtrays or even liners for the individual desserts.

The Flan is best prepared a day in advance and allowed to chill. Unmold an hour or so before guests arrive and continue to chill. Orange segments make an attractive garnish for this cooling dessert.

This is a casual and fun splash to be enjoyed by adults or even teenagers. For the younger set, substitute a fruit punch for the Sangria.

White Sangria

SERVES: 8
Preparation time: 15 minutes
Chilling time: 4–6 hours or overnight

White Sangria is a light and refreshing drink to serve in the summer or year round for those who prefer white wine.

The Ingredients:

2 bottles dry white wine
¼ cup Grand Marnier (or brandy)
¼ cup superfine sugar
10 strawberries, hulled and halved
1 navel orange, unpeeled and sliced
1 lemon, unpeeled and sliced
1 ripe pear, cored and sliced
1 peach, peeled and sliced
½ cup seedless grapes
2–3 cups chilled sparkling water
Ice
Garnish: Mint sprigs

The Steps:

1. Combine wine, Grand Marnier (or brandy), and sugar in a very tall pitcher and stir with long wooden spoon.
2. Add cut-up fruits, cover with plastic wrap, and allow to marinate in refrigerator for 4–6 hours or overnight.
3. At serving time, add chilled sparkling water and ice; serve in large goblets, topping each serving with sprig of mint.

Variation:

Add sparkling water to taste. I prefer the Sangria without the bubbles, but many prefer it with them.

Make-It-Easy Tips:

√ Superfine sugar is used because it dissolves faster in cold liquid. Regular sugar may be used if superfine is unobtainable.

√ To peel a peach easily, drop into boiling water for 1 minute, remove, and the peel will slide off easily. A few frozen unsweetened peaches may be substituted.

√ Ice cubes, frozen with a slice of lemon peel, make an attractive addition to the Sangria.

Sour Cream–Avocado Dip

YIELD: 3 cups
Preparation time: 10 minutes
Chilling time: 1 hour

The Ingredients:

2 ripe avocados
1¾ cup dairy sour cream
2 ripe tomatoes, roughly chopped
4 scallions, roughly chopped (green and white parts included)
4 teaspoons lemon or lime juice
4–5 shakes Tabasco, or to taste
Accompaniments: Nacho Chips or vegetable crudités (raw vegetables for dipping).

The Steps:

1. In food processor or blender, combine avocado with sour cream, tomato, scallions, lemon juice, and Tabasco and blend until smooth. Chill for 1 hour.
2. Serve chilled sauce with nacho chips or vegetable crudités.

Variations:

The sauce may be used as a topping for pita bread that has been stuffed with chopped tomatoes, cheese, chicken, and lettuce for a lunch or supper dish.

It can also be used on tacos or tostados as a substitute for guacamole.

Make-It-Easy Tips:

√ The sauce should be prepared the same day it is to be served.

√ Avocados will ripen in a brown paper bag or dark place in a few days. Once ripe, refrigerate until ready to use.

Paella

SERVES: 8
Preparation time: 20–25 minutes
Cooking time: 25–35 minutes

Paella, a saffron-flavored rice dish from Spain, is a mixture of many ingredients—chicken, meat, seafood, and vegetables. This Make-It-Easy version can be varied with additional seafood, sausages, and vegetables, as you like, since there is no one traditional Paella. Each region in Spain emphasizes the ingredients that are most readily available.

The Ingredients:

- 4–5 tablespoons good olive oil
- 1 large onion, roughly chopped
- 1 green or red pepper, sliced thinly into julienne strips
- 1 teaspoon freshly minced garlic
- 8–10 chicken thighs (or combination of thighs and breasts, cut into pieces)
- 2 cups raw rice

½ cup dry white wine or dry vermouth
1 cup cubed baked ham (or 2 broiled and sliced *chorizos*—Spanish sausages; or 2 broiled and sliced sweet or hot Italian sausages)
½–1 teaspoon saffron flowers (or a healthy pinch of saffron powder), to taste
3½ cups chicken broth, hot
½ teaspoon paprika
Pinch of thyme
Pinch of ground coriander seed (optional)
1 dozen cherrystone clams, scrubbed
8–10 medium shrimp, shelled and deveined
8–10 frozen artichokes, thawed
1 cup frozen peas, thawed
Garnish: Freshly chopped parsley, pimiento strips

The Steps:

1. Heat 3 tablespoons of olive oil in very large deep skillet and sauté onions and peppers over medium heat, until soft. Add garlic, stir well, and remove to platter with slotted spoon.
2. Add 1–2 tablespoons olive oil and sauté the chicken over medium-high heat until golden. Remove and set aside with cooked vegetables.
3. Remove skillet from heat; add rice and stir well to coat grains with oil.
4. Return skillet to high heat, immediately add wine, and stir well to deglaze pan, incorporating browned particles from bottom of pan into sauce.
5. Return chicken and vegetables to pan and add ham or sausages. Dissolve saffron in hot broth and pour into pan. Bring to boil, add paprika, thyme, and optional coriander; cover and simmer for 10 minutes.
6. Add clams; recover and cook an additional 10 minutes.
7. Add shrimp, artichokes, and peas, and continue to cook until shrimp are pink, clams are totally open, and rice is tender.
8. Taste for seasonings, adjust as necessary, and serve Paella immediately, garnished with freshly chopped parsley and strips of pimientos.

Variations:

Additional seafood such as scallops, lobsters, snails, or mussels may be added to the Paella, depending on cost factors. Add seafood gradually, timing accordingly.

Sautéed pork, bacon, or other ethnic sausages (such as Polish *kielbasa* or Portuguese *linguica*) may be substituted for the ham.

Peas may be omitted if desired or replaced by other green vegetables.

Saffron, the world's most expensive herb, is made from dried orange-red stigmas of autumn crocuses. To avoid bitterness, leaf saffron is first dissolved in liquid. Less expensive powdered saffron may be substituted. Mexican saffron, *achiote*, can be used as a substitute for color but not for flavor. The saffron available at local East Indian groceries is more economical than the kind available in spice departments of markets.

Make-It-Easy Tips:

√ The garlic is not sautéed to avoid the bitter taste that often accompanies browned garlic.

√ If using sausages, prick all over and boil or broil them to release excess grease; then slice.

√ To easily clean clams, place in a bowl of cold water with a sprinkling of oatmeal. The clams will eat the oatmeal and spit it out along with any accumulated sand and dirt.

√ Remember, do not eat unopened clams since it is likely that they were not alive before cooking and therefore might be spoiled.

Green Salad with Lime Dressing

SERVES: 8
Preparation time: 10 minutes

The Ingredients:

2 large heads romaine lettuce, washed and dried
½ pound piece jicama, peeled and cut into matchstick strips

Dressing:

¾ cup olive oil
¼ cup fresh lime juice
2 tablespoons sugar

¼ teaspoon ground ginger
Pinch of cayenne
Salt and freshly ground pepper to taste

The Steps:

1. Break lettuce into small pieces and place in salad bowl; top with jicama.
2. Combine dressing ingredients together in screw-top jar and shake.
3. Pour dressing over greens, toss well, and serve immediately.

Variations:

Substitute sliced water chestnuts or shredded Jerusalem artichokes (sunchokes) for jicama

Substitute lemons and lemon juice for limes and lime juice.

Make-It-Easy Tips:

√ Store limes away from direct light. If yellowing, use as quickly as possible; the juice will still be good.

√ Jicama is a Mexican root vegetable that resembles a potato yet tastes like a sweet water chestnut. Recently it has become popular as a *crudité*, a raw vegetable used with dips.

Make-It-Easy Flan

SERVES: 8
Preparation time: 15 minutes
Cooking time: 35 minutes
Chilling time: 4–6 hours or overnight

A traditional flan has a caramelized top. Here there is a sprinkling of brown sugar, which melts into the creamy and delicious finished dessert.

The Ingredients:

8 teaspoons brown sugar
2 cups whole milk
2 cups half-and-half
6 eggs

½ cup sugar
½ teaspoon salt
2 teaspoons vanilla extract

The Steps:

1. Preheat oven to 350°. Lightly butter 8 oven-proof custard cups.
2. Place 1 teaspoon brown sugar in the bottom of each custard cup.
3. In medium saucepan, heat milk and half-and-half together just until bubbles form around edges of pan.
4. In large bowl, beat eggs slightly with whisk or electric beater. Add sugar, salt, and vanilla.
5. Add small amount of hot milk to eggs, whisking constantly; gradually add remaining milk and whisk until smooth.
6. Pour into prepared dishes, set them in larger roasting pan, pour boiling water to ½″ in bottom of pan, and bake for 30–35 minutes, or until inserted knife comes out clean.
7. Remove from pan, allow to cool, and then chill for 4–6 hours or overnight.
8. To serve, run small knife around edge of dishes to loosen. Invert on small plates, and shake gently to loosen, allowing brown sugar to cover top and sides.

Variations:

Flan can be served as is from the cups, without inverting.

A real caramel topping can be prepared by heating 1 cup brown sugar in a heavy saucepan over medium-high heat stirring constantly until a syrup is formed. Quickly pour the syrup into little dishes, using pot holders to hold them and protect your hands from the hot syrup. Proceed with custard.

Flan can also be prepared in a 9″ pie plate or round baking dish; cook for 5–10 minutes longer, or until set.

Make-It-Easy Tips:

√ A few tablespoons of the hot milk must be added to the egg mixture in Step #5 to prevent curdling of the eggs. Once they are warmed, the rest of the hot milk can be safely added.

√ The water bath in Step #6, also called a *bain marie,* promotes even cooking.

√ Time baking carefully. Too long a time and the custard will be curdled; too short, and the custard will not set.

Guess Who's Coming to Dinner

SERVES: 4
Tossed Salad with Pine Nuts and Mushrooms
Scallops of Veal in Madeira Sauce
Brown Rice Primavera
Cheesecake Pie

"Elegant and understated" is the theme for this dinner. It's an occasion for bringing out the good china and silverware, finest tablecloth and napkins, and sparkling glassware. A simple and lovely floral arrangement makes a fitting centerpiece, especially when placed atop a mirror to reflect its color.

Napkins may be folded simply, but napkin rings are an elegant touch. As a pretty and quick alternative, fold both ends of the napkins into the center, leaving a ½″ opening. Accordian-pleat from left side in 1½″ fold. Secure them in the center with a decorative clip, ring, or festive colored ribbon, and then flare into a flower shape. (See illustration.)

The cheesecake for dessert is made well ahead of time, and the first steps for the salad can also be completed in advance. Assembling the ingredients for the veal and rice early will allow you to prepare them quickly and easily. Only the salad should be wilted in this menu, not the cook!

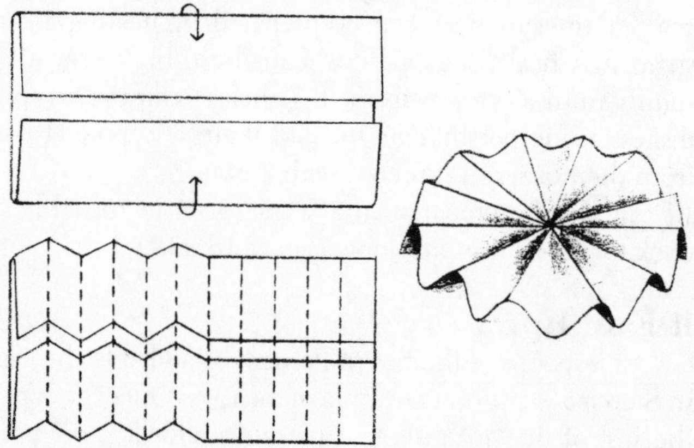

Flower
1. Fold both ends in toward the center leaving a ½″ opening. 2. Crease, accordion-style from left in 1½″ pleats. 3. Secure in center with decorative clip or ribbon; flare into a circle.

The veal is pounded, seasoned, and floured before dinner. The salad is served as a first course while the rice finishes simmering. After the salad, let people know you're about to prepare something special—which you are—and will be back in just a few minutes—which you will. Guests and your spouse or dinner companion will have a little time to chat. At this time, add the broccoli to the rice. While it cooks, continue preparing the veal through Step #4. Toss the final ingredients into the rice, and finish cooking the veal while the rice sets. In 5 minutes or less, the rice and veal are ready for the serving dish and platter. Arrange them attractively, and prepare for your guests to be thoroughly delighted.

Tossed Salad with Pine Nuts and Mushrooms

SERVES: 4–6
Preparation time: 15 minutes
Cooking time: 5–10 minutes

The unique flavor of raspberry vinegar makes this "warm" or "wilted" salad a wonderful first course as well as a side dish.

The Ingredients:

2 heads Boston lettuce
½ cup sliced water chestnuts
⅓ cup walnut oil
½ pound mushrooms, thinly sliced
¼ pound pine nuts
⅓ cup raspberry vinegar
Salt and freshly ground pepper to taste

The Steps:

1. Wash and dry lettuce and break into small pieces. Slice water chestnuts and place in salad bowl atop lettuce.
2. In skillet, heat 2 tablespoons oil and sauté mushrooms for 2 minutes or until lightly golden.
3. Add pine nuts and continue to sauté until golden brown.

4. Remove from heat; add remaining oil and raspberry vinegar, stirring constantly.
5. Season to taste with salt and pepper; pour over lettuce and serve immediately.

Variations:

As substitutions: for Boston lettuce, use romaine or leaf lettuce; for water chestnuts, use jicama or Jerusalem artichokes (sunchokes); for walnut oil, use almond, hazelnut, or olive oil; for pine nuts, use slivered almonds.

Make-It-Easy Tips:

√ To prepare in advance: Chill lettuce in the morning. Sauté nuts and mushrooms an hour before, and reheat before deglazing with vinegar.

√ Select mushrooms with closed caps and no exposed gills. Brush them or wipe them clean with acidulated water (water plus lemon juice). Dry thoroughly before sautéing.

Scallops of Veal in Madeira Sauce

SERVES: 4
Preparation time: 10 minutes
Cooking time: 7–10 minutes

The high cost of veal reserves this elegant dinner for very special occasions. Pounded chicken breasts are a wonderful and less expensive alternative. Remember that this is a last-minute recipe. Assemble all ingredients in advance and be ready to serve immediately.

The Ingredients:

1½ pounds veal scallopine, sliced ⅜″ thick
Salt and freshly ground pepper to taste
½ cup all-purpose flour
2 tablespoons unsalted butter
2 tablespoons olive oil
½ cup Madeira wine

¼ cup chicken or beef broth
2 tablespoons unsalted butter
1 teaspoon lemon juice
Garnish: Freshly chopped parsley

The Steps:

1. Place veal between layers of waxed paper and pound with mallet, meat pounder, or side of cleaver until ¼″ thick.
2. Sprinkle with salt and pepper; lightly dip into flour, shaking off excess.
3. In large skillet, melt 2 tablespoons butter and oil together. When butter is hot and beginning to lightly brown, sauté single layer of veal scaloppine; brown 2–3 minutes on each side; remove to platter and brown remaining veal.
4. When all veal has been browned and removed, pour off all but a light film of fat and add Madeira, stirring and scraping up browned particles from bottom of skillet. Add broth and continue to cook over high heat for 1–2 minutes, or until sauce thickens.
5. Return veal to skillet, reduce heat to low and cook 1–2 minutes, just to warm scallopine, basting with sauce.
6. Remove scaloppine to platter with slotted spatula and arrange attractively. Add 2 tablespoons butter and lemon juice to sauce remaining in skillet, stir well to combine, and adjust with salt and pepper to taste. Serve immediately, garnished with freshly chopped parsley.

Variations:

Sautéed sliced mushrooms can be added to taste.
Dry Marsala or even port wine can be substituted for Madeira.

Make-It-Easy Tips:

✓ The butcher will often agree to pound the veal for you. Make sure it has been pounded to ¼″ so that it needs only a short amount of cooking to keep it tender.

✓ When browning veal, watch it carefully, regulating heat so that the veal browns without burning.

Brown Rice Primavera

SERVES: 4–6
Preparation time: 15–20 minutes
Cooking time: 50 minutes

The Ingredients:

1 tablespoon unsalted butter
1 tablespoon olive or vegetable oil
1 clove garlic, minced
1⅔ cups chicken broth
1 cup water
¼ teaspoon nutmeg
Salt and freshly ground pepper to taste
1 cup raw brown rice
2 cups tiny broccoli florets
1 cup cherry tomatoes, sliced in half
Garnish: Freshly grated Parmesan cheese

The Steps:

1. In large saucepan, heat butter and oil together; add garlic and sauté over low heat for only 1–2 minutes, until just soft.
2. Add broth, water, nutmeg, salt, and pepper. Bring to a boil, add rice, cover tightly, reduce heat, and cook over low heat for 40 minutes.
3. Place broccoli on top, cover, and continue to cook until all liquid has been absorbed, about 10 minutes.
4. Stir in tomatoes, cover to heat through, and serve hot, garnished with Parmesan cheese.

Variations:

Sliced mushrooms, grated carrots, julienned zucchini, minced scallions, or other chopped vegetables can be added to taste.

Beef or vegetable broth can be substituted for chicken broth.

Grated Monterey Jack cheese, Cheddar cheese, or even Swiss cheese can be used as alternative garnishes.

Make-It-Easy Tips:

√ Brown rice requires more liquid during the cooking process because of the longer cooking time.

√ Buy brown rice in small quantities since its shelf life is shorter than white rice's, due to the oxidation of the bran layer that covers the grain. For long storage, refrigerate.

Cheesecake Pie

YIELD: One 9″ pie
Preparation time: 10–12 minutes
Cooking time: 35 minutes
Chilling time: 5 hours or overnight

This recipe comes from an acquaintance, Judy Selzer, who finds it easier to bake cheesecake in a pie plate rather than a springform pan.

The Ingredients:

Crust:

1 cup vanilla wafer crumbs (about 25)
2 tablespoons unsalted butter, melted
1 tablespoon sugar

Filling:

12 ounces cream cheese
½ cup sugar
½ teaspoon vanilla
2 eggs

Topping:

1 cup dairy sour cream
¼ cup sugar
½ teaspoon vanilla

The Steps:

1. Preheat oven to 350°. Generously butter 9″ pie plate.
2. Combine crust ingredients in small bowl, mix well, and press into bottom and sides of pie plate.

3. With elecric beater or by hand, beat cream cheese with sugar and vanilla. Add eggs, one at a time, beating well after each addition. Pour into prepared crust and bake for 25 minutes or until firm. Cool 5 minutes.
4. Combine topping ingredients and mix well until smooth and creamy; place atop baked cheesecake and bake 10 minutes longer.
5. Remove from oven, cool, and chill at least 5 hours or overnight.
6. Serve cut in wedges.

Variation:

Crumb crust can be varied to taste. Substitute zwiebacks, graham crackers, gingersnaps, or even chocolate wafer crumbs.

Make-It-Easy Tips:

√ Cream cheesecake freezes successfully, wrapped securely.

√ The easiest method of slicing cheesecake is with dental floss. Take a long strand of tautly held waxed or unwaxed floss (not mint-flavored) and press it through the cake; pull it out without pulling it up again.

Emergency Substitutions

When You Are Out Of:	***Substitute:***
Buttermilk, 1 cup	1 cup fresh milk plus 1 tablespoon vinegar or lemon juice allowed to stand 5 minutes.
	1 cup plain yogurt.
Sour cream, 1 cup	⅓ cup melted butter plus ¾ cup sour milk. (To make sour milk, use ¾ cup whole milk plus 2½ teaspoons lemon juice or 2¼ teaspoons white vinegar. Let mixture stand 10 minutes.)
	1 cup plain yogurt or sour half-and-half (but only in cooked, not in baked dishes).
Light cream (18%), 1 cup	Add 3 tablespoons melted butter to ⅞ cup of undiluted evaporated milk. (Evaporated milk is homogenized milk dehydrated to half its original volume.)
Whole milk, 1 cup	½ cup evaporated milk plus ½ cup water =
	1 cup skim milk plus 2 tablespoons melted butter =
	1 cup reconstituted nonfat dry milk plus 2 tablespoons butter =
	1 cup skim milk plus 1 tablespoon cream = (or in baking substitute 1 cup fresh fruit juice).

Heavy cream (36%), 1 cup	¾ cup milk plus ⅓ cup melted butter (for baking and cooking only).
Half-and-half (10%), 1 cup	⅞ cup milk plus 1½ tablespoons melted butter.
Yogurt, 1 cup	1 cup sour cream or sour half-and-half (though they have a higher fat content).
Baking powder, 1 tablespoon	1 teaspoon baking soda plus 2 teaspoons cream of tartar (1 teaspoon baking powder = ⅓ teaspoon baking soda plus ½ teaspoon cream of tartar).
Unsweetened baking chocolate, 1 square	3 tablespoons unsweetened powdered cocoa plus 1 tablespoon butter or shortening.
Cake flour, 1 cup	¾ cup plus 2 tablespoons all-purpose flour plus 2 tablespoons cornstarch.
Self-rising flour, 1 cup	1 cup sifted flour plus 1¼ teaspoons baking powder and a pinch of salt.
Thickener	1 tablespoon cornstarch = 2 tablespoons flour + 1 tablespoon arrowroot = 1 tablespoon potato starch = 4 teaspoons quick-cooking tapioca = 3 egg yolks.
Honey, 1 cup	1¼ cup sugar plus ¼ cup water (liquid).
Light corn syrup, 1 cup	1 cup sugar plus ¼ of the liquid called for in the recipe boiled together until syrupy = ¾ cup honey = 1¼ cup molasses = ¾ cup maple syrup. Lower temperature to 350° with honey to prevent excessive browning.

Confectioner's sugar, 1 cup	⅞ cup granulated sugar whirred quickly through blender or food processor with 1 tablespoon cornstarch.
Superfine sugar	Grind granulated sugar in food processor or blender, pulsating until as fine as necessary.
Breadcrumbs, 1 cup	¾ cup cracker crumbs.
Cayenne, ⅛ teaspoon	4 drops hot pepper sauce.
Lemon juice, 1 teaspoon	½ teaspoon vinegar.
Canned tomatoes, 1 cup	1½ cups fresh chopped tomatoes, simmered 10 minutes.
Jerusalem artichokes	Water chestnuts = jicama.
Pine nuts	Slivered almonds.
Dry mustard, 1 teaspoon	2½ teaspoons prepared mustard.
Raisins or dried currants (for baking), *1 cup*	1 cup finely chopped soft prunes or dates.

Index

DISCARD